War Machines

TEXAS A&M UNIVERSITY
★ 71 ★
MILITARY HISTORY SERIES

War
Machines

Transforming
Technologies
in the U.S. Military,
1920–1940

TIMOTHY MOY

TEXAS A&M UNIVERSITY PRESS : COLLEGE STATION

Library of Congress Cataloging-in-Publication Data

Moy, Timothy.
    War machines : transforming technologies in
the U.S. military, 1920–1940 / Timothy Moy.—1st ed.
      p. cm.—(Texas A&M University military history series ; 71)
  ISBN 1-58544-104-x (cloth : alk. paper)
    1. Military weapons—United States—History—20th century.
2. Technology and state—United States—History—20th century.
3. United States. Marine Corps—Weapons systems. 4. United
States. Army. Air Corps—Weapons systems. I. Title. II. Series.
U800.M64 2001
355'.07'0973—dc21   00-010344

Contents

Illustrations

Preface

I first noticed these connections as a child. In the midst of a common boyhood fascination with World War II airplanes, I found that when looking at a photo of an unfamiliar American airplane I could guess with a high degree of certainty whether it had been used predominantly by the Navy or the Army Air Forces. I could not, at the time, explain how I could tell; heavy bombers were easy, of course, but even fighters had distinctions about them that seemed to reflect their services. Some airplanes simply "looked Navy" and others "looked Air Force."

Only years later did I realize that one big giveaway was the shape of the engine space. Navy planes generally had large, cylindrical cowls to accommodate their big, air-cooled, radial engines; Army Air Forces fighters (with some exceptions) had liquid-cooled, in-line engines that permitted a sleek, pointed nose. But why was this so? Part of the answer, I learned, was that individual airplane companies develop certain design preferences over time. The Navy got most of its fighters from a small set of companies (Grumman, Chance-Vought, and so on), whereas the Army Air Forces got most of its fighters from a different set of companies (Lockheed, North American, Curtiss, and so on). But the look and feel of Navy and Air Force fighters was also shaped by a mundane socio-technical fact: air-cooled engines were easier to maintain and repair. At sea for extended periods, tied to long and sometimes tenuous supply lines, the Navy opted for the simpler and more rugged radial engines, and that is part of what gave the F4F Wildcat, the F6F Hellcat, and the F4U Corsair that barrel-nosed Navy look. The Army Air Forces, on the other hand, unencumbered by trying to maintain an air force for carrier operations, opted for the higher performance but increased fragility of liquid-cooled, in-line engines, thus giving the P-40 Warhawk, the P-51 Mustang, and the P-38 Lightning that sleek Air Force profile.

Once you look for them, it is easy to find these sorts of connections between the design of technologies and the special characteristics and concerns of the organizations that create them. Such connections can exist even for machines that are theoretically unrestricted by any technical requirements whatsoever. A fellow *Star Trek* fan once pointed out that the 1960s version of the starship *Enterprise* looked like it had been designed by Chevrolet, the early 1980s movie *Enterprise* looked like it had been designed by BMW, and the late 1980s–early 1990s *Star Trek: The Next Generation Enterprise* looked like it had been designed by Mazda.

It goes without saying that their environments shape technologies. Aircraft designers in the 1940s worked within complex technical restrictions, and the various artists at Paramount were, despite their twenty-fourth-century vision, bound to the industrial and aesthetic milieu of the twentieth. But do these connections go farther? Is there more to the relationship between technology and institutions than the shape of an engine cowl or a science-fiction spaceship? Can entire technological systems bear the imprint of the institutional identities that created them?

It was these sorts of questions that brought me, a historian of science and technology, to look at the U.S. Army Air Corps and the U.S. Marine Corps during the years between the world wars. Originally, I had intended to focus on what I thought would be the most fertile historical period for studying the relationships between military institutions and technology: the early Cold War era. However, as I read the literature on science, technology, and the military during and immediately after World War II, I could not shake the feeling that I was already looking at a well-organized political, industrial, and bureaucratic apparatus—something that clearly had not sprung spontaneously into existence in the mad rush after Pearl Harbor. Rather, this machine appeared to have been operating for some time, wanting only fuel. The enormous influx of wartime dollars sent the machine, already extant and carefully tended by skilled operators, into high gear. In search of the genesis of this machine, I began looking back into the 1920s and 1930s.

I quickly found that the interwar decades were a much better period for examining this relationship. The dynamic between technology and institutional identity was easier to see in that era because it was uncomplicated (compared to the Cold War period) by the extraordinary experiences of World War II. In the days before radar, missiles, and nuclear weapons there was much less of a consensus on the relationship between technology and war. Consequently, the unique cultures and characteristics of individual institutions were able to play much larger roles in shaping technology for military purposes. The interwar years were uncertain and precarious times, filled with opportunity and risk, and the field was wide open.

The book that has resulted is a somewhat hybrid study. It is about agencies within the U.S. military, but it is not strictly a work of military history. Rather, it is an analysis of the relationships between technology, politics, and culture that happens to focus on military organizations. So, while I hope the book will be useful to scholars of military history, my primary intention has been to illuminate a broader dynamic between institutions and the technologies they envision.

Acknowledgments

It is a pleasure to thank the many people who have helped bring this book to fruition. I am intellectually indebted to the work of several historians of technology and culture, including Thomas Hughes, Donald MacKenzie, and Joseph Corn; of historians of military culture such as Michael Sherry and Craig Cameron; and of political scientists such as Barry Posen and Carl Builder, whose focus is on military institutions.

I am personally indebted to many people who have supported and guided my research on this project. John Heilbron, Roger Hahn, and Gene Rochlin at the University of California–Berkeley, and Dan Kevles at Caltech, directed the dissertation version of this research, which was supported by the Institute on Global Conflict and Cooperation of the University of California and by the Office of Air Force History. In addition, a large number of people helped me with my archival research: Richard Kohn, Herman Wolk, Maj. Michael Wolfert, and the staff at the Office of Air Force History; the staff at the Air Force Historical Research Agency at Maxwell Air Force Base, Alabama; Tom Crouch, Gregg Herken, Dom Pisano, David DeVorkin, and the staff at the Smithsonian Institution's National Air and Space Museum; Brig. Gen. Edwin Simmons (USMC, retired) and the staff at the Marine Corps Historical Center; Lt. Col. Donald Bittner (USMC, retired) and Kerry Strong at the Marine Corps University Archives in Quantico, Virginia; Dean Allard and the staff at the Naval Historical Center; Lt. Gen. Victor Krulak (USMC, retired); the staff at the Marine Corps Command Museum in San Diego, California; and the staffs at the Manuscripts Division at the Library of Congress, the National Archives and Records Administration in Washington, D.C., and the Washington National Records Center in Suitland, Maryland.

Several colleagues I first met as a graduate student have also influenced this work. My thanks go especially to Dominique Pestre, Glenn Bugos, and Peter Neushul for numerous enlightening conversations. My very warm thanks go to Jessica Riskin and Christopher Kutz, whose readings of the manuscript improved it enormously.

Paul Kennedy and Mark Shulman taught me much about doing political and economic military history while I was a John M. Olin Foundation postdoctoral fellow at the International Security Studies program at Yale.

I am deeply grateful to a number of my colleagues at the University of New Mexico. David Farber and Beth Bailey have been invaluable in helping me both broaden and focus my thinking on these issues; I cannot thank them enough. Durwood Ball generously took his blue pencil to an early version of the manuscript. I am also thankful to Linda Hall, Virginia Scharff, and Ferenc Szasz for their support and guidance.

The staff at Texas A&M University Press has been a pleasure to work with on this project. I would also like to thank the anonymous reviewers of the manuscript, whose insights and suggestions have helped me understand better what I wanted to say.

I would also like to thank my parents, David and Betty Moy, without whose support this work obviously would not have been possible.

Finally, my overwhelming gratitude and deepest affection go to Rebecca Ullrich, my wife, friend, and colleague. Rebecca's acute analytical sense and indispensable readings of the manuscript have been overshadowed only by her endless support, confidence, and love over the years. This book is as much hers as mine, and I happily dedicate it to her.

War Machines

Chapter 1

Culture, Technology, and Institutions

It looked like a video game. When the bombs started falling on Baghdad in 1991, Americans by the millions were captivated by nosecone and wing-camera footage of precision-guided "smart" bombs flying down ventilator shafts and through armored doors. They marveled at this latest illustration of American technological wizardry in the service of national security. If some of the wizardry later turned out to include a touch of the charlatan, no matter; technologies, made in America with wonderfully American names like Patriot, Tomahawk, and Maverick had become new American war heroes.

To say that the American military loves technology is to state the obvious. It is difficult to think of a military force, in this century or any other, which has been more intimately tied to its technology than the U.S. military since World War II. But while the American military establishment has had an extremely close relationship with technology, the origins, evolution, and nature of that relationship have varied enormously from one service to the next.

This book is a study of the relationship between technology and institutions. While it focuses on the U.S. Army Air Corps (predecessor of the U.S. Air Force) and the Marine Corps during the period between the world wars, it explores a relationship that is not unique to military agencies. Specific technologies mean different things to different institutions. In the 1980s, the electronic digital computer meant something very different to the blue-suited men from IBM than it did to the sneaker-shod kids at Apple. Although both were computer companies, and both dealt with similar conglomerations of silicon and electrons, they, like their creations, were instantly distinguishable from one another. For most of the twentieth century, even as uniform and rigid a technology as the baseball bat has meant something different for institutions as similar to one another as the home run-hitting Yankees, the base-stealing Dodgers, and the singles-hitting Red Sox. That single piece of hardware plays a different role in shaping the institutional identities of each of those organizations.

It is also the case that different institutions will shape technologies to their own ends and within the bounds of their individual, institutional cultures. A child can distinguish automobiles designed by different manufacturers. Likewise, the IBM personal computer and the Apple Macintosh, especially in their early incarnations, very much reflected the institutions from which they sprang.

The same is true for the relationships between technologies and military institutions in the twentieth century. The Air Force, for example, evokes images of pilots operating high-tech weaponry, striking swiftly and precisely from out of the blue to lay waste enemy installations and factories. For the Marine Corps, on the other hand, the fundamental icon is Iwo Jima, an image literally cast in bronze as the Marine Corps memorial in Washington, D.C. The vision of marines hitting the beaches in simple but rugged landing craft and then slogging their way ashore under enemy fire defines the Marine Corps as an institution. But much lies beneath these surface manifestations of how different institutions interact with technology. What role does technology play in shaping institutional behavior and serving bureaucratic ends? How do institutional cultures, in turn, shape attitudes about technology and technologies themselves?

The central argument of this book is that while airmen and marines have had different relationships with their machines, they have shared the historical dynamic that created those relationships. The images of precise aerial bombing and grueling amphibious landings both originated in the period from 1920 to 1940. During the interwar years, leaders of both the Army Air Corps and the Marine Corps carefully and deliberately wedded their institutions to visions of warfare that were based on new military technologies, and then staked their institutional survival on those images. Empowered and constrained by technology and culture, they recreated their agencies during the interwar years.

Competition and Culture

Sociologists and political scientists have long noted that institutions behave like organisms. In finite environments, both are driven by their innate penchant for self-preservation to interact competitively with one another. The precise form of that competition, however, can vary enormously. Organisms have many ways to compete for scarce resources. An organism's survival strategies might include killing its rivals, cooperating with them, stretching higher to gather more sunlight, or finding the underside of a slimy (but life-sustaining) rock that somehow went unnoticed by its competitors.

Institutions also compete in different ways. The venue of that competition can be a marketplace, a board meeting, or a congressional appropriations hearing. The form of the competition can be a zero-sum confrontation in which a victor triumphs at the expense of the vanquished, or it can be a remote interaction in which one or both agencies find new institutional niches in which to live and thrive. Throughout this book, the term *bureaucratic* will refer to this sort of institutional stress and competition. In no way should it be read pejoratively; it is exactly analogous to the terms *adaptive* or *selective* for organisms.

For organisms, both the form and content of competition are shaped by the characteristics of the species involved. A species' physical characteristics may enable it to compete extremely well in some ways and in certain environments but may prevent it from competing in others entirely. For example, a cheetah, with its swift legs and sharp teeth, may be a wonderful competitor on a grassy plain, a mediocre one on a mountaintop, or a rather poor one in an ocean. The same holds for institutions in their interactions with one another. As with organisms, the competitive behavior of institutions can be shaped by their material characteristics—how large they are, their command of material resources, and so on. But institutional behavior is also shaped by institutional culture.

Throughout this book, the term *institutional culture* will refer to beliefs, practices, and habits of mind that are shared by members of an institution. Membership in an institution—the Air Force, the Marine Corps, the New York Yankees, or Apple Computer—includes adopting some measure of the culture of the group which has been shaped over time by, among other things, the institution's genesis, its past experiences, and the leadership of strong individuals within it. Since its creation, Apple Computer has been a self-proclaimed corporate renegade. Steve Jobs, one of Apple's founders, openly indoctrinated his employees with an antiestablishment vision of how small computers could empower individual people. During the company's heyday in the 1980s, a homemade Jolly Roger flew over the corporate headquarters in Silicon Valley.[1] In a different realm, the New York Yankees are sluggers and champions—and have been since the days of Babe Ruth and Lou Gehrig. Even during the dark days of the early 1990s they remained the Bronx Bombers to their faithful fans. Like all institutional cultures, the cultures of Apple and the Yankees can change—Apple could become more corporate and the Yankees could become a hit-and-run team of heartbreak losers—but this would take time and considerable effort on the part of new institutional leaders.

The characteristics that stem from institutional culture can shape the way that institutions behave in a competitive world. Jobs's vision has predisposed Apple to compete in some ways in the computer market (targeting the educational, commercial art, and desktop publishing markets) and not in others (business applications and networks). When the Yankees have a bad season or need a new outfielder, they look to certain kinds of players for assistance. In much the same way, the Air Corps and Marine Corps, facing increasingly intense bureaucratic competition in the years between the world wars, saw their competitive options configured both by their respective material and technological circumstances, and by the institutional cultures within which airmen and marines brought those material resources to bear.

Doctrine and Technology

During the 1920s and 1930s the U.S. military endured severe bureaucratic pressure stemming from the return to normalcy and dwindling political enthusiasm for military matters. The spending cuts and force reductions that came at the end of the Great War were difficult but unsurprising. Much more threatening was the distinct turn in American politics back to its traditional rejection of great-power intrigue and the complexities that came with a long-term commitment to world affairs. Rejection of the League of Nations, increasingly protectionist trade policies, arms-limitation treaties, and government declarations outlawing war all boded ill for the bureaucratic fortunes of military institutions, and placed them in an increasingly competitive environment.[2]

For the most part, America's military agencies responded to this pressure by trying to carve out new institutional niches for themselves, primarily by articulating new military missions as the justification for their existence. This meant inventing entire new military doctrines—theoretical yet detailed visions of how war can and should be waged.[3] Air Corps and Marine Corps leaders in particular created whole new forms of warfare during the interwar years that profoundly shaped the face of battle for those who went to war again in 1941.

The 1920s and 1930s were also the heyday of American technological enthusiasm, when modern marvels like electrical appliances, radio, the automobile, and the airplane were transforming American society. In this atmosphere, military attitudes about technology became an unusually important facet of institutional culture. In many ways, the Air Corps and the Marine Corps were at opposite poles of a spectrum of technology and culture. Since its inception during World War I, the Air Corps had been built around a hallmark of high technology—the airplane—and the belief that the airplane represented the future of warfare. After the war, especially as doped canvas biplanes gave way to sleek metal monoplanes, the Air Corps began to regard itself as the most futuristic, even high-tech, branch of the military services. The Marine Corps, on the other hand, had always regarded itself as a simple, rugged, warrior force built around the "leatherneck" (later known as a "grunt") with a rifle. During the interwar period the Marine Corps came to epitomize a low-tech military culture.[4] Yet the Air Corps and Marine Corps, despite their very different attitudes about the role and importance of technology, developed their new doctrines around new, technologically informed visions of warfare that were nevertheless congruent with the preexisting cultures of their institutions.

Overview

In the case of the Army Air Corps, the new warfare involved the high-altitude precision bombing of enemy cities. Air Corps leaders crafted this form of strategic bombing in ways that harmonized wonderfully with the Air Corps's evolving institutional culture. Despite the atrocious casualty rates and gruesome deaths that had accompanied air combat in World War I, the air war was the only arena of war to emerge untouched by the de-romanticizing effects of modern military technology. Although the war in the trenches was almost universally condemned as dehumanizing and ignoble, the air warriors had been able to maintain an almost chivalric image of themselves as elite knights of the sky engaged in a form of single combat in which individual courage and prowess still carried the day. After the armistice, airmen continued to regard the Air Corps and air war itself as the most professional form of military service.

During the interwar decades the Air Corps's self-image also changed as aviation technology advanced. Biplanes gave way to monoplanes, wood gave way to metal, and engines became more powerful, propelling air-planes higher, faster, and farther. Likewise, the Air Corps's knights-of-the-sky image merged with that of Buck Rogers (who had been an Air Corps pilot in World War I, as every boy in the thirties knew). Strategic bombing, too, seemed precise, technological, and supremely professional—all in keeping with the Air Corps's institutional self-perception.

On the bureaucratic front, many Air Corps officers entered the inter-war period convinced that their institutional patron, the U.S. Army, did not appreciate the military potential of the airplane. Air Corps leaders, particularly the group of young officers surrounding Brig. Gen. William "Billy" Mitchell, became convinced that for the Air Corps to flourish, it needed to gain its independence from the Army. In the minds of Air Corps officers like Frank Andrews, Haywood Hansell, Benjamin Foulois, and Henry "Hap" Arnold, the key to independence was strategic bombing.

In order to articulate precisely how strategic bombing should work, these officers gained control of the Air Corps Tactical School (ACTS), the locus of airpower doctrinal development during the 1920s and 1930s. Never losing sight of their political and bureaucratic goals, the self-pro-claimed "bomber boys" at the ACTS realized that Mitchell's original idea of terror bombing civilian centers was politically unpalatable. They thus transformed his vision into the precision bombing of industrial facilities. With scientific precision, they argued, strategic bombing could instantly take away the enemy's ability to make war.

This image of an irresistible, devastating, and precise assault from the sky proved extremely popular among Air Corps theorists. In addition to justifying the Air Corps's bureaucratic existence, daylight precision bombing also conformed to the airmen's institutional self-image. Like the Air Corps's vision of itself, this form of strategic bombing was futuristic and high-tech. Like the Air Corps itself, it was precise, elegant, and even humane (for it could theoretically end war with a single, shattering bolt from the blue). And like the Air Corps itself, it held out the hope of recovering the military professionalism that appeared so threatened after World War I. Only highly skilled and technically proficient officers and crews would, after all, be able to operate the complex of technologies that comprised this intricate weapon.

However, by the early 1930s this technological weapon—the airborne bomb delivery system consisting of high-altitude, long-range bombers armed with precision optical bombsights—existed only in the airmen's imaginations. Consequently, the Air Corps spent much of the 1930s striving to make precision bombing a technological reality. An intricate network of agencies—academic institutions, private aircraft corporations and engineering firms, the National Advisory Committee for Aeronautics, and the Air Corps's own Materiel Division—helped the Air Corps acquire the machines it needed: large four-engine bombers from Boeing and Martin, and optical bombsights from Sperry and Norden.

The technology in turn reinforced the Air Corps's institutional self-identity. The Norden bombsight, for example, would become a central part of the Air Corps's high-tech image. Air Corps leaders were enamored of the bombsight's "top secret" mystique, a reputation carefully cultivated by Norden's public relations people. But they were especially captivated by the machine's supposed ability to put a bomb in a pickle barrel from twenty thousand feet. With its gyroscopic stabilization, clockwork rate mechanism, and high-powered optics, the Norden bombsight—like the sleek and shiny bomber aircraft themselves—reflected the Air Corps's bomber culture in a way that wedded the institution to the machines.

At the other end of the spectrum of technology and culture was the U.S. Marine Corps, whose new warfare was amphibious operations. Despite an impressive combat record in World War I, the Marine Corps also faced serious bureaucratic threats during the interwar years. Since its creation during the Revolutionary War, the Marine Corps had never found a single coherent mission to justify its existence. For most of its history, the Corps's diverse yet disjointed duties had included serving as ships' guards, consular guards, military police, shore parties, and standard infantry. In fact, the marines' strong record as infantry during World War I led many policy makers to wonder whether the Army should absorb the Marines Corps.

During the 1920s, therefore, several rising young marine officers began searching for a new mission that would continue to legitimize the Marine Corps's position as a quasi-independent agency within the U.S. Navy. Fortunately for them, a strategic possibility quickly presented itself. The Treaty of Versailles and the naval arms limitation treaty of 1920 combined to create new and difficult strategic commitments for the Navy. In the event of war with Japan (considered a serious possibility by naval planners since 1901), the Navy anticipated quickly losing control of the Philippines. The ensuing campaign—a long, arduous, "island hopping" war waged across the Pacific—would require securing small islands for use as temporary naval bases along the way. Precisely how and by whom these "advance bases" were to be captured was not clear, and it was in this strategic uncertainty that marines sensed their opportunity.

For the ten years from 1922 to 1932, Marine Corps leaders fought to secure the "advance base mission" as their institution's *raison d'être*. The grueling and difficult nature of this future warfare dovetailed perfectly with the Marine Corps's self-image as a simple, rugged, yet elite corps of American warriors who were always the "First to Fight." Led by officers like George Barnett, Benjamin Fuller, and John Lejeune—all of whom eventually became generals and Marine Corps commandants—marine planners articulated the doctrine for amphibious assaults and lobbied their military and civilian superiors to grant this job to the Corps.

Like their strategic bombing counterparts in the Air Corps, marine amphibious-warfare proponents appropriated their command and staff college to develop their new vision of warfare. The Marine Corps Schools (MCS) at Quantico, Virginia, was the traditional gateway for career marines to prepare for the upper echelons of leadership, making it the perfect place to train and indoctrinate up-and-coming officers in amphibious operations. By the early 1930s the MCS's curriculum, traditionally devoted to infantry operations, was completely recast to emphasize the amphibious assault. In 1934 the MCS issued a comprehensive manual that detailed the elements of amphibious warfare and later served as a blueprint for the early World War II Pacific landings.

Throughout this process, the Marine Corps's institutional culture shaped its technological choices. The hardware that could make amphibious warfare possible—from landing craft to combat rations—did not exist in 1930 and would have to be created. Reflecting the ideals of the Corps, marine planners opted for simple, rugged, low-tech machines. For example, the landing craft that the marines adopted—designed and produced by both the U.S. Navy and private boatyards—were emblematic of Marine Corps culture. Rather than exploring the bounds of 1930s high technology, such as hydrofoils or even helicopters, marines opted for landing craft that were simple, sturdy, graceless, and easy to produce in quantity—all in keeping with the marines' vision of landing under enemy fire and slogging their way ashore.

The similarities and contrasts between the Air Corps and Marine Corps stories illuminate the dynamic relationship between technology, culture, and institutions. The two institutions faced very similar bureaucratic threats and prospects during the interwar years. In both cases, relatively young and politically adept officers successfully thwarted the threats to their institutions by articulating new military missions for them. Both ultimately embraced new forms of warfare and new technologies that harmonized well with their distinct institutional cultures. But because those cultures were so different, airmen and marines forged different relationships between their services, their cultural identities, and the machines they created.

The World before the Complex

Throughout the Cold War era, historians and political scientists agreed that, for the most part, technological change provoked military innovation. In many instances since World War II, the development of new military technologies preceded any coherent need for them. Thermonuclear weapons, multiple-warhead nuclear missiles, lasers, and quantum electronics are only a few examples.[5] One prominent observer of technology and the military during this period noted that "military requirements tend to become after-the-fact rationalizations of technical ideas cooked up at a relatively low level in the military-technical-contractor bureaucracy."[6]

The impression that the military would do the research and development (R&D) first and ask questions later became so pervasive after World War II that leaders in the engineering community actually started warning their colleagues against getting too caught up in the Pentagon's technological enthusiasm. Because of the dramatic wartime successes of the atomic bomb and radar, military "operational users" had come to hold technology in too high a regard. One engineer warned members of his professional society: "This regard has led to the almost blind acceptance of new ideas or gadgets presented. It is literally possible to find some operational user who will be intrigued by any suggestion. Unfortunately there is no library of disproven ideas to which one can refer and no substitute for sound judgment. It is therefore necessary to consider the enthusiasm of a non-technical military user for paper ideas with some caution."[7]

To be sure, this technology-driven dynamic prevailed through much of the Cold War period because of America's vibrant, influential, and well-funded military R&D community. This network of federal research centers, military contractors, and academic laboratories has provided the military a nearly constant flow of new technical ideas that has served as grist for the mill of military innovation.

Before World War II, however, the relationship between science, technology, and the military was very different. Before mushroom clouds and radar blips had burned their images onto the palimpsest of American political culture, there was no aggressive military R&D establishment; Dwight Eisenhower's warning about a military-industrial-academic complex in 1960 would have made little sense thirty years earlier. Consequently, the motive forces for military innovation during the interwar years were less technical and industrial and more cultural and bureaucratic.

Back to the Future

Understanding this genesis of the American military's technology-based culture is fundamental to our understanding of the history of technology and the military in the twentieth century. Despite our widespread image of the new vistas of military technology for the twenty-first century, it is the situation between the world wars that most resembles the situation for the near future. Beginning in the 1920s, new military doctrines and technologies arose in a context of great technological enthusiasm and social apprehension. Evangelists of many creeds saw the salvation of world peace in arms limitation treaties, international renunciations of war, and several super weapons that once again made war too horrible to contemplate as an instrument of foreign policy. This was also a time of considerable anxiety about the future of the military in America. Men and women in uniform who had just helped make the world safe for democracy came home to a United States that had no obvious enemies and a deep isolationist tradition. Clearly, the military services would have to adapt to the nation's new role in the world, and that evolution would hold both danger and opportunity. It is a situation that the United States finds itself in again today.

During the 1920s and 1930s the American way of war and the institutions that wage it were fundamentally recast by leaders who understood and harnessed the strategic, bureaucratic, cultural, and technological forces at their disposal. That story, and America's technology-based military itself, began in those difficult decades between the world wars when victorious institutions like the Air Corps and Marine Corps came home from the war in Europe to fight for their lives.

Part 1

Precision Bombing

Chapter 2

The Bombers' Vision

Aerial bombardment has been the heart and soul of the U.S. Air Force. Based on an image carefully created and cultivated during World War II, the Air Force has identified itself as the military service with both the ability and the responsibility to bring down devastation from the sky, and to do so accurately and irresistibly. It matters not whether the vehicle of destruction was a high-altitude bomber with a human crew or an inertially guided intercontinental ballistic missile, or the instrument of destruction a high-explosive "dumb" bomb, a precision-guided "smart" bomb, or a thermonuclear warhead. Since the 1920s America's airmen have very deliberately created and embraced a bomber culture that has profoundly shaped the evolution of their service, of the U.S. military as a whole, and of the entire American aviation community. In fact, this bond between the Air Force and bombing has appeared so deep and abiding that it is tempting to imagine that strategic bombing was the service's only proper destiny.

However, the historical relationship between the Air Force and strategic bombing was hardly preordained. It resulted instead from a confluence of contingent forces that, in the decades prior to World War II, combined to make high-altitude precision bombing against logistical centers the most attractive mission to Air Corps leaders.

The first of these forces was a set of severe bureaucratic stresses that threatened the Air Corps's political welfare during the 1920s and 1930s. At a time when Americans largely turned away from Wilsonian globalism and military budgets concurrently declined, Air Corps leaders realized that their agency's well-being depended upon their ability to articulate and promote a distinct and well-defined mission—one that would be simultaneously attractive enough to justify congressional appropriations and specialized enough to keep it within the Air Corps's purview.

It was a difficult balance. Until 1947, what is today the U.S. Air Force was part of the U.S. Army. The Army Air Service began as part of the Signal Corps during World War I—a clear reflection of the widespread belief at the time that the airplane's primary military value would be in reconnaissance. Although the Air Service moved out from under the Signal Corps before the end of World War I and received some autonomy as the Army Air Corps in 1926, it remained subordinate to the Army's hierarchy until after World War II. For all of the interwar period, the chief of the Air Corps answered directly to the Army chief of staff, and indirectly to the general staff and the secretary of war.

In order to patch together any kind of political consensus for a new mission in life, the Air Corps had to find a job that was reasonably well integrated into the rest of military thinking. At the same time, that mission somehow had to be tailored to the Air Corps's unique strengths to prevent some other agency (like, for example, naval aviation) from stealing it away. This was a tricky bureaucratic problem, and one that strategic bombing eventually solved beautifully.

The second set of forces that helped wed the Air Corps to long-range bombing was the congruence between the image of strategic bombing and the institutional culture developing in the Air Corps in the decades following World War I. The public embraced images of chivalrous warriors riding their winged steeds into the wild blue—and the Air Corps did, too.[1] After the war, airmen came to regard aerial combat as the most honorable and professional form of the military art. The sleek and futuristic airplane, they felt, epitomized the modern military. Air Corps leaders became convinced that strategic bombing, in spite of its threat to civilians, would recover the military professionalism that had been lost in the mindless slaughter of trench warfare. Precise and technological, bombing came to fit neatly with the Air Corps's institutional identity.

Finally, the Air Corps became attached to strategic bombing during the interwar years because of several crucial technologies that made, or appeared to make, the strategic-bombing vision technically feasible. After the bureaucratic front had been secured, Air Corps leaders carefully encouraged the development of those elements of the bomb delivery system—consisting of aircraft, ordnance, bombsight, and crew—that would make strategic bombing possible.

Although it is possible to list individually these various forces drawing the Air Corps and strategic bombing together, they interacted profoundly with one another during the interwar decades. The Air Corps's bureaucratic difficulties deeply influenced the articulation of the strategic-bombing vision, for example, just as that vision greatly shaped the Air Corps's technological demands. Nor, of course, were these forces inexorable. Air Corps leaders made conscious and well-informed choices that served to identify their service with strategic bombing—a fact that is clearly illustrated by the other possibilities that they considered and rejected in favor of bombing. After casting about for a well-defined and technologically feasible mission during the 1920s and early 1930s, Air Corps leaders found that their branch's bureaucratic difficulties, its articulation of a strategic-bombing vision, and its institutional culture made daylight precision bombing appear the most profitable and obvious course to pursue.

The Stifled Promise of World War I

On one hand, the aviators' experience during the war had been one of the only bright spots in an otherwise horrifying and dehumanizing endeavor. The war in the air had appeared more gallant and noble than the indiscriminate slaughter of the ground war. The airmen saw it as a form of combat, perhaps the only one, which still rewarded courage and skill.

On the other hand, World War I was an extremely frustrating enterprise for American airpower enthusiasts. While German, British, and French air forces conducted daring bombing raids deep into their respective enemy's territory, the U.S. Army Air Service entered the war too late to compile a comparable record. The Americans dropped only 138 tons of bombs (the British delivered 543 tons in the summer of 1918 alone), a number so small that it was often converted in service histories to 276,000 pounds,[2] and plans for larger American bombing raids were cut short by the armistice.

While British aviators were honored in the spring of 1918 with the elevation of their service from the Royal Naval Air Service and the Royal Flying Corps to a totally new and independent Royal Air Force (RAF), their American counterparts had to be satisfied with being shuffled from Signal

Corps control to being managed by the general staff. The RAF's bureaucratic emancipation brought with it the privilege of independent planning and operations. In contrast, the Army Air Service muddled through the war distributed piecemeal among the various ground units and employed mainly in support of ground operations: as reconnaissance for the infantry, spotting for the artillery, and, when necessary, preventing enemy planes from harassing the troops.

The Air Service's ability to bring large numbers of airplanes to bear had also been unimpressive. Although it enlarged its inventory from several hundred to over 6,200 airplanes by war's end, approximately 4,800 of those planes were produced in France. American industry contributed only 1,216 airplanes, and almost all of those were of foreign design.[3]

Though frustrating, the Air Service's wartime accomplishments left the airmen's hopes for military aviation undimmed. Like much of the rest of the country, they embraced a brand of technological enthusiasm that historian Joseph Corn has called the "winged gospel," a creed of aviation that bespoke "the wondrous transformations which would occur if people only believed in and accepted the airplane."[4] Theirs was a nearly utopian vision in which the airplane would bring a new era of peace, harmony, culture, and humanity.

Perhaps the clearest articulation of this vision of air warfare came from Leighton Brewer, a decorated American fighter pilot who after the war became a Yale- and Harvard-educated English literature professor at Boston University. Brewer's best-known work was his 1934 epic poem, *Riders of the Sky.*[5] For air warriors like Brewer (who returned to military service during World War II), the peaceful and civilian winged gospel held out the promise of a new and higher form of combat that could recover the honor and valor of military service that had been so stained in the trenches of France. In *Riders of the Sky,* aerial combat became a contest between gallant and professional knights of the sky, and the airplane became a military technology that (unlike most others of the Great War) restored a measure of chivalry and humanity to warfare. A hostile sky was more than merely contested airspace, it was "[T]hat bright station where a glorious few—/Knights of the world's last knighthood—venture forth/To tilt for life and death among the clouds."[6]

The moral code of this new knighthood was clear from its wartime tales. The airplane bestowed upon foes a bond of brotherhood that transcended even the demands of war. Among the best-known expressions of airborne chivalry, celebrated in song and story, was the tradition of flying low over the crash site of a vanquished foe and dropping a wreath of flowers.[7] Another was how, according to Brewer, World War I aces would duel one another in the sun:

> Until, with ammunition drums exhausted,
> As Hector and great Ajax from the heat
> Of combat costly presents interchanged
> And noble words; no longer enemies,
> But side by side like undivided comrades
> They flew, and waved in friendly courtesy.[8]

Brewer also described how the legendary Baron Manfred von Richtofen had nobly spared the life of an outmatched novice:

> Yet once, they say, he let an enemy
> Escape: some dashing boy tricked into battle
> With the Kaiser's kingly ace; who found himself
> With hopelessly jambed gun, helpless before
> That nerveless hand and that unerring eye.
> Perhaps in admiration for a spirit
> Whose skill matched not his quality of courage,
> Perhaps a magnanimity of soul
> Remindful of the Nibelungenlied;
> But he withheld the sting of his Spandaus,
> And let him go.[9]

Although these tales of valor were cliched and romanticized, if not occasionally fabricated entirely, they reflect a pervasive image of the airplane and airpower between the wars—an image as powerful within the Air Corps as it was without. For the military disciples of the winged gospel, the airplane was a transforming technology, and the men who rode it into battle were a special breed of warrior. They believed that they and their higher form of combat had outgrown the earth-bound confines of traditional military institutions.

Precisely this belief—that the revolutionary potential of the airplane was stifled within the U.S. Army—led officers like Billy Mitchell to conclude after World War I that military aviation deserved and required an independent service organization on a par with the Army and Navy. Before the war, then-Captain Mitchell (along with 1st Lts. Henry H. Arnold and Benjamin D. Foulois) had argued just the opposite. Mitchell told the House Committee on Military Affairs in 1913 that "it would be a mistake to start a separate corps" for military aviation, since the Air Service's position within the Signal Corps provided everything the airmen needed at the time. Moreover, Mitchell noted, "The offensive value of this thing has not yet been proved."[10] After the war, however, Mitchell reversed positions completely.

One flight over the lines gave me a much clearer impression of how the armies were laid out than any amount of traveling around on the ground. A very significant thing to me was that we could cross the lines of these contending armies in a few minutes in our airplane, whereas the armies had been locked in the struggle, immovable, powerless to advance, for three years. To even stick one's head over the top of the trench invited death. This whole area over which the Germans and French battled was not more than sixty miles across. It was as though they kept knocking their heads against a stone wall, until their brains were dashed out. They got nowhere, as far as ending the war was concerned.

It looked as though the war would keep up indefinitely until either the airplanes brought an end to the war or the contending nations dropped from sheer exhaustion.[11]

Although the war ended far more from exhaustion than airpower, Mitchell became a convert to the belief that the airplane heralded a new era of military art: "The air force has ceased to remain a mere auxiliary service for the purpose of assisting an army or navy in the execution of its task. The air force rises into the air in great masses of airplanes. Future contests will see hundreds of them in one formation. They fight in line, they have their own weapons and their own way of using them, special means of communications, signaling, and of attacking."[12]

Mitchell was especially critical of the way air units had been organized during the war— distributed as accessories to ground units. Such organization, Mitchell realized, cemented the airplane's subservience to ground forces and therefore kept it from realizing its true potential as an independent weapon. He concluded that the only hope for American airpower, and hence the nation itself, was for the Air Service to gain its independence from the Army.[13]

It was a tall order. The Air Service entered the return to normalcy very much a part of the ground-based Army. Through most of the 1920s the officers who held the post of chief of the Army Air Service had begun their careers as ground officers, and most of them entered the office not knowing how to fly. The selection of Air Service leadership, coupled with the distribution of air units throughout the ground Army, led Mitchell and his followers to regard their branch as the captive of outsiders—especially the infantry, which they considered to be a conservative and short-sighted bureaucracy unwilling or unable to appreciate the military value of this wondrous new technology. Airmen soon came to see their branch as the unwanted and ill-treated stepchild of the War Department and decided that their most fruitful recourse was to run away from home.

Mitchell's Martyrdom and Testament

Mitchell's call was quickly taken up by other airmen, but never as forcefully or brazenly. Shortly after the war, Mitchell's continuous and public criticism of the War Department general staff and even the chief of the Air Service earned him the eternal animosity of his superiors and the admiration of many younger officers. He never missed an opportunity to point out that the Air Service's chief—Maj. Gen. Charles T. Menoher, a former infantry officer—was not a pilot and consequently had no understanding of military aviation. The on-going feud eventually drove Menoher to resign the post in 1921.

Menoher's replacement was Maj. Gen. Mason Patrick, another nonflier but a masterful administrator who had directed the Air Service toward the end of World War I. Patrick, however, turned out to be more independent than either Mitchell or the general staff had expected. He refused Mitchell's demands for special command prerogatives as senior flying officer in the Air Service, upon which Mitchell threatened to resign. Patrick called the bluff by accepting the resignation, which Mitchell quickly withdrew. Then, at age fifty-nine, Patrick earned his wings in his spare time, thus making Mitchell the second senior flying officer in the service and earning Patrick a loyalty from the junior officers that Menoher never had. He then dealt with Mitchell largely by sending him on numerous projects and inspections far from Washington.[14]

Patrick's major aim was to bolster what he perceived to be an Air Service rapidly deteriorating from obsolescent airplanes and the lack of a coherent policy for using them. As eager as Mitchell to develop the military potential of aviation, Patrick was far more tactful and politically skilled. He gradually convinced Secretary of War John Weeks to investigate the possibility of increasing the size of the Air Service and segregating all air units from ground organizations and into a special reserve force.

More importantly, Patrick started educating the general staff in a concept that would later prove central to the bombing advocates: the distinction between air *service* and air *force.* The air service, as conceived by Patrick and his staff officers (including bombing proponent Maj. Carl Spaatz), comprised aviation that worked directly in conjunction with ground troops, including aerial reconnaissance, artillery spotting, and close ground support. Air Force (and the term was often capitalized), on the other hand, comprised aviation that was capable of working independently from ground forces, including pursuit (combat with enemy aircraft), attack (combat with enemy ground forces), and especially bombardment. "These branches of aviation," explained Spaatz, "strike independently at enemy centers such as cities, factories, railroad yards, docks, etc., without regard to location or operation of ground troops. In other words it is a 'Force' within itself; i.e., 'Air Force.'"[15]

In 1923 Patrick recommended that the War Department recast the Air Service as an organization composed of 20 percent air service and 80 percent air force. Secretary of War Weeks quickly established a board, directed by Maj. Gen. William Lassiter, to consider Patrick's proposal. The Lassiter Board recommended that the War Department increase the Air Service's size along Patrick's guidelines (to twenty-five hundred planes from about fourteen hundred, and to four thousand officers from about nine hundred). Although the board failed to endorse all of Patrick's proposed reorganization, it did accept the central distinction between air service and air force, and the tenet that bombardment and pursuit units should be available for strategic missions that might be completely independent of ground forces.[16]

In response to the Lassiter report, the House of Representatives appointed its own committee, chaired by Rep. F. H. Lampert of Wisconsin, to investigate the Air Service's organization in 1924. The Lampert Committee's key witness was Mitchell, then serving as assistant chief of the Air Service. Mitchell's testimony included a blistering indictment of his superiors, and he accused the War and Navy Departments of strangling the Air Service out of fear that it might put them out of business. "The organization that we have in this country now ties aviation to older existing agencies, which it promises either to completely supplant or put entirely out of business," Mitchell told the committee. "The result is that all the organization that we have in this country really now is for the protection of vested interests against aviation. That is about the size of it."[17]

Mitchell also accused the Army both of threatening uncooperative airmen with disciplinary action if they spoke their minds under oath to the committee, and of being totally incapable of formulating an intelligent policy for military aviation.[18] Mitchell's charges, which were thinly substantiated and clearly insubordinate, seemed out of line even to the spectacle-hungry press. Warned the New York Times: "If General Mitchell does not use more discretion in carrying on his campaign for aviation before the investigating committee, he will injure his cause and forfeit the respect of his supporters, besides inviting discipline by them."[19]

Just as the Lampert hearings were ending, Weeks announced that Col. James E. Fechet would replace Mitchell as assistant chief of the Air Service. While it was true that Mitchell was up for a scheduled rotation, his reassignment to San Antonio, Texas, was widely regarded as disciplinary.[20]

From Fort Sam Houston, Mitchell, now accustomed to making headlines, continued to issue increasingly radical statements to the press. Finally, when a Navy aircraft disappeared over the Pacific in September, 1925, and the dirigible Shenandoah crashed over Ohio killing fourteen aboard a few days later, Mitchell told reporters that the accidents were the "direct result of incompetency, criminal negligence and almost treasonable administration of the National Defense by the Navy and War Departments."[21]

Weeks, Patrick, and especially Pres. Calvin Coolidge had had enough. Mitchell was charged and tried in a widely publicized court-martial; the charge was insubordination, and there was never any question, even among Mitchell's closest supporters, of his guilt. Spaatz, for example, later recalled: "All of us who were friends of his—admired him—felt that the court martial was justified. He brought it on himself and I think he did it deliberately. We hated to see him court martialed, but at the same time, had no quarrel with the administration of military justice as it applied to him."[22]

Mitchell was found guilty, relieved of his command, and reduced to half pay. He resigned in February, 1926.

Patrick, meanwhile, was working the situation with much less fanfare but considerably greater success. While Mitchell had called for independence, Patrick told the Lampert Committee that some sort of unified air force would probably exist some day, but that the current situation hardly called for such a "radical reorganization." Instead, Patrick suggested an evolutionary Army Air *Corps,* whose position within the War Department would be similar to that of the Marine Corps within the Navy.[23]

In response to the Lampert hearings (and perhaps hoping to draw attention from Mitchell's impending court-martial), President Coolidge in the fall of 1925 appointed yet another board to examine military aviation affairs, this one under an old friend, Dwight W. Morrow. In four weeks of hearings, the Morrow Board called many of the witnesses who had recently appeared before the Lampert Committee, and unsurprisingly heard much of the same testimony. The board distinguished itself, however, by managing to release its report two weeks before the Lampert Committee.

Although the councils drew on almost identical evidence, the Lampert and Morrow studies came to very different conclusions. The Lampert report argued for creating an entirely new military hierarchy in the form of a unified Department of National Defense. The new department would subsume the Army and Navy, as well as a newly independent Air Force, which would be coequal with the two older branches.[24] The Morrow Board, on the other hand, recommended a reorganization very much along the lines Patrick had suggested: an Air Corps within the War Department, a new assistant secretary of war for aviation matters, greater representation for aviation on the general staff, extra flight pay, and a five-year expansion program.[25]

The eventual legislative compromise came after a bruising struggle between three separate bills, and finally resembled Patrick's proposal much more than Mitchell's. The Air Corps Act of 1926, based mostly on the Morrow Board's report, created an Army Air Corps with an increase in size from 900 to 1,514 officers and from 9,760 to 16,000 enlisted men. The personnel expansion was to come largely at the expense of the rest of the Army, since the act made no allowance for an overall increase in the War Department's size. A five-year plan set a goal of eighteen hundred serviceable airplanes. The act further required that the Air Corps chief, two of the corps's three brigadier generals, and 90 percent of the officers be certified pilots—a clear nod to the aviators' contention that only a flyer could truly understand aviation issues.[26]

The Air Corps's frontline bureaucratic battle was granted a temporary cease-fire by the Air Corps Act and its five-year plan. Satisfied, Patrick retired the following year. However, many airpower enthusiasts were not content with the creation of the Army Air Corps. They still wanted an air force independent of the Army. Earlier in the 1920s, Mitchell and his followers had promoted several aerial duties as grounds for autonomy. Mitchell had at first argued for a Department of Aeronautics, pointing to the great benefits of airborne communications, supply lines, transport, and the vulnerability of ships to attack by enemy aircraft.[27] To prove the point, he had staged several highly publicized demonstrations of airplanes' abilities to sink old warships, including the captured German battleship *Ostfriesland.*

After his court-martial and resignation, however, the direction of Mitchell's thinking changed. In a preface to his World War I memoirs, Mitchell tried a new argument for an independent air force:

War itself is a continuance by physical means of an altercation between nations, and its object is to impress one's will upon the enemy. This can only be done by seizing, controlling or paralyzing his vital centers, that is, his great cities and the sources of raw materials, his manufactories, his food, his production, his means of transportation and his railways and steamship lines.

. . . Air power can attack the vital centers of the opposing country directly, completely destroying and paralyzing them. Very little of a great nation's strength has to be expended in conducting air operations. A few men and comparatively few dollars can be used for bringing about the most terrific effect ever known against opposing vital centers.

The power of airplane bombs, and the use of chemical weapons will unquestionably decide a future war.[28]

Mitchell used the terms *vital centers* or *nerve centers* seven times in the four-page preface.

Rather than an air force devoted to communication, supply, or even attacking ships, Mitchell now proposed an air force whose primary mission was to attack logistical hubs far behind enemy lines. He contended that massive attacks on these vital centers would so panic the population and disrupt industrial activity that it would completely strip the enemy nation of its ability to wage war, thus providing a quick and relatively inexpensive victory (measured in both lives and dollars) to whomever had the aerial resources to strike first.

The image of a lethal bolt from the blue was not original to Mitchell. The first expressions of this idea had come from across the Atlantic.[29] One source of inspiration was RAF general Hugh Trenchard, who greatly shaped the bombing arm of the RAF in the years after the war. Mitchell had met "Boom" Trenchard during the war and greatly respected him and his ideas on aerial warfare. He was particularly taken with Trenchard's conviction that airplanes were inherently offensive weapons, and that the bomber in particular could exert a psychological, or "moral effect" that was "out of all proportion to the [physical] damage which it can inflict."[30]

Mitchell also admired Italian air force proponent and agitator Giulio Douhet. Douhet's 1921 *Command of the Air* portrayed naval and ground forces as essentially defensive factors in any future war, with all offensive operations assumed by the air force. Bombers, Douhet argued, would be certain to reach their targets—he, too, called them "vital centers"—and cause such widespread destruction among enemy forces and cities that victory could come in a matter of days, long before any ground forces even got within striking distance of one another.[31]

Mitchell corresponded with both Trenchard and Douhet, and by 1927 the three had arrived together at a vision of air warfare that would greatly affect their respective military services. Mitchell's court-martial had served to radicalize him and his followers, and lend his emerging ideas on strategic bombing the credence of a martyr's testament. Mitchell became an icon to his disciples, a mythic symbol of everything airpower could be but had not yet achieved. In the memory of Hap Arnold, a prominent Mitchell follower who would later command the Army Air Forces during World War II:

> There were three Billy Mitchells: there was the man they court-martialed, not personally known to the public, who wouldn't rest until

he became a martyr; there was Mitchell the air prophet, not in the sense of popular but of highly scientific forecasts. And then there was the third Mitchell, who included the first two, but added something. This was the Billy the public loved, and whom the Air Corps loved. Quite aside from his fine war record and his leaping mind, this Mitchell was the hero who had always had the American public on his side—the dashing, colorful doer-of-deeds who cut red tape, defied the stuffy boss, snapped his fingers in the face of authority, cried, "What, I can't sink your ships?" and sent them to the bottom; exposed the evil interests, paused in the midst of it all to marry the charming girl, and in short, did everything Billy did. After he had gone too far, for a man in uniform, and his superiors had crushed him, the public and the Air Corps still loved him, and Billy, in civs, went right on fighting.[32]

The School

In early 1920 the War Department authorized the Air Service to establish several service schools, the most important being the Air Service School at Langley Field, Virginia. From the outset the school was conceived as a gateway for up-and-coming officers to enter the ranks of higher staff work and leadership positions within the Air Service. As the coursework and personnel at the school evolved, the name was changed to the Air Service Field Officers' School in mid-1920, then to the Air Service Tactical School in the fall of 1922, and finally to the Air Corps Tactical School (ACTS) in 1926.[33]

In 1922 the ACTS curriculum covered twenty subjects in 1,345 hours of instruction. The courses emphasized tactics and techniques, with 160 hours each devoted to observation, pursuit, and bombardment aviation, and 136 hours to combined air tactics. Not surprisingly, technical issues commanded a great deal of the students' time, with 200 hours of coursework on aeronautical engineering. There were also courses on supply operations, navigation, meteorology, and photography.[34]

However, as is common with military schools of this type, the curriculum was shaped as much by the students as the faculty. A student one year might be an instructor the next, and vice-versa. So, although the school existed ostensibly to educate its students, it also explicitly served as an incubator for new military doctrine.

During the 1920s, the ACTS thus became the place where Air Corps leaders (many of them part of Mitchell's circle) worked out the intricacies of their new form of warfare, and then spread the gospel among those officers passing through the school as students. The ACTS curriculum thus clearly reflected the thinking of the Mitchell camp—and how that thinking changed.

Throughout the mid-1920s, Mitchell voiced the belief that the primary mission of an air force was to maintain aerial supremacy through the use of pursuit (fighter) aircraft to control the contested airspace, thus allowing friendly observation and transport operations while denying those same operations to the enemy. "Pursuit aviation," he explained in 1920, "is the basis of an air force, just as infantry is the base on which an army rests."[35] During that same period, the primary texts at the ACTS likewise identified the maintenance of aerial supremacy as the principal job of the Air Service. A 1923 ACTS text, "Fundamental Conceptions of the Air Service," explicitly identified air supremacy as the Air Service's primary mission; the text suggested, à la Mitchell, that this required considerable independence from the Army, since the Air Force "operates more or less independently of the ground troops."[36]

Conversely, the ACTS courses in bombardment during this period clearly identified bombing as a secondary Air Service function. The text used in the bombardment course, for example, gave strategic bombing a lower priority than even the support of ground troops, declaring that it "must not take precedence over the support of ground operations." It even questioned the morality of targeting civilian population centers.[37]

But as Mitchell's thoughts turned to the image of an enemy country laid waste by massive bombing attacks against its vital centers, his vision of strategic bombing and its central role in Air Corps identity gradually dominated the thinking at the ACTS. By the summer of 1925 (after Mitchell had been "exiled" to Texas), the spirit of the school was already turning away from aerial supremacy and toward strategic bombing. However, the school's conception of bombing vital centers differed in one significant way from that of Mitchell, Douhet, and Trenchard. Rather than emphasizing the terrorizing effects of bombing, ACTS officers began making the doctrine more palatable to American audiences by arguing that future bombardment would be accurate enough to make the material effects—the actual destruction of enemy factories, railways, and so on—its principal military value. In July, the school's commandant, Maj. Oscar Westover, objected to one bombardment text's assertion that the psychological effect of bombing industrial centers was far greater than its physical effect—an assertion that Trenchard made often.[38] Westover argued, somewhat optimistically: "This is an old saying completely out of date. While it may have been true during the war, the school holds that it is no longer true. Bombing has developed to the point where it is accurate and destructive."[39]

The following year, the school's Combined Air Force text drew Air Corps thinking farther away from the aerial superiority mission, and at the same time laid down what would become another fundamental tenet of American bombing doctrine. Whereas aerial superiority had made pursuit aviation the core of the air force, the 1926 text stated that bomber technology would soon make it impossible for pursuit aircraft effectively to stop a concerted bombing attack. Once the fighters were in the air, at least some bombers would always get through. The only way to "defend" against enemy bombers, the text argued, was to destroy them on the ground, presumably by preemptive bombing.[40] Gradually, bombardment aviation was becoming the central component of the concept of air forces.

During the next several years, these two principles—that the bomber will always get through and that it has the ability to destroy materially an enemy's ability to wage war—became central to Air Corps bombing doctrine, just as bombing became central to the Air Corps's institutional identity and its quest for bureaucratic independence. By 1930, for example, ACTS students were learning, in language that clearly echoed Mitchell's, that "*Bombardment aviation, under the circumstances anticipated in a major war, is the basic arm of the Air Force. . . .* There will probably be certain vital objectives comparatively limited in number which, if destroyed, will contribute most to the success of combined arms of the Nation. . . . [B]ombardment aviation can operate at distances far beyond the front lines of the ground forces and against objectives outside the immediate concern of an army or even a group of armies . . . to secure the desired results against the *vital* objectives."[41]

The course also made clear that the proper use of bombing was strategic rather than tactical. Although situations might arise that required bombers to attack ground units close to the front, the ACTS regarded enemy ground forces as unsuitable targets, too "tactical" to reap the maximum benefits of bombardment.[42] The school's doctrine writers increasingly held that vital centers far behind enemy lines were the only proper targets for air force bombing.

During the 1920s, strategic bombing became the warfare of choice at the Air Corps Tactical School. Driven by the desire to find an independent mission for an independent air force, and by the vision of airpower that Mitchell articulated after his court-martial, ACTS theorists gradually abandoned aerial supremacy as the Air Corps's primary mission in favor of the strategic bombing of an enemy's industrial infrastructure. The school's doctrine as of 1930 served the Air Corps's bureaucratic needs well.

It is easy to see how this vision also harmonized with Air Corps's culture at the time. With strategic bombing, the knights of the sky offered a technologically advanced and humane escape from the horrors of trench warfare. Future wars would be won not by the brute force of attrition, but by the expert application of a wondrous new technology in the hands of highly trained military professionals. The problem was that in the late 1920s the necessary technology existed only in the airmen's dreams.

Chapter 3
The Bombers' Technology

Long-range bombing proponents within the Air Corps were captivated by aviation technology, and the futuristic vision of strategic bombing that they advocated reflected that enthusiasm. Nevertheless, their conception of strategic bombing in 1930 was considerably beyond the technological capabilities of the day. In order for the strategic-bombing vision to perform its military and bureaucratic functions, the Air Corps had to make it technologically feasible. This meant designing, developing, and producing a delivery system—a technological system that would accurately and reliably place bombs on target in spite of vigorous enemy defenses.

Broadly conceived, the bomb delivery system was a colossal network of machines and objects, including bombs, bomb racks, defensive machine guns, radios, navigational slide rules, and insulated flight clothing—not to mention the production engineering needed to manufacture all of that hardware. At its simplest level, the system consisted of a relatively fast, high-altitude, long-range airplane, and a precise optical bombsight.

Organizations

During the interwar decades, the Air Corps gradually acquired a diverse network of organizations that formed the nucleus of what would later become a military-industrial-academic complex. Although technical expertise (and the concomitant authority to set the research and development agenda) was distributed among the Air Corps, civilian government agencies, private industry, and educational institutions, the Air Corps itself provided much of the direction for aeronautical research and development.

Materiel Division

The heart of the Air Corps's own technical expertise was its Materiel Division. When the United States entered World War I, the Army had no in-house organization for aviation R&D. At the time, the Army Aviation Section's Engineering Organization in Washington, D.C., consisted of one junior officer and five civilian engineers. However, with the wartime emergency, the War Department established McCook Experimental Field outside of Dayton, Ohio—then the hub of the nation's nascent aircraft industry. By Armistice Day, McCook sported a dynamometer laboratory building, a propeller test lab, a small wind tunnel for calibrating airspeed instruments and studying small airfoils, and several workshops. It employed fourteen officers and 1,335 civilians.[1]

At first, the Signal Corps's Science and Research Division supervised the wartime work at McCook, since the Signal Corps was the Air Service's parent organization. After the war, McCook became the headquarters of the new Engineering Division, which directed research and development for all aspects of military aviation technology, including aircraft, engines, cooling systems, superchargers, propellers, and flight equipment. The Engineering Division was also responsible for testing new airplane prototypes, and thus became the Air Service's primary liaison to industry and its other R&D sources.

With the reorganization of Army aviation under the Air Corps Act of 1926, the Engineering Division expanded into the Materiel Division, which moved the following year to larger facilities at nearby Wright Field.[2] The impressive facilities at Wright Field served not only the Air Corps's technical needs but also its unending quest for good publicity. The Materiel Division conducted popular tours of the forty-six-hundred-acre facility, which housed public viewing areas and a museum to showcase Wright's large wind tunnels. The highlight of the tour was the world's largest propeller test bed and its six-thousand-horsepower motor, which was literally more powerful than a locomotive.[3] These formidable furnishings attracted so much attention from industry that the division had to fight off legislation authorizing Wright Field to perform aircraft and equipment tests for private individuals and corporations.[4]

Through the middle 1930s, the complement at Wright Field hovered around ninety officers and one thousand civilians. Development work on the varying flight operations was directed from project offices. The bombing office, for example, usually consisted of one officer, a civilian engineer, and a stenographer. The project offices were the central points of contact between the division and private contractors, and the engineers who worked in those offices would later remember fondly the casual and open flow of ideas. A contractor could easily see or phone the project engineers at Wright to discuss some technical matter, or, if necessary, talk it over with the chief of the Air Corps. Conversely, lieutenants and junior engineers had relatively easy access to company presidents.[5]

By 1939, the number of personnel at Wright had grown to about two thousand (including more than seventeen hundred civilians), and the facilities included separate labs for aircraft, power plants, propellers, armament, photography, flight equipment, materials, aeromedicine, and airborne radio.[6] Just as significant, several of the key bomber proponents who would later lead the Army Air Forces during World War II, including Air Corps generals Hap Arnold, Benjamin Foulois, and Carl Spaatz, commanded the Materiel Division during the interwar years.

National Advisory Committee for Aeronautics

In 1929 the publisher of *Popular Mechanics* magazine asked Assistant Secretary of War F. Trubee Davison to see if the Air Corps might be interested in helping to dispel some popular misconceptions on the dangers of lightning to airplanes in flight. The magazine had already secured the use of the Outdoor Lightning Laboratory of the Ohio Insulator Company in order to conduct tests. When asked, Maj. L. W. McIntosh of the Materiel Division informed Assistant Secretary Davison that such an investigation appeared too general for Air Corps purposes, and added that "if any particular Government support is to be given, it should be through some highbrow outfit, such as the N.A.C.A."[7]

Since its creation in 1915, the National Advisory Committee for Aeronautics (NACA) had served as the basic research arm of Army and Navy aviation.[8] Although NACA was charged with advising and coordinating aeronautical research for all of the federal government, its ties to the Air Corps and the Navy's Bureau of Aeronautics were particularly close. Of the seven permanent seats on NACA's twelve-man Executive Committee, four were held by representatives of the military—including the Air Corps chief and the chief of the Materiel Division, who were always members.[9] Air Corps and Bureau of Aeronautics personnel served on all NACA technical committees, and the military aviation branches maintained close contact with NACA and each other through a constant and vigorous exchange of technical information.[10]

Throughout the 1920s and 1930s, NACA's Executive Committee made a habit of formally asking the Air Corps for prioritized lists of important research projects, and the Air Corps was happy to provide them. Sometimes the Air Corps would transfer funds to NACA for the service, but usually not. In this way, the Air Corps benefited from the enormous amount of NACA research in such areas as the effect of certain fuels on spark plug insulation, the aerodynamic behavior of engine nacelles, techniques for spot welding, the development of new instruments, the pattern of ice formation on the wings and fuselage, and the theoretical and empirical relationship between propeller tip speed and efficiency. The Air Corps also received crucial flight characteristic data on the large bombers of the middle 1930s from NACA's wind tunnels.[11]

To no one's surprise, the Air Corps lobbied hard and successfully in helping NACA muddle through its sundry bureaucratic adversities during the interwar years. In 1925 and 1937, Congress considered legislation to absorb NACA into the Department of Commerce, and in 1932 lame-duck president Herbert Hoover tried to reduce it to a branch of the Bureau of Standards. The Air Corps chiefs consistently supported NACA's independence, often with letters drafted by NACA secretary John F. Victory.[12] In all cases, NACA emerged victorious; the Air Corps was hardly willing to let go what it practically considered to be a basic research branch of the Materiel Division.

Private Industry

From its inception through World War II, the American aviation industry enjoyed and suffered a symbiotic relationship with the military, with practically no boundary between the two. Both the Wright brothers and Glenn Curtiss ran flight schools that trained pilots for the military. Military pilots often shuttled back and forth between industry and the service. Army pilot Reuben Fleet left the service and started a company that became Consolidated Aircraft. Eric Nelson likewise left the Army, became an executive at Boeing, and was joined there by Army aeronautical engineer Charles Monteith. Harry Sutton, a military test pilot, became Fleet's vice president at Consolidated. Some, like James Doolittle, Leigh Wade, and Joseph A.

Cannon, performed flight tests for private aircraft companies while still serving in uniform.[13] For the aircraft industry, the revolving door was already spinning early in the twentieth century.

As far as the Air Corps was concerned, private industry was a priceless source of technical innovation. Research and development on civilian transports often translated into military advances, especially for large, heavy bombers. Boeing's large and successful Monomail transport plane, for example, was easily redesigned as the B-9 bomber. Likewise, the 1935 Douglas B-18 bomber was essentially a militarized version of its successful DC-2 transport.

Through its development contracts with aircraft and engine companies, the Air Corps came to rely on industry to perform the bulk of aeronautical R&D. By the early 1930s, the Materiel Division, though still central to the Army's aviation technology establishment, had relinquished the aircraft design business to private industry.

For the most part, the partnership between the Air Corps and industry was a happy one. The aircraft companies were able to amortize their development costs into their production contracts, and by the late 1930s occasionally enjoyed War Department patronage under special contracts that sidestepped the requirement of competitive bidding. The Air Corps benefited from an almost continuous supply of technically advanced materiel, from improved materials and components to entire airplanes.

The depth of this symbiosis was best illustrated by the Air Corps's primary tension with the industry: the issue of sales abroad. Private companies exist to make money, and profit always comes from having a large number of customers. The Air Corps, on the other hand, was not always at liberty to spend money, and it never wanted any of its international rivals to have airplanes as good as its own. After 1924, when the Curtiss Corporation was discovered to have sold several aircraft engines to the British without notifying the Air Service, all contracts required War Department approval for foreign sales. The Air Corps eventually adopted a policy of not allowing the foreign sale of state-of-the-art aircraft—that is, aircraft that had been in production for less than one year.[14]

But the industry found itself in dire straits during the commercially lean years of the late 1920s and early 1930s. With the Air Corps and the Navy cutting back on new purchases, several companies sought approval to sell state-of-the-art airplanes abroad. How the Air Corps handled such requests reveals much about how it valued the industry's well-being. In the spring of 1934, after having lost on a competitive bid to produce its YB-10 and YB-12 bombers for the Air Corps, Glenn Martin asked permission to sell his bombers to Brazil, China, and the "U.S. Soviet of Russia." Martin pleaded that

> From the beginning, this Company has maintained secrecy as far as possible on all features pertaining to the above airplane, in the interest of the U.S. Government. We have, up until now, consistently refused lucrative foreign markets for this airplane, believing the U.S. Government preferred the exclusive use of the ship and would negotiate additional business with this Company to a sufficient extent to prevent serious disruption of our skilled personnel. . . .
>
> Since our specifications are disclosed by public bidding and since we are greatly in need of work to keep our shop open and avoid the laying off of part or all of our 2100 employees, we respectfully urge the State Department to give us permission at an early date to sell our airplanes [abroad].[15]

Under the letter and spirit of the Air Corps's policy, the requested relief was impossible. The bombers were then still service test models, and had been in production less than a year. "They represent," warned Air Corps chief Benjamin Foulois, "the most advanced bomber development in the world today."[16] Remarkably, Foulois nevertheless recommended that the War and State Departments approve the sale:

> The shortage of aircraft in the Army Air Corps is fast becoming critical. This is particularly true with respect to bombardment aircraft. With no further business in sight, The Glenn L. Martin Company is faced with a shut-down on completion of its present contract with the Army Air Corps. This shut-down would throw approximately two thousand aircraft workers out of employment and remove one of the most important aircraft manufactures from the field.
>
> Though I am loathe to recommend it, if the Air Corps cannot be equipped with the Martin Bomber which is by far the most efficient airplane of its type in existence today, in justice to the Glenn L. Martin Company and to keep these facilities available for national emergency

permission should be given them to sell their bomber to any other customer, foreign or domestic, who desires to purchase it, and all government restrictions as to its sale abroad should be removed.[17]

A similar request from Lockheed for foreign sale of its Electra transport was approved a short time later despite charges that the company had been dealing secretly with German airplane magnate Anthony Fokker to convert the Electra into a bomber, and that blueprints for the prototype had been back-dated and smeared with grease to make them appear older.[18]

The Air Corps's protection of the industry is as revealing as it was far-seeing. Foulois and others believed that the military threat of state-of-the-art aircraft in the hands of potential enemies was less grave than the threat of losing any of the large aircraft companies to economic ruin. They were probably right.

Academe

Aeronautical research and development gradually moved from the workbench to the laboratory during the interwar years, and the American aviation enterprise gradually demanded more academically oriented aeronautical engineers—people who could discuss fluid dynamics and mechanical stresses in quantitative terms. The Air Corps was no exception.

But aeronautical engineering was an extremely new endeavor in the 1920s and had found little room in the academy. In 1922 only five universities offered courses in aeronautical engineering, and only two granted degrees.[19] In 1926 the Daniel Guggenheim Fund for the Promotion of Aeronautics, built largely on the enthusiasm of Guggenheim's two aviator sons, deliberately set out to change that. With $2.8 million in hand, the fund endowed seven major schools for aeronautics in four years: at Stanford, the California Institute of Technology (Caltech), the University of Michigan, the Massachusetts Institute of Technology (MIT), the University of Washington, the Georgia School (later Institute) of Technology, and the University of Akron. All of the Guggenheim schools but the last (which focused on lighter-than-air flight) were very successful, and they formed an educational establishment that remained central to American aeronautics through World War II. Caltech's Theodore von Kármán— brought to Caltech with Guggenheim funding—and his group played major roles in the development of several of Douglas's large transports. Stanford's propeller research became a centerpiece of NACA's work on the subject. The school at the University of Washington developed close ties to Boeing in Seattle, and practically every Boeing model underwent some wind-tunnel testing at the school. Michigan and MIT concentrated on producing engineers for consumption by industry and government. By 1942 a majority of the nation's senior aeronautical researchers were Guggenheim graduates; NACA's Langley Laboratory alone employed fifteen MIT alumni.[20]

The Materiel Division, of course, kept in close touch with the goings-on at Caltech, Stanford, and MIT. Air Corps officers reported regularly on academic research projects of interest, and the chiefs of the Air Corps and the Materiel Division were often invited to visit the facilities.[21] The Air Corps began sending Regular Army officers to these schools in 1937 for graduate training, and over the next two years thirty of them took courses in aeronautical engineering, meteorology, and mathematics at Caltech, the University of Michigan, Stanford, and MIT.[22]

The research performed at colleges and universities during the 1920s and 1930s probably was not critical to the development of bombardment aviation in the Army Air Corps. The very basic research typical of academe had a less immediate impact than the development work performed by the aircraft companies, and the most important of the basic work could as easily have been done by NACA. However, the academic production of aeronautical engineers was absolutely central to the Air Corps, and was beyond the capabilities of the Materiel Division, NACA, or the industry. Without the universities and the help from Guggenheim, the military and civilian industry would not have had the engineers they needed. And without the engineers, the enterprise literally would not have gotten off the ground.

The Network

The decentralized character of Air Corps R&D during this period makes it extremely difficult to identify any coherent research policy. With so many actors, it is impossible to distinguish a single research program, or even perhaps a clear research establishment. This difficulty, coupled with the low funding levels compared with expenditures in World War II, have left the impression that research and development for military aviation was practically nonexistent before Pearl Harbor.

The schematic diagram, however, tends to conceal the interaction between seemingly disparate parts. The primary factor promoting close communication was the simple fact that the administrators of these various entities—the Materiel Division, NACA, the aircraft companies, and the universities—were often the same people. The Air Corps and Materiel Division chiefs were always members of NACA's Executive Committee, as were prominent members of the industry. The assistant secretary of war responsible for aviation, F. Trubee Davison, was one of the Guggenheim Fund trustees for the duration of the fund's existence.

This constant exchange of information meant that Air Corps leaders were always aware of the latest technical possibilities, and NACA, the universities, and industry were ever mindful of the Air Corps's needs. Certain bomber proponents, like Hap Arnold, were also extremely interested in technical matters, and made every effort to enhance the Air Corps's technical capabilities by increasing engineering staffs and promoting new ideas themselves.[23]

Thus, despite the seemingly disjointed nature of the Air Corps's R&D establishment, it was possible to promote coherent, and sometimes detailed, research programs. As strategic bombing became the Air Corps's raison d'être, it also became the priority for just about everyone else in the business.

Early Bombers

The technological problems facing bomber development were easy to delineate. Successful bombers had to be fast, or at least fast enough to prevent attacking pursuit planes from flying circles around them. They also had to have the range to be able to attack distant targets. If war broke out with Japan, American bombers would likely have to cover thousands of miles of Pacific before reaching their targets. Against a European enemy, or perhaps Great Britain, bombers might have to fly across the entire Atlantic to wreak their havoc. Finally, the bomber would have to carry enough bombs to attack the enemy's vital centers to good effect. Precisely how much was enough, however, no one knew.

But aside from these obvious goals, the aspiring bomber designer of the 1920s had little to go on. Strategic bombing had no precedents, so there were no ground rules by which to decide how much was enough.

Nor was there any a priori method by which such parameters could be calculated. Designers were further confounded by the fact that, as with all engineering development, designing the optimal machine entails a series of trade-offs. In the case of the bomber, increasing load tends to decrease speed and range, and vice versa. And without a general idea of how bombing would be done, it was impossible to know confidently which compromises would be advantageous and which would be disastrous.

In the face of such unknowns, the Air Corps's Materiel Division engineers at Wright Field adopted what would become a classic research strategy: work on those areas that will be likely to help no matter how doctrine evolves later. General improvements, such as increasing aircraft speed, range, load, and other performance characteristics could be derived in several ways.

One method for increasing speed was to reduce drag on the airframe. The most immediate way of reducing drag was to remove unnecessary protuberances or structures that might interrupt the airstream. Most World War I–era aircraft were externally braced biplanes with struts and wires that supported their wings. These proved to be prime sources of drag in flight. Designers during the 1920s therefore worked hard to remove external wing braces by cantilever design (in which the wings are supported by internal structures) or monocoque construction (in which they are supported by the skin of the aircraft itself). Further general improvements came with the conversion from biplanes to monoplanes, with the additional speed more than compensating for the reduced lift. By the mid-1930s, drag was cut enormously by installing retractable landing gear, despite the newer gear's greater production and maintenance costs.

Another way to increase speed was to improve engine performance. At the beginning of World War I, the most powerful engine in general use was about eighty horsepower. At war's end, the best practical engines put out about 400 horsepower. Over the next ten years engine power rose to 500 or 600 horsepower, with even higher energy engines on the way.[24]

High altitudes are another place to go for better aircraft performance. As the air gets thinner, drag decreases and an airplane gains about 1 percent in speed per thousand feet of altitude. Moreover, being able to fly several thousand feet higher than your adversary carries obvious tactical advantages. The problem is that aircraft engines tend to choke for lack of oxygen in the thin air at high altitudes. The Materiel Division focused its attention on engine superchargers—blowers that compress the air before it enters the combustion chamber, thereby restoring some of the engine power otherwise lost at high altitudes. Superchargers were first developed in France during World War I, and the information was shared with American engineers. General Electric first produced them in the United States, and tested them at the top of Pike's Peak during the war. Mounted on a 350-horsepower Liberty engine, the supercharger delivered sea-level power at fourteen thousand feet. Although the armistice temporarily halted further development, improvement of the supercharger was a high priority in both military and civilian aviation from 1919 until the jet engine made it unnecessary after World War II.[25]

Another area ripe for general improvement was propeller technology. While in the air, the optimal pitch of the propeller blades varies from one flight environment to another. One pitch bites the right amount of air for takeoff, another is used for high-speed flight, and still other pitches are needed for optimal performance at different altitudes. Through World War I, propellers consisted of a single piece of solid wood with blades locked at a fixed pitch. This fixed pitch was a necessary compromise between the various optimal pitches, and thus pulled the plane through the air at less than peak efficiency most of the time. In the mid-1920s, Frank Caldwell of the Hamilton Standard Company began experimenting with a propeller hub and removable metal blades that permitted the ground crew to change the pitch before takeoff, set in anticipation of the plane's most likely maneuvers for that flight. In 1928 Caldwell produced a two-position hub that allowed the pilot to switch between a high and low pitch setting in flight. And in 1934, Caldwell's group devised a feedback governor that automatically varied the pitch to maintain a constant number of revolutions per minute, thus keeping the propeller at nearly the optimum speed for all maneuvers. This same device was later modified to allow "full feathering," meaning that the propeller blades on a dead engine on a multiengine aircraft could be rotated so that they would ride edge-on into the wind, almost eliminating their drag and making the job of the remaining engines a little easier.[26] Virtually every military aircraft from the early 1930s through World War II benefited from the performance of Hamilton Standard variable-pitch propellers.

This sort of development work, including other all-purpose innovations like wing flaps and gear brakes, consumed the majority of the Materiel

Division's resources during the 1920s. From 1920 to 1929, the division devoted an average of 52.9 percent of its yearly "Experimental Development" budget toward all-purpose developments, while spending an average of 33.7 percent on new airplane models.[27] Work on new aircraft was also hindered by the existence of Great War surplus and a Congress disinclined to spend precious dollars on new models when perfectly good old ones were already in stock. The bomber proponents in the Air Service were able to acquire a few new types during this period, though far fewer than they sought.

Martin Bombers

The most successful American bombers produced in the early 1920s came from the Glenn L. Martin Company. The Martin series of early bombers—all strut-braced biplanes with seventy-one foot wingspans and two four-hundred-horsepower Liberty engines—could carry fifteen hundred pounds of bombs at about a hundred miles per hour.

At the time, the War Department regularly farmed out production contracts of the same model to manufacturers not responsible for the original design. Companies like Curtiss and Aeromarine therefore produced many of the Martin bombers. Although substantially identical, these planes bore different designations—MB-2, NB-2, and NBS-1. Some 130 of this standard bomber were built.[28]

The NB-2 was the aircraft that Billy Mitchell used in his bombing test against battleships at Hampton Roads, Virginia, in the summer of 1921. But the airplane's performance fell far short of the big, fast heavies that bomber proponents envisioned. By then, however, Mitchell had something else in the works.

The Barling Bomber

Walter Barling was a British airplane designer who had helped design an immense but unflyable bomber during World War I. He had also met Billy Mitchell, who persuaded him to emigrate to the United States after the armistice. After Barling arrived in America in 1919, Mitchell met with him again to ask if he could design a bomber that could single-handedly sink a battleship. Barling quickly sketched out a preliminary design.[29]

Mitchell, keenly aware of the value of large aircraft for public relations, was impressed by the sheer size of Barling's model and took it immediately to the Materiel Division. The division, at Mitchell's urging, began soliciting bids for construction of the plane in May, 1920. The Witteman-Lewis Company of Teterboro, New Jersey, won the competition with a bid to build two of the bombers for a total of $375,000. The company in turn hired Barling to serve as the project's chief engineer. Although technically an employee of Witteman-Lewis, he reported directly to the Materiel Division.

Before Witteman-Lewis began fabricating the prototype, Barling built a scale model of the bomber, now dubbed XNBL-1 (Experimental Bomber, Long-Range-1) in 1921 at the Engineering Division's facilities at Wright Field. Wind-tunnel tests there in early 1922 indicated that, with slight adjustments to the tail and rudder, the airplane should be capable of ninety-six miles per hour—one mile per hour faster than required in the Air Service specification.

So close was Barling's relationship to the Materiel Division that, when the time arrived to build the prototype, the division insisted on coproducing the bomber with Witteman-Lewis. The company contracted to fabricate the parts in New Jersey and then ship them to Wright Field, where members of the Materiel Division staff would assemble them. This arrangement caused numerous complications. For example, no single part could be more than thirteen-and-a-half feet tall since all of the pieces had to fit through the railway tunnels between New Jersey and Ohio. Barling shuttled frequently between Wright and Teterboro, trying to coordinate the construction and to incorporate last-minute design changes. Upon arrival in Dayton, some of the parts were found to be incompatible, which meant they had to be redesigned and reproduced at considerable expense. The cost of the project soared and the Materiel Division and Witteman-Lewis eventually agreed to reduce their goal to only one prototype at a cost of $525,000.

By April, 1923, all of the parts were ready for assembly at Dayton. The plane took thirty-four engineers ninety-four days to assemble. It was twenty-eight feet long with a 120-foot triplane wingspan and a total of six four-hundred-horsepower Liberty engines. Three of the engines were mounted on either side of the fuselage, two serving as tractors and one as a pusher. The tail alone had a forty-five-foot span, larger than the wingspan of a typical World War I fighter. The upper wing, the largest, was so long that it could not be attached to the fuselage within the hangar; the aircraft had to be moved outdoors for final assembly.

Inside the cockpit, two pilots sat side-by-side. Behind them sat a flight engineer whose job was to monitor the six engines. The aircraft could continue in flight for a short time if one engine went out—provided that the engineer was willing to crawl out on the wing to fix it. Below the pilots sat the bombardier, who peered through the bombsight and informed the pilots of necessary course changes by means of a pencil, a piece of paper, and a rope and pulley.

Perhaps the most innovative design element of the Barling bomber was its specially designed landing gear. At forty-seven thousand pounds loaded, the airplane would have crushed conventional landing gear. Moreover, the optimal angle for the forward gear was different for taxiing and landing. During landings, the gear needed to be farther forward to absorb the shock of hitting the ground, whereas while taxiing, the wheels needed to be shifted back to take pressure off the tail skid. Barling therefore designed an adjustable four-wheel truck for the forward gear. Before landing, one of the pilots would reach down and lower the forward section, causing those wheels to touch down first, absorbing the shock through oil-cylinder dampeners. Shortly thereafter, the two wheels immediately behind would touch down. A similar arrangement is used today in large passenger jets.

The bomber first flew on 22 August 1923. In front of many local spectators and the press, the airplane soared over Wright Field for about half an hour, not climbing much above two thousand feet, and landed easily. The takeoff and landing runs were much shorter than feared. The year before, Air Service chief Mason Patrick had told a congressional committee that the plane might have to be floated by barge down to Houston because that city had the only runway in America long enough to accommodate the huge bomber's anticipated long takeoff and landing rolls.[30] In its first flight, however, the bomber lifted off easily within 320 yards. Overall, the aircraft was capable of carrying a two-thousand-pound load at ninety-seven miles per hour for about twelve hundred miles.

Just as important as the airplane's military flight characteristics was its potential to sell Mitchell's strategic bombing vision to the public. The aircraft was a futuristic behemoth, and Mitchell was keenly aware of its public relations ability to serve both as crowd-pleasing spectacle and hard, mechanical evidence that strategic bombing was a technological reality. Consequently, Mitchell had the Barling bomber spend most of 1924 performing at air shows and air races around the Midwest, including an appearance at the Pulitzer races in St. Louis. He also used the bomber's large cargo capacity to set combination weight and altitude records.[31]

But these demonstrations revealed a serious deficiency: The bomber's six engines were not up to the task of driving its extreme weight to altitudes expected for combat operations. When the plane tried to fly to Washington, D.C., to appear in an air show later that year, it could not clear the Appalachians and had to turn back to Wright Field. By the time it landed, the Barling bomber project was dead.

Congress had been unaware of the bomber project until just before Witteman-Lewis began manufacturing the parts in 1922. When he found out about it, the chairman of the House Subcommittee on Military Appropriations, Rep. Daniel R. Anthony, was furious. He protested both the plane's high cost and the fact that his committee had not been notified of the unusual expenditure. When the project failed to produce a usable bomber, congressional criticism intensified, and Mitchell's boss, General Patrick, was left trying to disown the entire venture. Testifying before Anthony's subcommittee for the 1925 appropriations bill, Patrick could do no more than give the project faint praise. When Anthony asked his general opinion of the bomber's military value, Patrick could only say that is was "quite a unique plane."[32] He also pointed out that the contract had been let a year before he became the Air Service's chief and said that he had no intention of ever building another plane like it.[33]

With funds for further development cut off, the prototype flew very little in 1925 and 1926, and was retired to its specially built hangar in the summer of 1927. That fall it was dismantled and warehoused at Wright Field. When Maj. Hap Arnold became commander of Wright Field in 1928, he came across the crated and decaying airplane. Eager to rid the Air Corps of the embarrassing monument, he asked for permission to scrap it. Due to continuing congressional concerns over the project's management, the War Department refused the request. Undeterred, Arnold then sought permission to dispose of the "XNBL-1," not identifying it as the Barling bomber. Permission was granted, and Arnold had the remains burned forthwith.[34]

Cyclops and Condors

After the failure of the Barling bomber, the Air Corps turned back to more conventional designs. In 1927 and 1928 it flight-tested two new biplane bombers, the B-1 Super Cyclops from Keystone (a newly formed corporate descendant of Huff-Daland) and the B-2 Condor from Glenn Curtiss. Both were considerably larger than the Martin bombers, with eighty-five- and ninety-foot wingspans, respectively. Both were powered by two six-hundred-horsepower engines, could carry about twenty-five hundred pounds of bombs a distance of 700 to 800 miles, and could reach top speeds of 120 to 130 miles per hour. The Condor was the first bomber to incorporate a tail wheel in place of a skid to assist in braking.[35] Later improvements on the Keystone extended the range just past 850 miles—a little better than the Condor.

By 1928, the Air Corps's best was still far short of the ideal bomber envisaged by the bombing advocates. But even though the desired airplane was still lacking, the technical outlook was improving—if only because aircraft designers had more to go on. Biplane designs, for example, were clearly on the way out; the necessary struts and braces created too much drag for the extra lift they delivered. Multiple engines, although more expensive to procure and maintain, held out the promise of both greater range and improved odds of making it home should an engine fail in flight.[36] Fabric covering was also giving way to metal skins. The decreased drag was more than worth the added weight, and damaged metal was far more likely to hold an aerodynamic contour than damaged cloth. And new alloys, like the industrially developed duralumin, seemed to be getting lighter all the time.

Improved materials and techniques came so quickly during the 1920s that some aircraft became obsolete before they made it to prototype. For bombers, the time from design to production could be as much as five years. With aircraft technology so much in flux, bomber procurement remained low through the end of the decade.

Still, biplane bombers like the Cyclops and Condor served the bombing enthusiasts in one crucial respect. Flying out of airfields throughout the country, pilots, bombardiers, and gunners were training daily in the use of machines and techniques for strategic bombing. The Second Bombardment Group, the Air Corps's primary operational bombing wing, produced a small cadre of airmen with groundbreaking experience in finding their targets, flying the approach, dropping their bombs, and protecting one another with defensive fire.[37] To be sure, neither the technology nor the doctrine was yet up to the challenge of enemy fighters, or even of enemy cities, but these early bombers accomplished their mission of keeping the idea of strategic bombing politically and bureaucratically viable.

Early Bombsights

Getting the bombs to their target was only half the job; delivering them accurately onto their targets was the other. This was an extremely difficult technical problem, one that was not truly solved until the development of "smart" ordnance that is guided by radar, laser, or video. For conventional "dumb" bombs, like all of the ordnance used through World War II, the challenge consisted of finding a course that would bring the airplane directly in line with the target, and then determining precisely when to release the bombs so that they fell directly on the target.

Theoretically, the "bombing problem" might seem trivial. Given the aircraft's altitude and ground speed, the range to target, and the acceleration due to gravity, Galilean calculations provide a perfect solution. Under real, and particularly wartime, conditions, however, the problem is nearly impossible, in part because it is extremely difficult to measure the necessary parameters to sufficient precision.

The most difficult variable to measure is ground speed. Since ground speed is actually the resultant vector of true airspeed and wind, one way to calculate this would be to measure its component vectors. Like altitude, airspeed can be calculated by sampling the air rushing past the airplane. The force of the airstream will vary with the airspeed, yielding indicated airspeed. Then, by factoring in the variation due to decreasing pressure at higher altitudes, the pilot or bombardier can determine the true airspeed.

Winds were a much more difficult matter. Under wartime conditions envisaged in the 1930s, it was generally impossible to have accurate wind data in the vicinity of strategic targets at the moment of the bombing. Presumably, wind data would be plentiful where the planes took off, but extrapolating this data to the target proved to be far too imprecise for the purposes of dropping bombs from miles up.

The effect of air resistance could also be troublesome. Ballistic data could be compiled from repeated tests at various altitudes and velocities, but over the course of a fifteen-thousand-foot drop, two bombs of identical design might land hundreds of feet apart due to slight irregularities in the bomb casings, uneven loading of the charges, or a bent stabilizing fin. A salvo of bombs could also be thrown off target if the airplane's attitude deviated even slightly from that held during practice runs. A subtle tilt of the aircraft's nose or a heavy gust of wind at the moment of release could result in bombs falling far from their targets.

Bombsight development suffered during the 1920s for a variety of institutional reasons. For much of the decade, the Air Corps devoted little attention or resources to the problem, preferring instead the more exciting issues of aircraft design. An Air Corps Bombardment Board complained in 1928: "[I]t matters not one whit whether the plane costs $50,000 and the sight $1,000, or whether the sight costs $50,000 and the plane $1,000. It is the combination of bomb sight and airplane which makes the hit. The Board feels that if the bomb sight development had been encouraged as well as experimental airplane development, the status of national defense would be in far better condition than at the present moment. As it is now, our most destructive weapon is impotent at service altitudes; and at the altitudes at which we now operate is handicapped at least 50 per cent by the crude sights employed."[38] Yet, later that same year, a memo from the Air Corps chief's office plainly stated that "[bomb]sights are not an integral part of the airplane nor is such a condition desirable," and suggested that all bombsight development be sloughed off to the Ordnance Department.[39] Finally, bombsight development within the Air Corps also suffered when the Materiel Division's chief engineer for bombsight design, Captain Henry B. Inglis, walked through the revolving door and took a more lucrative position with Sperry Gyroscope in 1928.[40]

Moreover, what had been true for bombardment aircraft was also true for bombsights. While the Air Corps's vision of bombing was still being debated during the early 1920s, its demands for bombsight accuracy were also unclear.

Bombsight designers could draw some suggestions but little encouragement from the airmen's World War I experiences. Most bombing missions had been conducted at relatively low altitudes and speeds, and thus made relatively low demands on bombsight accuracy. Bombing "low and slow" also left a great deal of discretion to bombardiers, who, with practice, learned to judge when to release their bombs at least as accurately as the mechanical bombsights available at the time.[41]

Still, these early sights employed the same basic principle used to aim bombs twenty years later: If the altitude is known, the range to target can be measured not as a linear distance but as an angle from the vertical. With a right angle at the ground, a sighting angle at the airplane, and the altitude-side in between, a right triangle is thus defined with the range as one leg.

The devices used during the war to aid the bombardier's judgment were extremely rudimentary. The earliest bombsights consisted of little more than a pair of nails along the fuselage, set at the correct "dropping angle" to the vertical. Flying at a predetermined altitude and speed, the bombardier simply let the bombs drop when the target was lined up with both nails.

These sights were clearly not up to the task of realizing the Air Corps's vision of strategic bombing. In addition to relying greatly on the personal skill of individual bombardiers, these early sights required the aircraft to drop the bombs from a predetermined altitude and velocity. Their inability to correct for drift (the effect of crosswinds) also forced the aircraft to fly a course either directly with or against the wind.

Sights developed by war's end, and improved during the early 1920s, used a more direct and reliable method of determining ground speed, thus allowing bombers to fly at variable altitudes and speeds. By using a telescope to sight on the target, the bombardier could determine ground speed by measuring how the telescope's angle to the vertical changed over a set period of time. This became known as the "timing method" of determining the dropping angle. Many of the Materiel Division's bombsight designs in the early 1920s used this method.[42]

These early bombsights suffered from several sources of error. In addition to the inaccuracies that could result from the optics or mechanical drives, bombs could also be thrown off target by the pilot's failure to fly the aircraft directly over the target. Even the best pilots were able to "eyeball" a flight path that took them only to within several degrees of a correct dropping point.[43] Even worse, determining ground speed by measuring angles completely placed the accuracy of the drop at the mercy of the bombardier's ability to compare the line from the aircraft to the target against the vertical. If, at inopportune moments during the timing interval, the aircraft pitched, yawed, or accelerated, the bombardier's angular measurements, and thus the bomb load, would be thrown far off. At the low altitudes and speeds of World War I, such errors in calculation might not have translated into large errors in where the bombs fell, but at the higher altitudes and speeds envisioned in the later 1920s, they certainly would. At 120 miles per hour and an altitude of 1,000 feet, a discrepancy of ten miles per hour in the ground speed measurement would only throw a bomb off target by about 100 feet; but that same discrepancy would translate into a 400-foot miss when bombing from 10,000 feet. Rigidly mounted bombsights simply would not permit a sufficiently accurate determination of ground speed for anything more precise than area bombing. If bombardiers were to have even a hope of hitting individual buildings, the bombsight would have to be independently stabilized.

Thus, for much of the 1920s and into the 1930s, the Air Corps's conception of strategic bombing was simply beyond its technological ability. Neither the aircraft nor the bombsights were up to the task of delivering the aerial devastation that Air Corps leaders envisioned. Perhaps even more importantly, the technology of the era failed to provide the bureaucratic armament the airmen needed to convince the rest of the military community, much less the rest of the government, that strategic bombing was a job that was both practicable and the sole responsibility of the Air Corps.

Chapter 4

Political Opportunities and Daylight Precision

As of the early 1930s, the bomber advocates' quest to devote the Air Corps to strategic bombing had been a mixed success at best. Air Corps Tactical School theorists had developed only a general outline of how bombing could win future wars which, though captivating to the technologically enthusiastic, was far too shallow in the technical details necessary to make it a bureaucratically secure military mission. Worse yet, the technology coming from the engineers at the Air Corps's Materiel Division was nowhere near capable of making even that vague vision a reality.

But in the early 1930s, through fortune good and bad, the clouds began to clear as several disparate trends converged to place the bomber even more firmly at the center of the Air Corps's existence.

Watershed, 1933

A variety of political developments during the mid-1930s served, sometimes inadvertently, to advance the cause of strategic bombing. First, as part of the New Deal, the Roosevelt administration diverted $15 million of Public Works Administration money to military aviation in 1933, divided evenly between the Navy and the Air Corps (amounting to roughly 30 percent of the annual Air Corps budget at the time).[1] Over the next few years, the Air Corps spent almost all of that windfall on development and procurement of bombers and attack aircraft.[2]

Second, a long-standing tension between the Air Corps and the Navy came to a head in 1933. At no time would American airpower be more important than during an invasion of the United States. Whether the enemy came by sea or air, the air force would have to control the skies over the coasts. The coastline, however, represented an infinitesimal but well-guarded dividing line between the jurisdiction of the Army and the Navy.[3]

Traditionally, the job of guarding America's coasts from invasion had been easily divided by the two services: The Navy took responsibility for defending the sea lanes along the coast, while the Army controlled a network of artillery emplacements and fortifications that were the nation's shore defenses. There had been little room for interservice rivalry on this matter, since no scenario anticipated the Navy sailing ashore or the Army marching into the ocean.

The military airplane changed all this. If Mitchell's bombing tests had shown anything, it was that airplanes could play a vital role in defending America's coasts from an invading fleet. However, with airplanes as a major component of coast defense, the line of demarcation between the ocean and the land vanished, especially if the invading force came by air. No realistic plan for air defense could expect Navy planes to attack the invaders only as far as the shoreline, and then hand the targets off to their Army colleagues; nor could Army fighters wait patiently for the attackers to cross the beach before engaging them.

The only alternative was to allow Army forces into what had been traditionally Navy territory, and vice versa. The ensuing turf battle lasted for more than twenty years. The coast-defense mission was particularly lucrative during this period due to its inherently defensive nature; it resonated better than offensive missions (like strategic bombing) with an isolation-minded public and Congress.

The war over coast defense was waged in the Joint Army–Navy Board, in the Congress, at times in the Oval Office, and more often in the press. Despite all the rhetoric over the proper use of aircraft in future wars, the debate boiled down to the simple fact that Navy aviators did not want the Air Corps flying over the water, and Army airmen did not want the Navy flying over the ground.

When naval aviation champion Rear Adm. William Moffett wrote a nationally distributed newspaper article arguing that carrier-based airplanes were better able than land-based planes to defend the coasts, he asserted very optimistically that the "extreme mobility of the aircraft carrier" meant that "bombing aircraft can shell shore positions without any chance of their mobile base being struck in return."[4] Five days after Moffett's article appeared, Maj. Carl Spaatz responded with an article entitled "Airplane Carriers Impotent against Shore-Based Aircraft."[5] Spaatz argued that aircraft carriers were fatally handicapped by their inability to launch more than one plane at a time (as opposed to an airfield), and that unlike Air Corps bases, the Navy's floating aerodromes were susceptible to sinking. He also argued that a coast-defense system based on aircraft carriers would require an additional set of ships to protect the carriers themselves, conveniently overlooking the bomber proponents' usual argument that airplanes, presumably even carrier-based airplanes, could defend against anything. Spaatz suggested to his superiors that the article would better illustrate the aircraft carrier's vulnerabilities if accompanied by a photo of a carrier with a formation of bombers superimposed above it.[6]

Such bickering had continued throughout the 1920s, and repeated efforts to untangle the two services' responsibilities for coast defense had ended in failure, a casualty of irreconcilable differences. But when the argument spilled over into the Oval Office in the summer of 1930, President Hoover directed the new Army chief of staff (CSA), Gen. Douglas MacArthur, and the new chief of naval operations (CNO), Adm. William V. Pratt, to settle the issue once and for all.[7]

The best that MacArthur and Pratt could do was to come to a "gentlemen's agreement," binding during the two chiefs' tenures, that essentially awarded the aerial coast defense mission to the Air Corps. In his next annual report, MacArthur described the arrangement:

> Under [the MacArthur–Pratt agreement] the naval air forces will be based on the fleet and move with it as an important element in performing the essential missions of the forces afloat. The Army air forces will be land based and employed as an element of the Army in carrying out its missions of defending the coasts, both in the homeland and in overseas possessions. Through the arrangement the fleet is assured absolute freedom of action with no responsibility for coast defense, while the dividing line thus established enables the air component of each service to proceed with its own planning, training, and procurement activities with little danger of duplicating those of its sister service.[8]

The Air Corps thus obtained its much-desired temporary restraining order against the Navy. For the next several years, the MacArthur-Pratt agreement provided the Air Corps not only with a bureaucratic raison d'être, but also with an excuse to promote long-range bomber development. During those years the airmen often made the intriguing argument that, in order to defend the coasts, they needed a bomber with the range to fly from coast to coast.

However, when Pratt was replaced as CNO on 1 July 1933, the new Navy leadership decided to rescind the agreement.[9] Colonel Oscar Westover, the assistant Air Corps chief, was quickly assigned the task of trying to negotiate with the new Navy leaders to keep the Air Corps from losing this crucial bureaucratic foothold, but to no avail. Westover glumly reported that "the discussions led nowhere."[10] With the coast-defense mission back "in play" and far from secure, the Air Corps had to come up with another job.

The following year the Air Corps unexpectedly became involved in a frustrating venture that made its misfortunes front-page news. On the morning of 9 February 1934 the Air Corps chief, Maj. Gen. Benjamin Foulois, received a phone call from Second Assistant Postmaster General Harlee Branch, asking him to come over to the Post Office Building. Foulois, who had no idea what the Post Office needed from the Air Corps, went to the meeting unprepared for the Postmaster General's request for the Army to take over all airmail service in the United States.[11]

A Senate committee had uncovered evidence that former President Hoover's postmaster general had illegally funneled airmail-delivery contracts to several private airlines. The investigation promised to be an enormous embarrassment to the Republicans, and the new president wanted to showcase the matter by canceling the contracts and turning over all airmail delivery to the Army Air Corps on at least a temporary basis. Typically, Franklin Roosevelt had directed the Post Office to discuss the matter with the Air Corps directly, without bothering to inform Foulois's superior, General MacArthur.

Foulois called back to his office to get several aides to join him, and then spent three hours with postal officials discussing the problem. Foulois eventually concluded that the Air Corps should be able to handle the job. When asked how long it would take to prepare to take over the mission, Foulois, unaware that Roosevelt wanted the transition to begin as soon as possible, answered casually, "I think we could be ready in about a week or ten days."[12] Before Foulois could even inform MacArthur of the discussion, Roosevelt issued an executive order canceling the existing contracts and directing the Air Corps to begin carrying airmail ten days later.

Foulois quickly learned that an organization equipped and trained to bomb, strafe, and dogfight might not be skilled at hauling mail. In ten frantic days of training pilots and servicing airplanes, it became clear that the Air Corps was not well prepared for the job. One particular problem was the Air Corps's paucity of "blind flying" instruments, especially necessary for long-distance airmail flights in bad weather or darkness. On the day President Roosevelt ordered the Army to carry the mail, the Air Corps possessed only 274 directional gyroscopes and 460 artificial horizons—and few of those had been installed in airplanes because they were being stockpiled in case of war.[13]

The political dimensions of the episode made the job even harder. Prominent Republicans, of course, were highly critical of Roosevelt's actions and eager to see the Air Corps fail. Furthermore, several famous pilots, including World War I ace Eddie Rickenbacker and Charles A. Lindbergh, were advisers or executives for some of the impugned airlines, and they publicly warned that the Air Corps was in no position to safely and reliably deliver the mail.

For the most part, they were right. Three days before the Air Corps was to start airmail service, three inexperienced pilots were killed in two separate training accidents. On the first day of service, bad weather grounded almost all flights along the eastern seaboard. The third day of operations, 22 February, was the nadir. One pilot got lost and died in a crash, another was killed in training, a third got lost and was badly injured in a crash landing, and a fourth got lost in a snowstorm and bailed out. The next morning, a pilot on a ferry flight to Langley Field drowned after ditching his plane in the Atlantic. At the end of the first business week of airmail service, the Air Corps death toll stood at six after tallying about a dozen crashes since training began.

Republican congressmen joined Rickenbacker's condemnation of the operation as "legalized murder" and a shaken Roosevelt privately blamed Foulois for misleading him and taking unnecessary risks. The crashes were front-page news.

After two weeks of relative calm, disaster struck again on 9 and 10 March. One pilot died by flying into the ground in a snowstorm. A few hours later, another crash killed a crewman. That night, two more aviators died in a crash on takeoff from Cheyenne, Wyoming. Later that night, three more planes crashed in separate accidents, but with no fatalities.

Roosevelt was livid. He called MacArthur and Foulois to the White House for a tongue-lashing that Foulois described as "the worst I ever received in all my military service."[14] Roosevelt asked when airmail delivery was going to stop killing pilots. "Only when the airplanes stop flying, Mr. President," Foulois replied. Roosevelt then showed the two officers a letter instructing the Air Corps to fly the mail only when safety was virtually guaranteed. The letter also pointed out that the Air Corps would be relieved of carrying the mail as soon as legislation authorizing new contracts was passed. Roosevelt dismissed the two with several more reminders to "stop those killings," and released the letter to the press.[15]

Since safety is never guaranteed in aviation matters, the president's letter placed the onus of all future accidents personally upon Foulois. Mail flights were suspended for over a week. More instruments were installed in Army airplanes, and the Air Corps reactivated some reserve pilots who had retired to private life as airline pilots. Many of them had been flying the same mail routes before their contracts were canceled.

The Air Corps resumed flying the mail on 19 March and started turning the routes back over to commercial airlines in the middle of May. From the time the flights resumed until the last Air Corps mail operation on 1 June, the Army lost only one more pilot. In all, the venture had cost twelve lives and sixty-six airplanes. Billy Mitchell lamented, "The Army has lost the art of flying. It can't fly. If any army aviator can't fly a mail route in any sort of weather, what would we do in a war?"[16]

Ironically, the airmail fiasco provided an unexpected boost to the Air Corps. For several months, the Air Corps's dearth of experienced pilots and up-to-date equipment was front-page news, and almost no one was willing to blame all of this on the Air Corps itself. Aviation proponents were quick to argue that the difficulties flying the mail were a direct result of insufficient funding and support from the War Department. In the wake of the disaster, the War Department and Roosevelt launched special investigations into Air Corps matters.

In April, 1934, the War Department formed a special board under Newton D. Baker, a former secretary of war, to report on the overall fitness of the Air Corps. Although the board included several prominent civilians (like Lindbergh) and Air Corps chief Foulois, it was mostly composed of general staff officers who were well versed in the official War Department position on Air Corps independence. In fact, many of those officers had been the architects of that policy.

After hearing two months of testimony from what by now had become an almost standardized cohort of witnesses, the Baker Board recommended a reorganization that followed very closely a War Department plan that had been developed the previous year but had gone nowhere. The report recommended creating a General Headquarters (GHQ) Air Force—a large operational force encompassing all aviation within the Army. No longer would aviation units be scattered among ground forces. The GHQ Air Force would be commanded by an officer who would report directly to the Army chief of staff.[17] The Baker Board also recommended increasing the Air Corps's stock of serviceable airplanes from eighteen hundred (authorized in the Air Corps Act of 1926) to 2,320. The crisis that created the board received only passing mention: The report noted dryly that Air Corps equipment was "not easily adaptable to air mail work."[18]

Although the Baker Board's recommendations disappointed those flyers intent on liberating the Air Corps from the Army, it proposed an agency that air force advocates had been agitating for since World War I: an independent organization that concentrated all Army airpower under one commander rather than having it distributed among ground units. The GHQ Air Force would be the unified combat arm of the Air Corps.

At about the same time, Roosevelt formed a special commission to investigate both military and civilian aviation. Chaired by newsman Clark Howell, the Federal Aviation Commission also heard testimony from the nation's aviation experts. Although somewhat more sympathetic to the air force advocates than the Baker Board, the Howell Commission concurred with the Baker Board's recommendations: GHQ Air Force, 2,320 airplanes.[19]

With two studies recommending it, the GHQ Air Force was a done deal. The War Department created it in March, 1935, leaving only observation planes under the command of the ground Army. Command of the force was given to a bomber advocate, Col. Frank Andrews, who was temporarily promoted to brigadier general for the posting.[20] The GHQ Air Force was in many ways a compromise between the views of the general staff and the air force advocates. While giving the Air Corps a unified air force capable of missions independent of the ground Army, it also tied that force more closely to the Army general staff. Still, the new force, in addition to bestowing semantic recognition of the air force concept, further paved the way for the Air Corps to develop its doctrine and tactics independent of ground concerns.

The Best Defense

The GHQ Air Force was the striking force the Air Corps had been waiting for, but the existence of a strategic bombing force seemed contradictory to American military policy. The military's fundamental mission is to defend the United States, and this limitation to defense was usually taken literally; offensive operations of the sort seen in World War I were exceedingly unpopular. This left bomber advocates plagued by the fact that bombing another country's cities was viewed by many as an offensive act.

Air Corps leaders went to great lengths to try to convince the general staff and congressional leaders that strategic bombing was actually defensive. The result was often intellectually acrobatic. Shortly after he took command of the GHQ Air Force, Andrews explained: "The mission of the Air Force, like that of the Army, is defensive. Its sole reason for existence is defense of our homeland. Let there be no mistake about that when I discuss striking the enemy and other offensive operations. An Air Force cannot dig trenches and erect barbed wire entanglements in the air. Though its mission is defensive, it operates only through the attack."[21]

Andrews further affirmed that attacks would only be made against aggressor nations, but argued that this sort of offensive defense could not wait for the enemy forces to attack before destroying them. "We do not wait until the enemy ground forces are ashore and able to maneuver," he explained, "nor do we wait for his airplanes to take the air before attacking them. In the former case they are too scattered and too well protected to be dislodged easily. In the latter case they are in three dimensional space and are elusive. As mosquitos are more effectively eradicated at their breeding places than in flight, enemy forces are more susceptible to Air Force action when they are concentrated than when they are deployed and in position to fight."[22]

Before the Air Corps would be able to eradicate the enemy in their nests, however, it had to have a firm idea precisely where those nests were.

During the early 1930s the bomber advocates at the Air Corps Tactical School (ACTS), which had been relocated to Maxwell, Alabama, fleshed out a doctrine for strategic bombing that the Air Corps later carried into the skies over Europe and Japan during World War II. The image they articulated further revealed their absolute faith in the power of science and technology to win the war of the future.

If the bomber had seemed a formidable weapon to ACTS theorists in the 1920s, by the early 1930s it had become invincible. First Lieutenant Harold L. George, chief of the Bombardment Section, told a Marine Corps Schools class in 1933 that pursuit and antiaircraft defenses would have little chance of stopping a bombing attack. Enemy fighters would be all but neutralized by the increasing defensive armament of American bombers, and antiaircraft artillery would "have to increase by leaps and bounds before it need be given serious consideration by air force commanders." He concluded that the strategic use of bombardment aviation meant that the air force should be regarded "not as an auxiliary but as a separate and distinct agent of national defense, a force capable of acting independently from ground troops."[23]

Another young ACTS bombardment instructor, 1st Lt. Kenneth N. Walker, helped the Air Corps chief's office draft a new field manual. Walker, who also was captivated by the power of bombing technology, realized that the bomber's growing invulnerability inadvertently solved another doctrinal problem. During the 1920s the ACTS usually envisioned strategic bombing as a nighttime operation. The cover of darkness would provide the bombers with much-needed protection from enemy fighters and antiaircraft guns when making attacks on industrial targets deep within enemy territory. As late as 1931, most bombardment training emphasized night operations, and the bombardment text stated that almost all raids would occur at night. The only exception was coast defense attacks, which required greater precision against ships.[24] But the darkness worked both ways, of course. In 1932, Walker and others at the ACTS began to assert that bombing missions must succeed in placing their bombs precisely on specific targets, a task that would be impossible in the dark. Moreover, with Air Corps theorists regarding the bomber as ever more invincible, Walker posited that American bombers would be able to attack in broad daylight: "To state that targets located at a considerable distance in hostile territory will usually be bombed at night is not a correct statement. Precision targets, which require accurate bombing will normally be engaged during daylight hours."[25]

That same year, the ACTS's air force course taught that "The Italians are exponents of large formations at night. . . . However, we do not subscribe to this idea at present. . . . When we arrive at our objective, the better the visibility, the better our chances of accomplishing our desired destruction."[26]

By 1933 this concept of daylight precision bombing from high altitude had become the warfare of choice for ACTS doctrine writers. The bombardment course that year synthesized all of the developments of the previous seven years: bombardment was the basic arm of the air force, its primary use was against strategic targets deep within enemy territory, centralized command was crucial, the bombers would irresistibly get through to their targets even in daylight, and bombing was accurate and destructive enough to strip the enemy of its war-making capacity.[27] Walker summed up the idea in what would become a credo for bomber enthusiasts: "A well-organized, well-planned, and well-flown air force attack will constitute an offensive that cannot be stopped."[28]

But there were a few voices crying in the wilderness. Among fighter pilots and instructors, the thinking at the school had taken a disturbing turn. Forsaking the aerial superiority role was bad enough, but claiming that the bomber was invincible meant that, as Douhet had argued, fighter aircraft were extraneous.

The most vocal of the critics was Capt. Claire L. Chennault, who was an ACTS pursuit instructor from 1931 to 1936 (before organizing and commanding the American Volunteer Group in China).[29] He noted in 1933 that the increasingly popular image of the bomber as invulnerable "establishes bombardment as the first exception to the ancient principle that 'for every new weapon there is an effective counter weapon,'" and warned that constantly improving radio and armament technologies were making it easier for defending fighters to locate and attack the bombers.[30]

Chennault's criticisms, though irritating to many of the bomber proponents, could not deter the true believers. Firm in their faith that American bombing technology was formidable enough to deliver bombs to their targets even in daylight, ACTS theorists worked to marginalize Chennault and turned their attention to the next theoretical problem: What precisely should be bombed?

How could precision bombing destroy an enemy's ability to wage war? In the crudest sense, it could kill or injure so many civilians and military personnel as to rob the enemy of its populace. But this would not have been elegant, humane, or scientific—and it certainly was not what Air Corps theorists had in mind. Rather, if precision bombing could disrupt that intricate network of industrial, political, economic, and social entities that allowed nations to wage modern war, it could surgically remove the enemy's will to resist.[31]

By the mid-1930s ACTS planners had decided that the enemy's industrial economy was the primary target. To figure out what needed to be bombed, they first had to identify the nodes of this fragile web of political and industrial control. As a consequence, they embarked on a fascinating foray into the realms of industrial economics, city planning, and even social psychology. One ACTS study, for example, focused on how modern communication systems had made governments much more sensitive to popular suffering. A few wisely cast monkey wrenches could bring the entire works to a halt.

> The tremendous growth of the means of communication during the past quarter century has greatly increased the homogeneity and sensitiveness of a nation and the influence which one part has upon the other. The telegraph, the telephone, the postal service, radio, and the public press reach every corner of a country, and the thoughts and feelings of one group are transmitted almost instantly throughout the nation. In spite of the most rigid censorship imposed during the World War, in all the contending nations the morale of the armies and of the civil population quickly exercised a profound influence each upon the other. . . . The decision of the commander . . . of the Central Powers in the World War to accept defeat, was largely based upon the condition and sufferings of the non-combatants at home. The employment of larger forces, the highly specialized development of commerce and industry, and of the means of communication, have intensified the effect of war upon a nation's population as a whole, and have increased the importance of the human element in war.

The ability of the airplane to annihilate time and space, and of an air force to strike directly the rear of the enemy's army, or the heart of his country, may have a profound effect upon his will to wage war.[32]

But what, precisely, should the targets be? What buildings, products, or services need to be denied to a population in order to transform an industrialized nation into a chaotic mass of humanity? Only by precise, scientific analysis, ACTS theorists believed, would Air Corps planners find the correct technical solution. As one ACTS instructor argued, "[T]he objectives to be attacked in this type of an air offensive are not to be selected on the morning of the attack. . . . Only by careful analysis— by a painstaking investigation, will it be possible to select the line of action that will most efficiently and effectively accomplish our purpose, and provide the correct employment of the air force during war. It is a study for the economist—the statistician—the technical expert—rather than for the soldier."[33]

The difficulty, however, was that few of the faculty at the ACTS had any background in the necessary social sciences. After World War II, Maj. Gen. Haywood Hansell Jr. recalled how, as a first lieutenant, he had struggled with the problem at the ACTS from 1935 to 1938. "It was essentially a problem for industrial economists," he wrote, "but no economists were available and no money was available to hire them, in view of the War Department's attitude toward such an approach. So the School did the best it could. It reasoned that other great nations were not unlike our own, and that an analysis of American industry would lead to sound conclusions about German industry, or Japanese industry, or any other great power's industry."[34]

Following this line of reasoning, ACTS bombardment theorists imagined how major American cities could be neutralized. They conducted a large study, for example, on how to bomb New York City, by analyzing maps of the metropolitan area's power grid, water supply networks, transportation infrastructure, and even the city's methods of importing and distributing food.[35]

These investigations of city-crippling tactics led to discussions of how to paralyze an entire nation's war effort, again furthered by studying the case of the United States. Recalled Hansell:

Our economy is highly specialized. For instance, the New England states make the great majority of our brass and copper items. . . . Likewise, almost all the shoes in the country are made in one locality. Most automobiles are made in one locality. Within each of these industries, there are in turn specializations. . . . An analysis of this great complexity indicates that munitions industries are especially sensitive to a relatively small number of plants, which make specialized parts, or systems which provide specialized service. The classic example of the type of specialization, and hence, vulnerability, literally fell into our laps. We discovered one day that we were taking delivery on new airplanes, flying them to their points of reception, removing the propellers, shipping the propellers back to the factories, and ferrying out additional airplanes. The delivery of controllable pitch propellers had fallen down. Inquiries showed that the propeller manufacturer was not behind schedule. Actually it was a relatively simple but highly specialized spring that was lacking, and we found that all the springs made for all the controllable pitch propellers of that variety in the United States came from one plant and that that plant in Pittsburgh had suffered from a flood. There was a perfect and classic example. To all intents and purposes a very large portion of the entire aircraft industry in the United States had been nullified just as effectively as if a great many airplanes had been individually shot up, or a considerable number of factories had been hit. That practical example set the pattern for the ideal selection of precision targets in the United States Tactical doctrine for bombardment. That was the kind of thing that was sought in every economy.[36]

It is easy to see how this image of warfare suited the Air Corps's high-tech, futuristic, and highly professionalized self-perception. While the search for "choke-point" industries continued into World War II, the idea that the precise destruction of wisely chosen targets—such as oil refineries or ball-bearing plants—could bring entire industries to a standstill with a single bombing attack was gospel at the ACTS by 1937. This articulation, coupled with its earlier vision of the devastating, precise, and unstoppable bolt from the blue, completed the Air Corps's strategic bombing doctrine.

By the late 1930s the ACTS bomber advocates had also completed their rout of the fighter pilots. The notion that the bombers were unstoppable had continued to gain favor at the school, much to the despair of pursuit advocates like Chennault, who finally retired in frustration in 1937. Well after World War II, Gen. Laurence Kuter, a former ACTS bombardment instructor, recalled how the bombers defeated the fighters at the school long before they ever faced one another in combat over Germany or Japan:

> There was a strong competition at that time between the fighters and the bombers, and Claire [Chennault] was the head of the fighters. Claire was not articulate. He saw the fighter as an offensive and defensive airplane, an all-purpose airplane, really. He wouldn't concede that bombardment or attack or observation or anything else might do more damage to ground targets. I think he took some untenable positions in support of the fighters, and he was supported only by [Earle] E. "Pat" Partridge, Hoyt S. Vandenberg, maybe Lotha A. Smith, whose name doesn't register very widely.
>
> Opposed to him was a very articulate group, Harold L. George, Odas Moon, Gene Eubank, Haywood S. "Possum" Hansell, and Ralph A. Snavely. I was in the group and took part in it. . . . We just overpowered Claire; we just whipped him.[37]

The fighters were defeated at the ACTS on both political and intellectual levels. As Kuter explained, the bomber advocates won more attention from the Air Corps chief, had greater leeway in personnel assignments, and, most importantly, garnered the greatest share of funding.[38] Throughout the late 1930s, as the Air Corps pleaded constantly for more heavy bombers, development and procurement of pursuit aircraft clearly took a backseat.

The fighters were defeated most clearly on the intellectual level. By 1937, standard bombing doctrine fully embraced the notion that the bombers were invincible. Hap Arnold told the 1936 Army War College class that because the bombers had grown in speed and range, "it is out of the question that pursuit can be so placed as to intercept all air raids."[39]

To a great extent, bombardment thinking at the ACTS had taken on an air of technological optimism that would prove extremely costly in the early years of World War II. In an interesting chain of reasoning, Haywood Hansell later recalled how the "bomber boys" (as he called them) were aided by their ignorance of new technologies for detecting the incoming bombers: "If our air theorists had had knowledge of radar in 1935, the American doctrine of strategic bombing in deep daylight penetrations would surely not have evolved. It would have been too easy to rationalize the power of the fighter defense against the medium altitude bomber. Our ignorance of radar was surely an asset in this phase."[40]

One infuriated fighter commander, unmoved by the "bomber boys'" ignorance, warned that the "recent academic tendency" to minimize or even entirely dismiss the importance of pursuit aviation "has led to the teaching of doctrines which have not been established as being true and might even be fatally dangerous to our aims in the event of armed conflict."[41]

Intellectually and politically, strategic bombing so dominated the Air Corps by 1938 as to become identical to it. A line of succession had formed in the Air Corps chief's office that ensured a bomber advocate would be at the stick for the foreseeable future. Moreover, the bomber boys at the ACTS had overthrown the air superiority mission and thoroughly routed the pursuit advocates. However, there was another participant not overjoyed by the turn of events at the school: the general staff, which in 1938 cautioned the school's commandant that ACTS textbooks did not represent Army policy. Official doctrine first had to be approved by the War Department and appear in field service regulations, training regulations, and field manuals.[42]

Until the War Department could be persuaded to accept the Air Corps's view of bombing, the subject would remain academic. Without the support of the general staff (which ultimately commanded the GHQ Air Force) and the secretary of war, no amount of theorizing could take the place of appropriations and airplanes. With the doctrine in place, Air Corps bombing enthusiasts in the latter 1930s turned to producing the spectacular technology that so far had flown only in their imaginations.

Chapter 5
A High-Tech Delivery System

By the mid-1930s the Air Corps's continuing interest in strategic bombing was spurring technological developments that made the mission appear more technically feasible and thus more bureaucratically viable. Driven both by Air Corps desires and the demands of the civilian air-transport market, aircraft producers had moved toward larger, multiengine, all-metal designs. Historian of technology Eric Schatzberg has argued that the move from wood to metal was driven more by ideology than technical imperatives. Although metal designs did offer certain technical advantages (especially in military aircraft, where metal surfaces were more likely to maintain their aerodynamic surfaces even when bullet-riddled), there can be little doubt that metal's appeal was due at least partly to its identification with progressive, high technology.[1]

The Coming of the Heavy Bomber

By 1930 the aging Keystone bombers were simply too primitive-looking to fulfill the Air Corps's rising expectations for high-technology strategic bombing. Theorists at the Air Corps Tactical School imagined large fleets of fast, large, long-range bombers. The biplane bombers of the 1920s represented the past, rather than the future, of aerial warfare.

The Air Corps began soliciting bids to replace the Keystones in 1930. The Materiel Division circulated a specification for an all-purpose, multiengine day bomber capable of carrying a two-thousand-pound bomb load two hundred miles at 150 miles per hour.[2]

Six designs were submitted in 1931, and several showed vast improvements over earlier models. The first to arrive was the Ford XB-906, a derivative of Ford's successful C-4A transport. Sporting three Pratt and Whitney 575-horsepower engines, it carried two thousand pounds of bombs internally, but never realized the great performance characteristics expected of it. Its top speed, for example, was only 144 miles per hour.[3]

Better still was the Boeing entry, the XB-901—later designated the B-9. After the 1930 success of its first commercial monoplane, the Monomail transport, Boeing crafted a bomber along similar lines. The B-9 had a single, low cantilever wing and stiffeners and bulkheads in a semimonocoque fuselage that carried the structural stresses of the wings internally and in the skin. Not surprisingly, the B-9 ended up looking very much like the Monomail, which was distinctive for its thin, cylindrical fuselage. Clocked at 186 miles per hour, the twin-engine bomber was sixty miles per hour faster than any bomber in service at the time, and the Air Corps immediately procured several for testing.[4] Other submissions came from Fokker, Douglas, and Keystone. The first two were eventually procured as dual bomber/observation planes, but the Keystone entry, with its biplane design, could not compete.

The Martin entry had failed to meet the official deadline. But when delivered in 1932, the XB-907, later renamed the B-10, turned out to be the fastest and most powerful heavy bomber in existence. The Air Corps board evaluating it found the B-10 "eminently suitable" for procurement and orders for additional Boeing B-9s were quickly canceled.[5]

Martin's B-10 was a great advance over the Keystone bombers it replaced. Its two Wright engines propelled it at 207 miles per hour and gave it a twenty-one-thousand-foot ceiling and six-hundred-mile radius. It carried a crew of four, 2,260 pounds of bombs, and mounted three machine guns for self-defense.[6]

The Air Corps loved the B-10, and, for a time at least, considered it the airplane that could make strategic bombing a political reality. The airplane's military capabilities were equaled by its public relations value. During the summer and fall of 1934 the Air Corps flew B-10s on several high-profile long-distance flights to demonstrate its ability to project airpower from coast to coast. Under the command of Col. Hap Arnold, ten B-10s flew from Washington, D.C., to Alaska and back. Arnold soon after led another such flight from California to New York City.[7]

In all, the Army purchased 103 B-10s, as well as thirty-two models with slightly larger engines, which were designated the B-12. But increased capability brought increased demand, and bomber proponents soon wanted an airplane that could carry a ton of bombs from coast to coast nonstop. General Foulois pointed out that, even with its spectacular performance, the B-10 was unable to reinforce rapidly either Panama or Hawaii since it would need to make refueling stops.[8] Even the B-10 was not enough.

Project A

While the Martin B-10 was still on order, bomber advocates had already begun working on its replacement. By mid-1933 the Materiel Division and Boeing were studying the feasibility of an enormous, ultra-high-tech, super bomber capable of carrying a two-thousand-pound load for some unspecified "maximum range."[9] After four B-10s made an impressive nonstop flight from Alaska to Seattle, the Air Corps specified the goal for Project A—a bomber that could carry two thousand pounds of bombs five thousand miles at two hundred miles per hour—then signed a contract with Boeing in April, 1934.[10]

Boeing immediately began working on the design, which it labeled the Model 294. The design team, headed by Jack Klystra, quickly realized that an aircraft able to deliver an enormous bomb load nearly twice as far as any existing bomber would require a radical design: a huge, four-engine, all-metal airplane.

Even while it was still on the drawing board, bomber advocates were singing Project A's praises and pinning the Air Corps's hopes for the future upon it. Bomber advocates Carl Spaatz and Hap Arnold made numerous visits to Dayton and Seattle to monitor Boeing's progress. After one such visit, Spaatz warmly predicted that because of Project A, "Air power is going to be an entirely different thing than what we have visualized it in the distant past and in the future is going to justify our most rosy dreams."[11]

The bomber's immense size continuously complicated the design process. Even getting components in the correct gauges proved to be a problem, since the plane required materials in sizes never before used for aeronautical work. Designing the engines was particularly difficult. The original design had incorporated experimental liquid-cooled, twelve-hundred-horsepower Allison engines. When these engines failed to materialize, Boeing had to switch to one-thousand-horsepower, air-cooled Pratt and Whitney engines. It also meant redesigning the engine nacelles, cowlings, and oil and fuel installations.[12]

The lower-powered engines proved fatal. The resulting aircraft, delivered in 1937 and dubbed the XB-15, was an all-metal, midwing behemoth with cooking, sleeping, and toilet facilities for a crew of ten that included, for the first time, an onboard flight engineer who could alleviate some of the burden on the pilot and copilot. The XB-15 was nearly 88 feet long, had a 149-foot wing span, and a wing area of 2,780 square feet. It was the largest military aircraft yet built. Despite its many innovations—an autopilot, deicing installations, fire-protection equipment, separate electric generators, wing passages to allow engine service in flight, airbrakes, and machine-gun turrets—the result was disappointing. Although it boasted a five-thousand-mile range, its four engines could drive its thirty-five tons at less than two hundred miles per hour empty and just 145 miles per hour with a two-thousand-pound load. Still, the XB-15 could carry an unprecedented eight thousand pounds of bombs.[13]

Although the Project A bomber went no farther as a military aircraft, it fared much better as a public relations vehicle. Perhaps its brightest moment came in the service of the American Red Cross. After an earthquake devastated an area of Chile in early 1939, the Red Cross asked President Roosevelt to have the Air Corps fly medical supplies into the region. The XB-15 took off for Chile several days later loaded with more than a ton and a half of bandages, ether, sulfa drugs, syringes, and surgical gloves. Upon returning to Washington, the pilot, Maj. Caleb V. Haynes, was greeted by a fifty-two-plane formation and a reception that included officials from the War Department, the Chilean government, and the Red Cross. The secretary of war personally awarded Haynes the Distinguished Flying Cross for his labors.[14]

The XB-15 eventually was scrapped in 1945, but Project A led directly to other, more successful, development projects, and the airmen's dream of a super long-range bomber would later be manifested in the B-29. More importantly, although the XB-15 was not the ultimate strategic bomber the airmen sought, Boeing's engineers knew the Air Corps desperately wanted a plane like it—and they now knew that they could make it.

The Flying Fortress

In early 1934, at the same time that Project A was gearing up, the Air Corps began looking for a more immediate replacement for the Martin B-10—a new bomber that could be in production within two years rather than Project A's projected five. This duplication of effort immediately caused consternation in the general staff. Some objected, for example, to the Air Corps's practice of submitting open-ended range specifications for its new bombers by adding the words "or more" to the range value. Complained one general staff officer:

> Where in coast defense, does the Army responsibility end and the Navy responsibility begin? How far to sea, in the absence of any naval protection (the extreme case) is it necessary for bombers to go to carry out air corps coast defense functions? How far over land is it necessary to go to perform bombing operations under our various war plans? This Division believes that these questions must be considered before specifications can be laid down. To specify that the range of the bomber at cruising speed shall be "1,000 miles or more, with full military load" leaves the door wide open for the construction of aircraft that will be very expensive and may be entirely unsuited to our actual needs.[15]

In particular, several general staff officers remained unconvinced that the Air Corps soon needed a bomber with range greater than that of the B-10's one thousand miles, which seemed more than adequate for coast defense. While long-term research projects like the XB-15 were worthwhile and relatively inexpensive, the effort and cost of development-for-procurement projects demanded much better justification.

Try as they might, bomber proponents could not provide one. The development of a long-range bomber was already in the works in Project A, so the future goal of being able to reinforce Panama and Hawaii with nonstop flights was already being addressed. And the Air Corps had no convincing argument to get around the thousand-mile range barrier.

In the end, however, the airmen found an arithmetic solution that got past the conservatives on the general staff. Rather than ask for a bomber with greater range, they asked for a bomber with greater endurance at cruising speed.[16] This simple mathematical maneuver was quite clever.

Greater endurance, one could argue, would give a coast-defense force the ability to patrol up and down the coast for longer periods of time. Switching to an endurance specification was little more than a method of arithmetically disguising how range would increase with speed. A one-quarter increase in desired range, for example, could be hidden in an increase in maximum speed from two hundred to 250 miles per hour, with the specification for endurance remaining numerically constant. And no one could argue with asking for more speed.

The Air Corps thus proposed a bomber with a top speed of about 250 miles per hour, conveniently out of reach for the B-10. Officially, endurance would remain at about six hours, yielding a range of more than a thousand miles at cruising speed with a bomb load of two thousand pounds. The general staff finally relented in the face of this line of reasoning. After all, it was always desirable to have bombers with a top speed as close as possible, or even greater, than that of the fighter aircraft trying to shoot them down.

Officially, the new bomber's endurance and bomb load would be about the same as that of the B-10. However, the bomber proponents at the Materiel Division made no secret of the fact that they really wanted a prototype capable of carrying its bombs more than two thousand miles. This information was of particular interest to Boeing president Clairmont L. Egtvedt, who already had the XB-15 design in hand and knew that four engines could go far indeed. Giving the Air Corps what it really wanted, Egtvedt reasoned, even beyond what it was allowed to ask for, would increase Boeing's chances of winning the contract, as well as establishing Boeing's supremacy in four-engine design.[17]

In May, 1934, Boeing learned that the Materiel Division would soon solicit designs for a new bomber to replace the B-10 in the short term. Even before being officially invited to compete, Egtvedt named twenty-three-year-old Edward C. Wells, fresh from the engineering program at Stanford, the head of a team tasked with designing an airplane that could carry two thousand pounds of bombs two thousand miles at well over two hundred miles per hour. By the time the Air Corps officially solicited Boeing in August, the design was finished.[18]

The competition had specified only a "multi-engine" model, and, as with Project A, Boeing immediately settled on a four-engine design. Construction of the Boeing Model 299, later dubbed the XB-17, began in August,

1934, and took almost a year. In an effort to reduce drag radically, all possible protuberances were removed or streamlined. The design incorporated internal bomb racks, enclosed machine-gun positions, and retractable landing gear.

The internal engineering was another example of what was becoming standard at Boeing: a semimonocoque fuselage, with the stresses carried mostly by the aircraft's skin rather than external spars. The fuselage was stiffened with longitudinal beams, rings of sheet metal, tubes, and corrugated metal sheets. The wings were likewise designed with the stresses very widely distributed: two main spars formed the leading and trailing edges, while truss-type ribs supported the upper and lower surfaces. This design later proved crucial in combat since the wings were able to take an enormous amount of damage without failure.[19] The sources of electricity needed to power several key systems—landing gear, flaps, bomb-bay doors—were deliberately decentralized. Several electric motors spaced throughout the airplane later helped prevent combat damage from forcing the aircraft to abort its mission.[20]

The airplane was designed with quantity production in mind. The circular cross-section fuselage, for example, was chosen for its ease of manufacture. The XB-17 was also designed so that it could be modified easily. By the end of World War II the basic design had undergone thousands of minor upgrades.[21]

The other major competitors, Martin and Douglas, derived their entries from preexisting models that had proven very successful. Martin submitted a significantly improved model built around the B-10 that featured better engines, improved landing gear, an automatic pilot, wing flaps, variable-pitch propellers, and better radio equipment. Douglas sent a two-engine derivative of its triumphant new cargo plane, the DC-2. Dubbed the XB-18, the "Bolo" was essentially a DC-2 with a bomber fuselage. Air Corps officials like Spaatz and Arnold frequently visited both the Boeing and Martin plants to monitor progress, and were very pleased with what they saw.

Based on advance reports, Air Corps officers proclaimed Boeing's Model 299, the XB-17, to be far superior to any American bomber yet seen, and many in the Air Corps were proclaiming the XB-17 victorious even before the competitive flight tests had begun. When the prototype was first rolled out to fanfare in Seattle, the *Air Corps Newsletter* enthused:

Hailed as the fastest and longest range Bomber ever built, a giant four-engine all-metal airplane, today was brought to light by the Boeing Aircraft Company of Seattle after more than a year of work on the project.

Known merely as the Boeing 299, the huge craft shortly will undergo test flights before being submitted to the United States Air Corps [*sic*] in open competition with other types at Dayton Ohio. These tests, it was announced, are expected definitely to stamp the plane as the most formidable aerial defense weapon ever offered this country, with far more speed and a substantially greater cruising range than any bomber ever before produced.

Military secrecy necessarily shrouds many details of the Model 299.[22]

Before Boeing delivered the airplane to Dayton, the Air Corps's assistant chief, Brig. Gen. Oscar Westover, tried to convince the general staff that the new bomber, although the most expensive military aircraft to date, was actually the most economical. Westover contended that even though the Boeing bomber cost almost twice as much as the smaller B-10, it was more than twice as useful. Since the XB-17's performance was much better than the cheaper B-10, it could, for example, carry a larger bomb load farther—a job that would require several B-10s. Moreover, the XB-17's greater range would allow it to quickly reinforce Hawaii, Alaska, or Panama, and perform the Army's much-publicized coast-defense mission.[23] The Air Corps deemed the mission of protecting America's shores paramount, thus earning the XB-17 a nickname that would survive through World War II: Flying Fortress, a moniker that also harmonized nicely with the Air Corps's belief in bomber invulnerability. But Mitchell's disciples knew that an aircraft like the XB-17 could do far more than merely guard the coastline.[24]

Westover's argument that the B-17 was more economical than the cheaper B-10 reveals more than lily gilding. His analysis makes sense only if one presumed very little in the way of friendly losses. In fact, one could come to precisely the opposite conclusion—that the older B-10 was more capable militarily—if one expected significant losses to enemy fire. Implicit in Westover's argument was the belief that the bombers were nearly invincible.

The Model 299 was completed in June, 1935, and underwent flight testing in Seattle before making a highly publicized, record-breaking flight from Seattle to Dayton in August, traveling the twenty-one-hundred miles nonstop at an average speed of 232 miles per hour. The Air Corps immediately asked the War Department to procure sixty-five Flying Fortresses for fiscal year 1936.[25]

The bomber enthusiasts were jubilant. At last they had an airplane to perform the mission that they had worked for years to claim as their own. The XB-17's four engines and all-metal sleekness gave it a technological appeal that was irresistible. The Air Corps's future seemed to ride on the wings of the Flying Fortress.

On 30 October 1935, the XB-17 took off for yet another flight test. At the controls was the chief of the Materiel Division's Flying Branch, Maj. Ployer P. Hill. Also on board were three other Materiel Division personnel, as well as Boeing's top test pilot, Leslie R. Tower, who had made the record-breaking flight from Seattle. Within seconds after leaving the tarmac, the Flying Fortress was a twisted pile of burning metal. Hill was killed outright; Tower, severely burned, died twenty days later.[26]

The ensuing investigation showed that the plane had taken off with the rudder and elevator controls still locked, leaving the pilots powerless to control the aircraft after it left the ground. The four-engine giant had climbed steeply, stalled, and crashed. But the aircraft itself was judged free of any mechanical or structural failure that could have caused the crash.[27]

Despite the XB-17's clean bill of health, the War Department reduced the Air Corps's procurement request to thirteen aircraft, and the Air Corps had to wait until the summer of 1937 to receive them. The general staff's reasoning was no comfort to bombing advocates. First, the adverse publicity of such a large, prominent machine "cracking up" was already evident. Because of this, the effect of any future accident would only be worse if the airmen continued to tout the Flying Fortress as their bread and butter.[28] For once, the Air Corps's romantic public image had become a liability.

Second, the War Department was still unconvinced that the Air Corps needed such long-range striking power. The B-17's great range made it seem, despite the rhetoric over coast defense, an inherently offensive weapon, and thus politically unpopular. The smaller Douglas B-18 was much more suited to a purely defensive role against enemy shipping, and could also perform the much-valued task of ground support.[29]

The gleaming, four-engine XB-17 Flying Fortress, rolled out with fanfare at Seattle, 1935. Even before competitive flight trials began, Air Corps bombing enthusiasts proclaimed it "the most formidable aerial defense weapon ever." Photograph courtesy of the National Archives and Records Administration

Third, the War Department had pledged to provide a certain number of aircraft to the Air Corps, and those targets obviously could be met much more economically with smaller, cheaper aircraft. The twin-engine Douglas B-18, although it carried a considerably smaller bomb load than the B-17, cost only about half as much. The B-18 Bolo thus became the official winner of the 1935 bomber competition.

Air Corps officials tried desperately to get the War Department to reconsider. Realizing that the general staff's decision was based largely on economic considerations, bomber advocates tried once again to argue that the B-17 was actually more cost-effective than its cheaper competitors. For example, Air Corps staff studies showed that it would take fifty squadrons of B-18s to do the work of only thirty-one squadrons of B-17s if an enemy fleet approached San Francisco. Moreover, the B-17s, with their greater range, would also be able to launch more attacks upon the enemy

527 89

The end of flight tests for the XB-17 prototype. The crash, which killed two pilots, was later determined to have been caused by ground crew error. It was nevertheless a substantial political setback for Air Corps proponents of strategic bombing. Photograph used with permission of the National Air and Space Museum

armada before it reached American soil than could the B-18s. In the hypothetical San Francisco scenario, each B-17 could deliver 32,400 pounds of bombs in the two days before the enemy arrived; each B-18 only 19,700.[30]

General Malin Craig, who had replaced MacArthur as Army chief of staff, was unmoved. Unless and until the international situation demanded them, the Air Corps did not need B-17s in large quantity. His thinking on this matter was typical of the period. The function of the peacetime military was to maintain a core of men and materiel that could be rapidly expanded in the event of national emergency. When the international situation demanded them, B-17s could then be produced and procured in quantity. For the time being, however, the B-18 was far more practical, and Craig directed the Air Corps to procure 350 of the Douglas aircraft and thirteen B-17s for mid-1937.[31]

The Flying Fortresses delivered that year were slightly revised editions of the original model and were designated Y1B-17. The airplane evolved gradually between 1937 and the coming of war. As engine power increased, the aircraft's maximum speed rose to 287 miles per hour and its bomb carrying capacity rose almost by half.[32] More machine-guns were gradually added to increase the bomber's defensive firepower. At times, development ideas came from unanticipated sources. For example, in 1938, during a test flight over Langley Field, a sudden storm caused a Y1B-17 full of performance-data instruments to stall. In trying to recover control of the aircraft, the pilot was forced to pull out of no fewer than nine spins. He eventually landed safely and the plane suffered only minor damage. The flight data later showed that the combined forces exerted on the airframe by the storm and the maneuvers should have torn the wings from the fuselage. Realizing that the aircraft's frame could take much higher forces than previously thought, Boeing's flight engineers upgraded the engines from 850-horsepower Wright engines to one-thousand-horsepower Pratt and Whitneys.[33] By the time the Germans invaded Poland, the B-17 had gone through four prototypes.

The B-17 also gave the Air Corps a new weapon for its public relations campaign. The sleek, huge airplane drew large crowds, and Air Corps officials never missed an opportunity to display it. The first production model B-17, delivered in March, 1937, after the long procurement battle with the War Department, spent several days on public display at Bolling Field within a week after arriving from Boeing. It attracted hundreds of spectators from the Washington, D.C., area. Four of the precious thirteen spent 16 May 1937 cruising in a great circle over Langley, Augusta (Maine), Cleveland, Pittsburgh, and Richmond. In all, the bombers made appearances over fifteen states and twenty cities in eleven hours. That fall, six B-17s flew in formation over the American Legion convention in New York City. In 1939, a B-17 graced the concourse at the Golden Gate Exposition in San Francisco. When the fair ended, the Air Corps fondly exulted that some five million people had "stood in the shadow of her wings or touched her gleaming silvery sides."[34] The airplane was celebrated as the acme of American airpower, and the public displays succeeded in wedding the Air Corps's public image to that of the large, high-tech bomber.[35]

The Air Corps also used B-17s in highly publicized "Good Will Flights" for the State Department. In February, 1938, six B-17s flew to Buenos Aires to celebrate the inauguration of Argentina's new president, Roberto M. Ortiz. Upon arrival, the commander of the flight, Col. Robert Olds, hand-delivered a greeting from President Roosevelt. Several days later the flotilla flew over the delighted crowd at the inauguration ceremony. When the Fortresses returned to Washington, Olds received the Distinguished Flying Cross. The B-17s made another Good Will Flight to Bogotá, Colombia, that summer.[36]

As for the official winner of the 1935 bombing competition, the B-18 enjoyed a short, uneventful career guarding the continental United States against attacks that never came. It was eventually phased out of its job as a bomber before Pearl Harbor. Its pilots described the Douglas bomber as having a "strong affection for the ground."[37] Despite its generally mediocre performance (the B-18 had a range of twelve hundred miles with full bomb load, a top speed of 215 miles per hour, and a cruising speed of 167 miles per hour), pilots and crew lauded its great reliability and appreciated its ability to get them home under the most adverse conditions.[38] Some B-18 pilots became quite fond, even protective, of their aircraft in a manner reflecting the utopian ideals of the winged gospel. One of them reminisced that he and his comrades were quite glad that this airplane never saw combat—not because of its poor performance, but because "it didn't seem right or fair that this amiable old airplane with whom we had enjoyed such a companionable relationship should be used as an instrument of violence."[39]

Such was not the fate of the B-17. American industry built 12,731 B-17s during World War II. More than half were built by Boeing, with Douglas and Lockheed splitting the remainder. At its peak, Boeing's Seattle plant was turning out sixteen bombers every twenty-four hours. In combat, the B-17 carried the brunt of long-range bombing duty and became one of the most commonly recognized aircraft of the war. As early as 1942, Hap Arnold told a West Point audience that the B-17's performance had vindicated the doctrine of long-range bombing, and that the Flying Fortress lay at the core of the Army Air Forces.[40]

Hitting the Target

The bomber, however, is only half of the bombing machine. A central element of the Air Corps's vision of futuristic bombing was its pinpoint precision. Any military force with large, fast airplanes could drop bombs indiscriminately on enemy cities. What made the Air Corps different was its mission of destroying only those facilities that underlay the enemy's ability to wage war—the individual buildings that house airplane or munitions factories, ball-bearing plants, railway centers, or oil refineries. This kind of precision in bombing, when coupled with the ACTS's doctrine of high altitudes and high speeds, required extremely precise mechanical bombsights.

The Air Corps's vision of strategic bombing had profound implications for the development of this particular technology. While several other nations engaged in high-altitude strategic bombing during World War II, no other nation sought the level of technical precision that the U.S. Army Air Forces achieved. Consequently, no other military force went to such great lengths in its attempt to acquire bombsights that could reliably place bombs on individually targeted buildings. How well the Air Corps succeeded in this quest was not well known until after the war was over. But the quest for this kind of precision, even if unattainable, was manifested clearly in the Air Corps's machines.[41]

By the early 1920s one large source of bombing imprecision was well known. At any given altitude and ground speed, there is only one point along a bomber's flight path from which a free-falling bomb will be carried by inertia and gravity precisely to its intended target. The simple bombsights of World War I could accurately tell the bombardier when the airplane had reached that crucial point in space, but only if the airplane was flying a straight and level course at the critical moment. The early bombsights designed by Georges Estoppey, for example, had no way of compensating if the pilot, thinking he was flying a level course, was actually pitching the airplane up or down by a degree or two. And from six or ten thousand feet up, a two-degree deviation from the straight and level would make a big difference in where the bombs hit the ground. For an airplane flying a hundred miles per hour at 6,000 feet, a pitch error of only two degrees would cause a dropped bomb to miss its target by 200 feet, and at 10,000 feet it would miss by 350.[42]

Even before the end of World War I, American engineers understood the magnitude of this problem and had a pretty good idea how to fix it. The answer, of course, was to find some way of independently stabilizing the bombsight against any unforeseen pitching or rolling of the aircraft.[43]

After experimenting with damped pendulums, the Materiel Division turned to stabilizing bombsights with gyroscopes.

In 1920 the center of American expertise in gyroscopic stabilization was the Sperry Gyroscope Company of Brooklyn, New York.[44] Sperry had designed and built gyro-damping systems to help stabilize naval artillery before the war. During the war, Sperry experimented with gyro-stabilizing entire airplanes.[45] During the twenties, Sperry became the prime contractor for Air Corps bombsights.

Three bombsight engineers formed the backbone of the Materiel Division's partnership with Sperry during the 1920s. Georges Estoppey was a Swiss immigrant who had designed simple bombsights for the Allies during the war. In 1921, after trying unsuccessfully to form his own company, Estoppey joined the staff of the Materiel Division (then still called the Engineering Division). Unfortunately, Estoppey apparently did not realize that as a Materiel Division employee he could not receive royalties for his designs—a misunderstanding that would cause both parties considerable heartache until Estoppey resigned in 1926.[46]

Alexander P. de Seversky was a Russian immigrant, military aviator, and later a very successful airplane designer. In 1921 he showed designs for a gyroscopically stabilized bombsight to the Materiel Division staff, who recognized its potential superiority over unstabilized models. Seversky was uninterested in actually building the sight; he wanted merely to sell the design to the Air Corps. The Materiel Division, anxious to have the prototype built under the direction of its designer, contracted with Sperry to build the prototype under Seversky's guidance.[47] The resulting device, tested the following year, provided much greater accuracy than its earlier counterparts. From 8,000 feet, the Seversky design (designated C-1) yielded an average error of 88 feet, as opposed to 178 feet for the Estoppey.[48] However, the stabilization mechanism proved to be so fragile as to require almost continuous adjustment and repair between trials.[49]

Undeterred, Seversky began redesigning the bombsight. But the Materiel Division had found Seversky difficult to work with. He seemed always to be holding out for more money, and interested only in selling his ideas to someone else to implement.[50] While Seversky continued to work on the C-1, the division contracted with Sperry in 1925 for more bombsight designs employing gyroscopic stabilization.

Henry B. Inglis was an Air Corps captain when he returned to civilian life in 1920 and joined the Materiel Division. Inglis's background in mechanical engineering and his interest in bombsights eventually led to him becoming the Air Corps's chief engineer for bombsight design. Inglis worked closely with Estoppey, Seversky, and Sperry Gyroscope, and designed several bombsights of his own along the way. Inglis's liaisons with Sperry became so close, in fact, that he left the Materiel Division for a job with Sperry in 1928.[51]

Despite numerous legal and financial tensions (often concerning possible sales to foreign governments), Seversky, Estoppey, Inglis, and Sperry Gyroscope developed several series of bombsight designs during the latter 1920s that employed not only gyroscopic stabilization, but also a new method of computing ground speed. The earlier timing method required the bombardier to keep the sight's crosshairs on target for a set amount of time in order to triangulate ground speed. Theoretically, however, the calculation could be done almost instantaneously. If the bombsight could measure the rate at which the bombardier needed to swivel the telescope to keep the reticle on target, it should require only a few seconds of tracking to measure the target's angular velocity, and thus the airplane's ground speed. The dropping angle could then be calculated as quickly as the bombardier could synchronize the target's apparent motion with a variable rate-drive gauge. This "synchronous" method of determining the dropping angle was incorporated into Sperry designs in the late 1920s.[52]

A Sperry-Inglis design, designated L-1, employed the synchronous method in 1928. The Materiel Division ordered five prototypes in April, 1929, and tested them along with further improved models from Seversky and Estoppey. By 1931 the Air Corps was considering three bombsight models: Inglis' L-1, Sperry's C-4 (based on Seversky's earlier C-models and the L-1), and Estoppey's D-7. All three had been developed under Materiel Division auspices, were independently stabilized, and employed the synchronous method of determining dropping angle. The radial errors of bombs dropped from 15,000 feet (the altitude anticipated in combat) were generally a respectable 200 to 300 feet.[53]

One other contender, oddly enough, came from the Navy. Since 1928, Air Corps bomber advocates had been hearing rumors about a gyro-stabilized sight developed for the Navy's Bureau of Ordnance that yielded unprecedented accuracy. The Materiel Division asked the Navy for a chance to inspect one of these sights, as well as the blueprints from its designer, a former Sperry engineer named Carl Norden.

Norden

Carl Lukas Norden emigrated to the United States from Holland in 1904. His newly minted degree in mechanical engineering from the polytechnic in Zurich landed him a job at Sperry Gyroscope, where he designed and developed gyrostabilizers for nine years. He left the company in 1913 on less-than-amicable terms, claiming that Sperry was not giving him sufficient credit for his contributions.[54] Norden's antipathy toward Sperry would inspire him greatly through the end of World War II.

By all accounts, Norden was a domineering, driven, and volatile man. A puritanical and impatient perfectionist, he often worked sixteen-hour days and showed an utter disdain for lesser minds. His son described him as "ruthlessly self-disciplined with outstanding powers of concentration." Navy officers secretly called him "Old Man Dynamite."[55]

During World War I Norden's consulting work on a catapult system for an experimental flying bomb for the Navy brought him to the attention of the Bureau of Ordnance as an expert on gyroscopic stabilization. When the war and the flying bomb project ended, the bureau put Norden to work on improving the Navy's wartime bombsight, the Mark III, by adding a gyrostabilizer.

It may seem odd today that the Navy was in the business of developing high-altitude bombsights. In the early 1920s, however, it was far from clear which branch of the service would have bureaucratic responsibility for strategic bombing. Moreover, a great deal of the discussion on the effectiveness of bombing centered on its value against naval targets. And, contrary to myth, the U.S. Navy was extremely interested in seeing airpower developed for this purpose. If airplanes could sink battleships, the Navy wanted to know about it.

After developing a stabilizer for the Mark III, Norden started designing a new, stabilized, timing-method sight, with the added feature of a "Universal Pilot Directing Device." Whereas most previous bombsight development had gone toward improving ranging (i.e., determining when to drop the bombs based on range and ground speed), Norden realized that greater accuracy would also come from helping the bombardier find the correct deflection.

Getting an airplane to fly straight and level over a relatively small target, especially at high altitude and with wind, was proving to be an extremely difficult task. Sperry, too, had confronted this problem, and had designed a series of pilot directors for the Army: an arrangement of lights by which the bombardier could inform the pilot when the bomber was on the correct heading. By the late 1920s Sperry's pilot directors had grown into full-fledged autopiloting systems that used gyrostabilizers to sense deviations in pitch and direction and correct them automatically. Following the typical pattern, as soon as Sperry's autopilot (known as the A-1) was ready in 1929, Air Corps chief Benjamin Foulois quickly arranged its presentation to the media in Washington. Again appealing to visions of a high-technology Air Corps, Foulois described the mechanical marvel: "The automatic pilot has arrived. Large airplanes may now be controlled by the untiring metallic arms of an ingenious mechanism—a mechanism which pilots transport airplanes straight and level and will hold them on course indefinitely."[56]

Although Foulois was careful to emphasize the civilian benefits of this new technology, it was clear that the Sperry autopilot's primary purpose was to guide Air Corps bombers smoothly and precisely to their targets.

Norden proposed coupling an azimuth gyroscope directly to the bombsight. As the bombardier kept the target in the crosshairs, the gyro would precess left or right if the plane was not precisely on target. All the pilot had to do was keep a flight-path pointer aligned with the course-indicator pointer and the plane would remain on a "collision course" with the target.

The new bombsight, designated Mark XI, was delivered to the Naval Proving Ground at Dahlgren, Virginia, in the spring of 1924. The sight was stabilized along two axes by two orthogonally spinning gyros. The range and dropping angles were determined by sighting on the target through a fore sight for a time period equal to half the time of fall from that altitude. As the bombardier kept the reticle for the fore sight on the target, a back sight would swivel at twice the angular rate so that when the time period was up the back sight was pointed at the correct dropping angle and then automatically locked at that angle. The bombardier then switched his eye to the back sight and dropped the bombs when the target came into the rear crosshairs.

The first results from this sight were disappointing, yielding an average error of 110 feet from an altitude of only three thousand feet.[57] Over the ensuing three years, Norden and the Navy Bureau of Ordnance worked on improving the sight and its pilot director. The Navy particularly wanted Norden to make the sight easier to use as virtually every report on the Mark XI noted how complex it was to operate. Norden worked strenuously to rearrange the controls to make the device more suitable for combat. By 1928 Norden's improved bombsight was delivering bombs within an error of about 2 percent of altitude. The Bureau of Ordnance considered the improvements sufficient to warrant a procurement contract of eighty bombsights at a cost of $348,800, including spare parts.[58]

To help Norden with the business end of the bombsight business, the Navy had encouraged him to collaborate with Theodore H. Barth, a former Army colonel with a flair for marketing. In many ways Barth was a perfect partner for Norden. In addition to being a skilled engineer, Barth was gregarious, patient, and stable. He had joined the Army during World War I and proved to be a skillful administrator managing the production of gas masks. The pair formed Carl L. Norden, Incorporated, in 1923.[59] With the austere Norden tackling the technical issues and the affable Barth running the business, the two men embodied an entrepreneurial team similar in style and potency to that of James Watt and Matthew Boulton two centuries earlier.

By 1929 word of the Mark XI's accuracy had filtered to Air Corps bombing advocates and the bombsight engineers at the Materiel Division were eager to examine Norden's creation. After some delay, ostensibly over security, the Navy Department permitted some Army bombardiers to observe the Mark XI in action and to examine it up close. Although the initial reports said the bombsight was "entirely too complicated," Air Corps officers recognized that the Norden sight was a superior application of gyro-stabilization.[60] No less important from an Air Corps perspective, the War Department—not wanting the Navy to hold exclusive rights to what might be the most accurate American-designed bombsight—convinced the Navy to let the Air Corps buy one in 1931.

The Air Corps's experience with the Mark XI mirrored that of the Navy: the sight was very accurate, but the constant use of both hands made it more difficult to operate than seemed necessary. Still, the Materiel Division was about to suggest procuring several more for service testing when word came down that Norden was working on yet another improvement.[61]

Pickle Barrel

As Mark XI development neared completion, Norden started working on another design that would provide at least the same degree of precision as the Mark XI but be simpler to operate. At the same time, the Navy decided that it might require two or three different kinds of bombsights with varying operational niches. The Mark XI would serve as an all-purpose high-altitude sight, but another sight might be necessary for very high-precision missions. The Navy's desires thus coincided nicely with Norden's and, in June, 1929, the Bureau of Ordnance contracted with him to develop another sight. Familiar with the Air Corps's relative success with Sperry's synchronous bombsights, the Navy specified that this new sight must use the synchronization method of determining dropping angle rather than the timing method. Norden, initially unconvinced that the synchronous method was better, took it upon himself to upgrade and convert the Mark XI timing sight.[62]

The new model, which employed an extremely precise mechanism for finding the correct dropping angle through synchronization, was finished in January, 1931. By far the most difficult technical challenge was to design a drive mechanism that would swivel the bombsight's telescope at a smooth, constant rate but still allow the bombardier to vary that rate in order to synchronize it with the target's apparent motion on the ground. The heart of Norden's rate mechanism consisted of two rapidly spinning disks mounted at right angles to one another. The larger of the two was driven at a constant rate. The second was driven by the first, its edge riding along the surface of the larger disk, like an old 45-rpm record rolling upright and in place on the surface of a spinning phonograph turntable. By varying the distance between the point of contact and the center of the large disk, the rate of rotation of the second disk could be varied with extreme precision.[63]

The bombardier synchronized the swiveling telescope with the target by turning a knob that varied the speed of the rate mechanism. When the telescope was synchronized, the bombsight thus had a measurement of the bomber's ground speed in terms of angular velocity. Then another motor, preset with the airplane's altitude and the time of fall of the bomb from that altitude, would move a pointer that stopped at the correct dropping angle. When the rate mechanism drove the telescope to that precise angle, the bombsight would automatically drop the bombs.[64]

The Navy's initial testing of the new Norden bombsight, designated Mark XV, in the summer of 1931 found it to be much simpler to use than the Mark XI and twice as accurate: From 4,000 feet, range deviation was about 35 feet, as opposed to 55 for the Mark XI.[65]

In 1932, Norden and the Navy tried to improve the bombsight's accuracy even further by developing a gyro-stabilized autopilot that would enable the bombardier to keep the aircraft straight and level during the bombing approach. Norden's Stabilized Bombing Approach Equipment (SBAE) eventually allowed the bombardier to fly the airplane directly using the bombsight.[66] The process of flying to the correct point in space, calculating the dropping angle, and dropping the bombs was thus almost completely automated.

Word of the Mark XV's accuracy quickly reached Army ears. When the Navy contracted with Norden for more Mark XVs in the summer of 1932, the Air Corps convinced the War Department to procure twenty-three of the new sights from the Navy for testing. Not surprisingly, the Air Corps chafed bitterly at having to procure bombing equipment from the Navy. It was simply intolerable to Air Corps leaders that they had to rely on Navy technology in their struggle to make strategic bombing their branch's bread and butter. Even worse, the Navy insisted on maintaining its exclusive contract with Norden, thus requiring that the Air Corps purchase its Norden bombsights through the Navy.

One battleground of the Air Corps's latest war with the Navy concerned autopiloting systems. Norden's SBAE underwent sporadic development over the next several years and eventually fell prey to Norden's old nemesis, Sperry. Sperry had also developed an automatic pilot system, the A-5, in the early 1930s, and many Navy pilots found it superior to Norden's. The A-5, the first all-electronic autopilot, used three vacuum tube amplifiers, one for each axis of flight, which boosted the signals from an arrangement of three gyroscopes. The amplified signals in turn controlled electrohydraulic servomechanisms, thus providing a very fast stabilization response.[67] Norden's SBAE, on the other hand, relied on older electromechanical switches to moderate the signals, and was considerably slower than the A-5 in responding either to gusts of wind or commands from the bombardier. Despite Norden's continuous attempts to make the Mark XV system compatible only with the SBAE, both the Army and Navy gradually came to favor the Sperry design. The issue was not

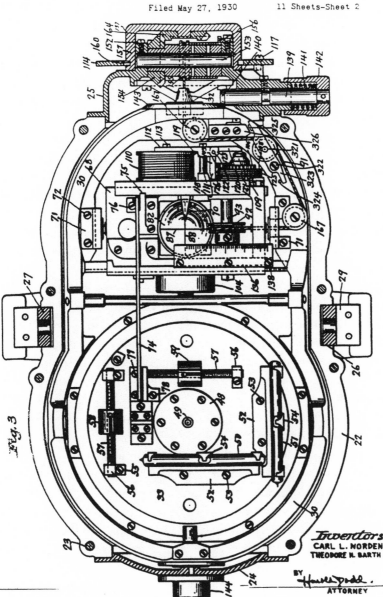

Cross-section view of the Norden "football." From Norden Bombsight patent, U.S. Patent Office, no. 2,428,678, 7 October 1947.

decided until early 1942, when the Air Corps contracted with the Honeywell Regulator Company to engineer an adapter system that permitted the Sperry autopilot to be used directly with Norden's Mark XV.[68]

Norden, however, remained victorious over the bombsight proper. Although Sperry had continued to improve its L-series and D-series bombsights through the middle 1930s, when it became clear that the Air Corps was committed to the Norden designs, the Sperry Company somewhat desperately secured permission to sell its bombsights to the Soviet Union in 1934.[69]

But the battle was not quite over. In 1936, with the Air Corps demanding increasing quantities of Mark XV bombsights from Norden through the Navy, Norden began having problems keeping up with the orders, which by then were reaching the hundreds. Although Norden and Barth had scaled-up production by purchasing a former motion-picture equipment factory, they were still manufacturing most of each sight by hand. In January, the Navy suspended all Mark XV deliveries to the Army until it could get its own orders filled.[70]

The situation was made even worse for Air Corps officers by the impression, probably accurate, that Norden was personally biased toward the Navy. Air Corps requests for improvements went unheeded, and Air Corps personnel visiting Norden's New York facility often received "a cold shoulder."[71] Even after the start of World War II, Air Corps officers felt shunned by Norden. Grumbled one Materiel Division officer after a visit:

> [A]s a result of this last trip, insofar as I am concerned, if I never enter the Norden factory again and deal with their high executive personnel, it will be too soon. It is not that I am rank conscious or ever stand on same, but in reality my reception at that Company was less than is offered to an ordinary seaman. It is my firm belief that the Army Air Forces can never expect any cooperation from this Company and it is my recommendation that we break all relations with this company insofar as possible and utilize Army facilities entirely.[72]

The situation was unbearable for the Air Corps. Having to procure Norden bombsights through the Navy was humiliating enough; the suspension of deliveries was intolerable. General Westover, who succeeded Foulois as the Air Corps chief, informed the Materiel Division that the

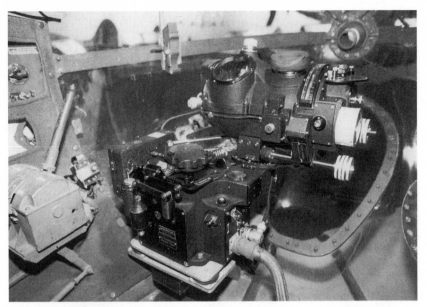

The Norden bombsight, ready for business. Photograph used with permission of the National Air and Space Museum

bombsight situation was "entirely unsatisfactory" and that the Air Corps must find other sources of bombsights. He even argued that the Air Corps might have to settle for sights less accurate than Norden's in order to cultivate more sources, but that "the objective to be attained, that of developing adequate sources available direct to the Air Corps, is deemed sufficiently important to warrant to some degree such concessions."[73]

Faced with this very substantive reminder of its bureaucratic vulnerability, the Air Corps immediately started casting about for alternative bombsight sources—sources that would be exclusive and loyal to the Air Corps. The obvious place to turn, of course, was back to Sperry Gyroscope, which had continued to work on new bombsights at its own expense. Desperate to free itself from the Navy-Norden cartel, the Materiel Division contracted with Sperry for a new sight designated the S-1.

Unfortunately, Sperry was simply unable to reproduce the performance of the Norden.[74] The Sperry sight was less accurate, required a longer bombing run (thus exposing the bomber to more enemy fire), and had poorer optics. Its electrical system was also more fragile than the Norden's,

The Sperry S-1 bombsight, a direct competitor of the Norden. Frustrated over their difficulty in securing Norden bombsights from the Navy, the Air Corps turned to Sperry for an alternative. Photograph courtesy of the National Archives and Records Administration and small voltage or current surges (common in combat situations) caused the unit to malfunction.[75]

Significantly, despite the Sperry bombsight's inferior performance, the Air Corps made it standard equipment alongside the Norden because Air Corps leaders were convinced the bureaucratic benefits of having an independent bombsight supplier was worth the trade-off in performance. The Norden was not officially declared superior to the Sperry until the Air Corps was able to secure its own sources of Norden bombsights—subcontractors Honeywell, the Victor Adding Machine Company, and the Burroughs Adding Machine Company—in 1943.[76]

The Norden, of course, went on to become one of America's most celebrated pieces of technology during World War II. Between July, 1939, and September, 1945, 43,292 Mark XV Norden bombsights were procured by the U.S. military—35,008 for the Army Air Forces and 7,920 for the Navy—at a cost, including production facilities, of about half a billion dollars.[77] Even more importantly, the Norden Company's carefully cultivated mystique surrounding the bombsight fit wonderfully with the Air Corps's high-tech self-perception. The bombsight's "top secret" reputation; its supposed ability to put a bomb in a pickle barrel from twenty thousand feet; and the rumor that the reticle was so fine that it required the especially delicate blonde hair from one Mary Babnick of Colorado were all images that, like those of the sleek and shiny B-17, reflected the Air Corps's bomber culture in a way that wedded the institution to those machines.[78]

Selling the System

By the mid-1930s the Air Corps's vision of high-tech precision bombing was beginning to look like a technological reality. The combination of the sleek, four-engine B-17 and the futuristically intricate Norden bombsight were physical manifestations of the bomber proponents' imaginings over the previous decade and a half. They were Air Corps politics and culture incarnate.

Even if the actual, technical precision of the delivery system was still unproved in combat, the bureaucratic power of this now-corporeal image was clear. In the summer of 1936, the Office of the Chief of Air Corps (OCAC) reincarnated the Air Corps General Board, which had existed since

1922 but had rarely met. The board's job was to coordinate efforts within the OCAC, the GHQ Air Force, the ACTS, and the Materiel Division for the overall "improvement of the Air Corps," but with a special eye toward the ways doctrine and organization would have to adapt to changing technology. The board was headed by Generals Andrews and Arnold, the commander of the GHQ Air Force and the assistant chief of the Air Corps, respectively.[79]

The board's first order of business was to outline a program for expanding the Air Corps to meet the targets proposed by the Baker Board and authorized by Congress: 2,320 serviceable airplanes. On the same day the board was authorized, it created a special sub-board, headed by Hap Arnold, to come up with a plan.[80]

Here was the chance to turn the Air Corps into the bombing force the bombardment advocates wanted. The plan Arnold came up with, called the Balanced Air Corps Program, recommended a five-year buildup to 2,708 airplanes—at an average annual cost of a little more than $100 million. The expansion would entail a significant increase in personnel and a distribution of combat airplanes that was heavily weighted toward bombardment.[81]

For the most part, the general staff supported the plan, especially after Secretary of War Harry H. Woodring made it clear that he supported an expansion of this sort. The plan eventually became known as the Woodring Program.[82] The general staff praised the plan as indicative of "a spirit of cooperation with the ultimate objective of the Army" and "arrived at after most careful study and thought."[83] The War Department approved the program in 1937 with only minor changes, downgrading the target number of airplanes to 2,358 but approving the $100-million-a-year price tag.[84]

Unfortunately for the bomber enthusiasts, the plan fell to pieces in the summer of 1938. There were some on the general staff, like Maj. Gen. Stanley D. Embick, the deputy chief of staff, who were still concerned that the Army might be losing control of its Air Corps by permitting such an expansion of strategic bomber procurement. When Arnold and the Air Corps chief, General Westover, began lobbying in the spring of 1938 for the development and procurement under the Woodring Program of bombers larger and more powerful than the vaunted B-17, the Embick faction bolted. Embick carefully maneuvered through the general staff and the secretary of war's office a restriction on the Air Corps that limited it to procurement of medium and light (that is, twin-engine) bombers.[85] "Estimates for aircraft requirements for FY1940 and 1941," Chief of Staff Malin Craig informed Westover, "will include no four-engine bomber types."[86] Approval for the Woodring Program was withdrawn in July.

Westover and Arnold were frantic. In a stony, three-sentence memo, Arnold complained that "the Air Corps is now without an objective," and urged General Craig to reconsider the restriction and restore the program. Arnold's final paragraph consisted of one gloomy sentence: "The necessity of an objective is axiomatic."[87]

Embick and the rest of the general staff were unmoved. Their reasoning was clear: "The rapid development of aviation which has made possible the procurement of combat airplanes possessing great speed, increased range of action and the ability to carry extensive destructive armament and bombs is fully appreciated. However, none of these improvements have changed the conception that the Infantry Division is the basic combat element by which battles are won, the enemy field forces destroyed, and captured territory held."[88]

The memo continued by citing evidence from Spain and China that "the air forces have been unable to gain, by themselves, a victory which has been lasting or decisive," and concluded with the observation that "The bulk of the Air Corps strength in airplanes should be of the type suitable for the close support of the ground forces in the accomplishment of their missions and therefore should be readily procurable in large quantities and at reasonable cost."

To provide a nucleus of trained personnel and remain adaptable to improving technology, however, the order permitted procurement of fifty-two B-17s and rescinded the restriction of further four-engine bomber development (but not procurement).[89]

The Air Corps's "Magna Carta"

That same month—September, 1938—two events helped to reverse the general staff's decision almost before it could be executed.

The first was that General Westover was killed when his plane crashed while on a routine flight in California. A week later, the assistant Air Corps chief and lifetime bomber advocate Hap Arnold was named as his replacement.

Second, two days after Arnold was named the new chief, Adolf Hitler and Neville Chamberlain signed the Munich Pact.

In the month following the inking of the Munich Pact, the conventional wisdom in Washington held that Hitler had been able to dictate terms to Chamberlain because of the threat of Luftwaffe bombing attacks on London. Although it is not clear where this idea came from, it is certain that Charles Lindbergh and the American ambassadors to England and France (Joseph P. Kennedy and William C. Bullitt, respectively) all believed it and made their opinions clear to President Roosevelt.[90]

On 14 November 1938 Roosevelt called his military leaders—including General Craig, Maj. Gen. George C. Marshall, the new deputy chief of staff, and General Arnold—to a meeting at the White House. There the military chiefs listened to the president outline a new national air defense policy that did far more than reinstate the Woodring Program of 2,358 aircraft. Roosevelt described a tremendous expansion of the Air Corps: He wanted an air force of 10,000 planes, with an industrial base capable of producing at least 10,000 more annually.[91]

Just about everyone at the meeting was stunned.[92] This was a far more massive buildup than the War Department, or even most in the Air Corps, had imagined. Roosevelt adviser Henry Morganthau, who was present at the meeting, recorded in his diary that the president saw "a huge airforce" as a necessary technological alternative to raising a huge army, which Roosevelt considered politically impossible in 1938. Morganthau also noted that the president's mind was firmly fixed on Munich as he announced the plan. Roosevelt argued: "When I write to foreign countries I must have something to back up my words. Had we had this summer 5,000 planes and the capacity immediately to produce 10,000 per year, even though I might have had to ask Congress for authority to sell or lend them to the countries in Europe, Hitler would not have dared to take the stand he did."[93]

Craig and Marshall were understandably concerned that such an expansion would come at the expense of the rest of the War Department. Marshall especially was committed to building a balanced military and not one that was air heavy.[94] Nevertheless, Roosevelt was undeterred. He wanted, as Arnold described it, "Airplanes—now—and lots of them!"[95]

Arnold was ecstatic, and later described that meeting as the Air Corps's "Magna Carta."[96] By the time Marshall became chief of staff the following year he had come to understand Roosevelt's desire for a strategic bombing force, and worked closely with Arnold to bring the plan to fruition.

Conclusion

The Air Corps underwent several more organizational changes before the United States entered the war. But by the time Germany invaded Poland, the Air Corps's fight for strategic bombing—precision bombing of industrial targets from high altitudes in the light of day—was pretty much over.

The war of strategic bombing was still ahead, however. Since then, military historians have long debated whether or not the strategic bombing offensive that the U.S. Army Air Forces waged against Germany and Japan was successful. For the most part, that debate has centered on military, economic, and technical considerations. However, the locus of these concerns should be the United States as much as Europe or the Pacific.[97] Strategic bombing's bureaucratic and cultural functions, including its role in shaping and reflecting the institutional identity of the Air Corps itself, is finally evident in the creation—largely based on the importance and uniqueness of strategic bombing—of an independent U.S. Air Force in 1947. In that sense, strategic bombing—including the culture, doctrine, politics, and technology that made it possible—was completely successful.

Part 2
Amphibious Landing

Chapter 6

Political Pressure on a Warrior Elite

The Air Corps's creation of precision bombing—a form of warfare that was extremely dependent on new technology—was a logical consequence of the Air Corps's futuristic institutional culture. As a service that regarded itself as high-tech, perhaps it is not surprising that they sought out technological solutions. At the other end of the spectrum, however, was the U.S. Marine Corps, an organization with an institutional culture a world apart from that of the airmen. Yet the Marine Corps, too, ultimately turned to technology to meet its interwar challenges. While the high-tech Air Corps created a high-tech form of warfare, the rugged, low-tech Marine Corps created a low-tech form of warfare. But low-tech is not no-tech; technology became as integral to amphibious operations as it was to precision bombing. And as they had for the Air Corps, the Marines' institutional self-perceptions profoundly shaped their vision of a new form of warfare and the hardware that would make it possible.

The flag raising on Iwo Jima's Mount Suribachi is the icon for the U.S. Marine Corps. On posters and postage stamps, in movies and monuments, this is the image of itself that the Marine Corps presents to the world. Since World War II, it has become almost impossible to think about the Corps and not imagine marines hitting the beaches and wading ashore under enemy fire.

Although its bureaucratic roots extend back to the Revolutionary War, the Marine Corps as we know it was created in the years between the world wars. Prior to World War I, no one associated the marines with amphibious landings, and had it not been for dire threats to its very existence in the 1920s, the Marine Corps might never have changed.

Marines coming home from World War I had a lot to be happy about. Serving as regular infantry, they had distinguished themselves in combat, especially at the battle of Belleau Wood during the Allied counterattack in June, 1918. That action brought widespread recognition to the Marine Brigade. Headlines in the United States blared, "Our Gallant Marines Drive 2½ Miles; Storm Two Towns, Capture 300 Prisoners."[1]

The press reports, of course, were exaggerated. The Marine Brigade had performed valiantly in the battle, suffering more than a thousand casualties (more than the Corps had lost in its entire previous history), but it was not the only American force participating. The marines' publicity in this battle was due in large measure to a fluke in military censorship.

Throughout the war, military censors had prohibited the press from identifying American Expeditionary Force (AEF) by unit number. However, the Marine Corps commandant, Maj. Gen. George Barnett, had convinced the AEF commander, Gen. John J. Pershing to allow the marines in France to keep their designation as "4th Brigade (U.S. Marines)." That additional parenthetical inadvertently allowed war correspondents to identify the Fourth Brigade by name, and dispatches explicitly noting the exploits of the "Marine Brigade" were allowed to pass the censors—to the growing resentment of their anonymous and unpublicized Army brethren.

Belleau Wood made matters worse. During the battle, Floyd Gibbons of the *Chicago Tribune,* a journalist known for his blood-curdling prose and fondness for the Marine Corps, filed an extraordinarily flattering account of Marine Corps contributions, and was then promptly wounded. A rumor quickly circulated that Gibbons had been killed. His friends at the censor's desk, thinking it might be Gibbons's last story, allowed it to go out virtually unaltered. The story left the clear impression among the American public that sharpshooting marines had single-handedly stopped the Germans at the gates of Paris.[2]

The marines demonstrated their traditional prowess as riflemen and infantry throughout the war, and their performance brought them considerable publicity in the 1920s; their exploits were glorified, for example, in movies like *What Price Glory* (1926).[3] But the public relations triumph also carried considerable cost, particularly a sour relationship with the

U.S. Army. The Army and Marine Corps had never been on very good terms, but the resentment born of World War I cemented a long-term hostility. The bickering yielded a series of public charges and countercharges regarding the marines' role at Belleau Wood, or even whether Belleau Wood could be considered a major engagement of the war. After the publicity battle subsided, many Army generals were left with the distinct impression that the Marine Corps would take any opportunity to denigrate the Army. Perhaps, some critics argued, the "Useless Sonsofbitches Made Comfortable" (a play on the U.S. Marine Corps's acronym) might best serve the national interest by becoming part of the Army.[4]

The notion of transferring the Marine Corps from the Navy to the Army was not a new one since many of the Corps's duties had always seemed like Army jobs. The idea seemed to merit serious consideration in the financially lean years after World War I.[5] If the marines' specialty was serving as infantry, why not make them regular infantry as part of the Army?

Since its creation in 1775, the Marine Corps had lacked a well-defined mission and therefore a justification for its existence in the U.S. military. The Corps traditionally had assumed numerous and disparate duties, including guarding ships, consulates, and embassies, and serving as boarding parties, shore parties, gun crews, and infantry. It was also called upon to quell unrest and protect American citizens and property in places like the Philippines and Nicaragua.

These multiple responsibilities had always caused problems in defining the Marine Corps's purpose, often leaving marine planners scrambling to protect their disjointed turf. In 1908, for example, Pres. Theodore Roosevelt decided to remove marines from naval vessels as part of his modernization of the military, thus eradicating one of their primary duties (as ships' guards) and radically weakening the Corps's link to its parent service, the prestigious (and bureaucratically secure) U.S. Navy. The removal of marines from the fleet prompted rumors throughout Washington that the Corps was soon going to be transferred entirely to the Army. The matter grew into a minor showdown between the president and Congress over control of military policy. Congress won, and marines were reinstated aboard Navy ships five months later. But the "ships' guard fiasco," as it became known to marines, emphasized the hazard of the Corps's jerry-rigged job security.[6]

In 1911 several young line officers, frustrated over Marine Corps headquarters' handling of the ships' guard issue and Pres. William H. Taft's appointment of a seemingly dilatory new commandant, organized to create the Marine Corps Association. Led by George Barnett, Benjamin Fuller, and John A. Lejeune (all of whom would later become Marine Corps commandants themselves), the association pledged to educate officers on the Corps's importance to the Navy and to fight all efforts to take away any of the Corps's missions. The association raised enough money in 1916 to create the *Marine Corps Gazette,* which quickly became the primary journal for discussing Marine Corps policy, training, techniques, and equipment.

In one of the first issues of the *Gazette,* another future commandant, John H. Russell, issued "A Plea for a Mission and Doctrine," in which he warned of the great dangers of taking on numerous, disparate duties. "In performing its 'Task'," wrote Russell, "the Marine Corps will, naturally, have many 'Special Missions' presented to it, in fact in years of Peace, they are apt to become so numerous that the impression is likely to prevail that such subsidiary work is not at all subsidiary but is, in reality, the Master Work of the Marine Corps. Such an impression is worse than misleading, it is dangerously false, and if allowed to permeate the service would result in its failure to properly prepare itself for the real issue and cause it to fight at an enormous and perhaps decisive disadvantage."[7]

It is not clear precisely which "real issue" or "decisive disadvantage" Russell was referring to here. He may have been considering not only the Corps's fight against foreign enemies in war but also its bureaucratic struggle against the other branches of the U.S. military. The lean budgets of the return to normalcy made the bureaucratic competition a matter of institutional survival. The Marine Corps desperately needed a mission.

Seizing the Beaches

If World War I exacerbated the Marine Corps's mission problem, it also delivered the promise of a solution. The Treaty of Versailles and the naval arms limitation treaties that followed in 1922 radically transformed America's military situation in the Pacific and created a possible mission for the marines.

Even before the United States entered World War I, some Navy and Marine Corps planners had recognized a special problem. Modern naval warfare required a network of bases to refuel and repair the fleet. Since all of America's potential naval rivals were a full ocean away, the demand for bases was even more acute. If the nation went to war, it would need to be able to establish and defend temporary "advance bases" to support the Navy in its progress across the ocean.

In the early part of the twentieth century the Navy and Marine Corps began considering the defense of advance bases as a possible new mission for the Marine Corps. As early as 1900 the Navy's General Board, the service's central planning entity, had suggested that marines take over the advance-base mission. But Marine Corps headquarters did not want to divert men away from other duties, and Congress was unwilling to provide the additional funding. Only a small cadre of marine officers showed any official interest.

In 1914, however, advance-base advocate George Barnett became commandant. Barnett had strong Navy ties, including a friendship with Assistant Navy Secretary Franklin D. Roosevelt, and soon surrounded himself with other allies, including John Lejeune. By 1916 Barnett had arranged to have an Advanced Base School added to the Naval War College. There, marine advance-base proponents like Dion Williams, Eli Cole, John Russell, and Robert Dunlap (all of whom later became generals) preached the importance of the mission and of the closest possible cooperation between the Corps and the Navy.[8]

In 1916 Lejeune alerted *Marine Corps Gazette* readers to the bureaucratic perils of not embracing the advance-base mission. In any war with another great power, Lejeune argued, all ground forces would have the ignominious job of waiting around until the great naval battles were over before they could begin the ground campaign.

In such a war the Marine Corps, if not assigned to Advance Base work, would in all probability be divided up into small detachments and either assigned to the vessels of the fleet, or held on shore in a state of inactivity as guards to navy yards, naval magazines, etc., while waiting for the war at sea to reach a decision. If, on the contrary, the Marine Corps be utilized as an Advance Base organization, it would have the opportunity to share with the Navy the glory always resting on those who strike the first blows at the enemy, and it also would have the satisfaction of feeling that it had an important, semi-independent duty to perform and that on the manner of its performance would largely depend the success or failure of the Fleet.

Surely, this is a mission which is worth while, and one which furnishes a spur to energetic effort and zealous labor in time of peace, so as to attain the true soldier's Elysian state, "preparedness for war."[9]

That same year, General Barnett told the House Naval Affairs Committee that "The fortification and defense of naval advance or temporary bases for the use of the fleet has been made the principal war mission of the Marine Corps."[10] On the eve of American entry into World War I, the Corps appeared dedicated to advance-base defense as the justification for its existence. At least, that is the way it looked on paper.

In reality, the Corps's commitment to the advance-base mission fell victim to headquarters' habitual unwillingness to abandon any of its traditional missions. Expeditionary duty to Haiti in 1915 and the Dominican Republic in 1916 sapped the Advanced Base Force (ABF) of personnel, and the use of marines as infantry in World War I had the consequence that the ABF had virtually ceased to exist by 1920.

Orange War

At the same time, however, a series of events was in motion that would bring the advance-base mission to the front of American military planning in the Pacific. At the turn of the century, both the War and Navy Departments reorganized their staffs to meet the enormous planning demands of modern warfare. The War Department created the general staff, and the Navy established the General Board. A Joint Army-Navy Board was formed in 1903 to coordinate planning between the two services, and was responsible for preparing joint war plans for almost every contingency imaginable. The Joint Board code-named each war plan by country and color. War Plan Tan covered armed intervention in Cuba, War Plan Green detailed the invasion of Mexico, and War Plan Red described war with Great Britain. After the Japanese attacked Russia in 1904, the Joint Board began drawing up War Plan Orange for war with Japan, America's most prominent naval rival in the western Pacific.

The early versions of War Plan Orange recognized that Japan's first target in a war with the United States would be the Philippines. Annexed by the United States after the Spanish-American War, the Philippines provided one of the few secure locations for an American naval base in the region. Prior to World War I, War Plan Orange was little more than a statement of principles: The fleet would cross the Pacific to relieve the defenders in the Philippines within three to four months; then, with the Philippines secure, the Army would go on the offensive.

More detailed plans fell victim to troubles within the Joint Board itself. When the board's inability to agree on a structure of overseas military bases led to an open dispute with Pres. Theodore Roosevelt in 1908, Roosevelt suspended the board for a year. President Woodrow Wilson suspended it again in 1913, and the board met only twice during World War I.[11]

The conclusion of the war brought with it revision of the world map and the need for drastically revised military plans. Despite President Wilson's objections, the Treaty of Versailles placed former German islands in the central Pacific, particularly the Marshall and Caroline Islands, under Japanese mandate. These island groups were directly astride U.S. supply routes to the Philippines, thus making any sustained defense of the Philippines in an Orange war an even more difficult proposition than before.

The Washington Naval Treaty, negotiated between 1920 and 1922, made matters even worse for the authors of War Plan Orange. Among other provisions, the treaty limited the number and size of warships of the signatory nations, primarily Great Britain, the United States, and Japan, to a ratio of 5:5:3, respectively. Japan accepted the inferior capital ship allotment in exchange for guarantees from the United States and Great Britain not to fortify their bases in the Philippines, Guam, the Aleutians, Singapore, Hong Kong, and several other locations west of Hawaii. That guarantee made defending the Philippines a virtually impossible task in the event of an Orange war.

The agreement ran counter to the judgment of many high-ranking Navy planners, who believed that war with Japan was inevitable. As early as 1920 the commander in chief of the Asiatic Fleet wrote to the secretary of the Navy and laid out in sweeping terms his reasons to expect a war with Japan:

> The relations between the United States and Japan cannot be said to
> be satisfactory. Incidents are daily created which cause irritation and

animosities, and unless the situation is cleared up, the two countries will probably drift into war. . . .

I do not believe that Japan wants to fight us; she would prefer to remain friendly, but I do believe that her one great ambition is to be in the East what the United States is in the West, and England is in Europe. She wants to lead Asia, and . . . she means to attain that object at any cost.

As England was the obstacle to Germany in realizing her ambition to dominate the world, so the United States stands across the path of Japan. . . . Like the Roman Catholic Church, Japan builds for the centuries. A nation which claims three thousand years of Imperial power in unbroken succession, can afford to wait patiently fifty or a hundred years to realize her ambitions. . . .

Unless there is a great change in our relations with Japan, when she is ready to try conclusions with us (and watchful and careful observers put the time at about one year hence) she will aggravate the United States beyond the point of tolerance, and we will be forced to deliver the ultimatum; then she will strike without further warning. Thus she will have the advantage of engaging in a defensive war. Our ships and our armies will have to carry the war overseas. The Japanese will not come to us.

It seems to me that the greatest danger of war lies in the conceit and the cock-sureness of the Japanese Military Party. It is impossible, of course, to know just how many of their General officers believe that Japan can defeat the United States, but a prominent Japanese has recently stated that Japan could easily take the Philippines in forty-eight hours.

We must be prepared.[12]

The Chief of Naval Operations circulated the report to all members of the planning staff.

The Joint Board was reorganized and reconstituted in the summer of 1919. Although it still had no executive functions or command authority, the board was given the authority to originate studies on its own initiative. The board's Joint Planning Committee immediately turned its attention to War Plan Orange.

Planning an Orange war was hampered by the vagueness of America's Pacific foreign policy, especially regarding the Philippines. What commitments would the United States make to defend Philippine sovereignty? What would American objectives be in an Orange war? What, in general, were U.S. interests in the region? As one Navy member of the Joint Board noted, "These questions are not for the War and Navy Department to answer, but for the State Department."[13]

No answers were forthcoming. Throughout the 1920s both Congress and the State Department toyed with the prospect of granting the Philippines independence, thus complicating the question of America's military commitment. The matter was not resolved until the Tydings-McDuffie Act, granting Philippine independence in 1946, was passed in 1934.

The only certainty regarding the Philippines was that, since it would not be fortified, it would be supremely vulnerable. With the Marshall and Caroline Islands mandated to Japan, the Orange planners were forced to consider a military option that appeared exceedingly ill-fated. In January, 1920, Adm. Robert Coontz, the CNO, informed General Barnett that the latest version of the Orange plan required "the capture of certain bases in the Caroline and Marshall Islands as the fleet advances across the Pacific."[14]

This simple statement radically transformed the advance-base mission. No longer was the objective merely to defend advance bases already established. Now the mission was to *seize* bases that might be defended by the enemy. In all likelihood this would entail an amphibious landing against a defended shore.

Both Coontz and Barnett knew well the most recent attempt of this sort of operation: the Anglo-French Dardanelles campaign in the summer of 1915. The landings at Gallipoli, made against initially modest Turkish opposition, had ended in unmitigated disaster and became a stark lesson in the futility of amphibious operations in an age of machine guns and long-range artillery. Militarily, Gallipoli had become synonymous with suicide.

Most British planners (including the farseeing Basil H. Liddell Hart) considered large-scale amphibious landings an impossibility as late as 1939. Many Americans agreed during the 1920s. According to one naval analyst at the time: "The chances for success of an invasion by forces transported overseas are becoming smaller and smaller. The greater facility of movement of forces on shore by railroad and motors; the rapidity of communication; the increase in power of mobile artillery; the increased efficiency of the submarine and aircraft, and the increase in size and effectiveness of regular armies and navies, have made invasion by sea almost an impossibility."[15]

The Navy's War Plans Division, however, could find no other means of successfully prosecuting an Orange war. Admiral Coontz informed the marines that War Plan Orange would, after its approval, become the basis for all naval planning. He also suggested that the Corps begin organizing expeditionary forces to carry out the new mission. In particular, Coontz recommended a force of six thousand to eight thousand men on each coast ready to embark within forty-eight hours. Although raising and training such a force would take a considerable period of time, Coontz believed "that if such a policy is decided upon, it will furnish a definite point of aim, which will permit of the logical development of the Marine Corps for the duties it will be called upon to perform under the War Plans."[16]

The first full interwar version of War Plan Orange was developed between 1920 and 1924. As expected, it outlined an offensive war, primarily naval, that required advance bases to secure the thirty-four-hundred-mile supply line from Honolulu to Yokohama. Since the Japanese were unlikely to leave potential bases vacant, the marines would have to take them by force.

Lejeune and Ellis

Meanwhile, General Barnett himself had come under fire. He had antagonized both Navy Secretary Josephus Daniels and Rep. Thomas Butler (father of Brig. Gen. Smedley Butler, who openly aspired to be the Marine Corps commandant), chairman of the House Naval Affairs Committee, over Marine Corps promotion policy. Under pressure from Daniels and Butler, Barnett retired in June, 1920, two years before the end of the usual second term as commandant.

Although Smedley Butler was the ranking officer, the outgoing commandant recommended John Archer Lejeune to be his successor. Lejeune, a stocky fifty-three-year-old southerner with a square, leathery face, juglike ears, and a shrewd political sense, was confirmed as commandant and quickly inaugurated several measures to enhance the value of Marine Corps stock within the U.S. military.[17]

A well-orchestrated public-relations campaign was among those measures. When Lejeune arranged to have marines guard the U.S. mail from 1921 to 1926, he repeatedly reminded the press that America's mail could not be safer. Headquarters publicized the marines' athletic events, especially their exhibition games with college football and baseball teams. The marines' public relations jewel, however, was their yearly reenactment of Civil War battles in the vicinity of Washington. Each year, Marine Corps headquarters invited the president and the press to observe marines stage the famous battles using modern weapons and tactics, demonstrating the enormous progress in the means of warfare in the twentieth century.[18]

But no public relations campaign could bring the Marine Corps bureaucratic security. Lejeune realized that the Corps's position within the military establishment rested legitimately in its military functions. As an advance-base proponent of long standing, Lejeune embarked on a mission to secure amphibious operations as a Marine Corps responsibility.

Lejeune reorganized the headquarters staff to reflect the new emphasis on missions and doctrine. In 1920 he added a new staff division of Operations and Training, which quickly became a locus of thought regarding Marine Corps missions. In 1921, although he had been unable to get a marine representative onto the Joint Board, Lejeune was able to assign Maj. Holland M. Smith to the Navy's War Plans Division and Col. Benjamin H. Fuller to the planning staff at the Naval War College. Both men were fervent amphibious operations disciples. The former would later command all marine amphibious operations in the Pacific in World War II, and the latter eventually became commandant. From these high positions in the Navy's planning staff, they were able to alert Lejeune to upcoming revisions in War Plan Orange and thus help provide opportunities for Marine Corps input.[19]

Lejeune had long understood the Marine Corps's bureaucratic need to link itself to amphibious operations. He openly told readers of the *Marine Corps Gazette* that embracing the advance-base mission was fundamental not only to national security, but to the Corps's budgetary security as well. Noting that appropriations always followed from "estimates of the situation," Lejeune argued that "In estimating the situation, the first thing to be considered is the *mission* of the military force concerned. The study of logic teaches us that the correctness of the conclusion depends primarily upon the soundness of the premises. The most important factor then in this estimate of the situation is the determination of the *true mission* of the Marine Corps in the event of war."[20] Lejeune had no doubt that the Corps's "true mission" had to be amphibious warfare—its bureaucratic existence depended on it.

Moreover, the hazardous and grueling character of the amphibious assault harmonized well with the Marine Corps's institutional identity coming out of World War I. One of the Corps's fundamental slogans— "First to Fight"—was actually a creation of public relations specialists in the Marine Recruiting Publicity Bureau during the war. The motto, taken from the "Marine Hymn," was extremely popular and helped make the marines the only service during the war that had little trouble filling its ranks with volunteers; not until the last few weeks of the war did the Corps accept draftees.[21] Amphibious operations fit perfectly into this image. Storming a hostile shore, facing enemy fire literally at the water's edge, was surely a job for the first to fight.

At headquarters, Lejeune assigned a great deal of the strategic and tactical staff work of amphibious warfare to Maj. Earl H. "Pete" Ellis, of the Operations and Training Division. A fragile, brilliant, thirty-year-old native of Kansas, Ellis had impressed Lejeune with his flair for strategic planning before World War I. Despite Ellis's long history of emotional disorders and alcoholism, Lejeune had the utmost confidence in his ability to turn War Plan Orange from a set of general principles into an operational war plan for marines.[22]

Ellis, obsessed with the problem, went into monastic seclusion in a small office in the headquarters basement, surrounded by maps and liquor. By early 1921 he had generated several versions of what became Operational Plan 712, "Advanced Base Force Operations in Micronesia."

This remarkable document—eighty pages of text plus long appendixes consisting of charts, schedules, and graphs—embodied a prescient and frighteningly detailed description of the conduct of an Orange war. Just as importantly, "Advanced Base Operations" articulated for the first time in operational planning documents how the Marine Corps was wedding itself to the amphibious assault.

Ellis introduced his study by explicitly acknowledging the importance of the advance-base mission both to an Orange war generally and to the Marine Corps specifically.

In order to impose our will on Japan, it will be necessary for us to project our fleet and land forces across the Pacific and wage war in Japanese waters. To effect this requires that we have sufficient bases to support the fleet both during its projection and afterward. As the matter stands at present, we cannot count upon the use of any bases west of Hawaii except those which we may seize from the enemy after the opening of hostilities. Moreover, the continued occupation of the Marshall, Caroline, and Pelew Islands by the Japanese (now holding them under mandate of the League of Nations) invests them with a series of emergency bases flanking any line of communications across the Pacific throughout a distance of 2300 miles. The reduction and occupation of these islands and the establishment of the necessary bases therein as a preliminary phase of the hostilities is practically imperative. . . .

The extent to which the Marine Advanced Base Force will participate in these operations will very likely depend upon the number of Marines available and *their military worth in Advanced Base Operations.* If skilled in ship-to-shore operations and inculcated with a high morale and offensive spirit they will doubtless be used to the limit—if only for the sake of general economy of lives.[23]

For Ellis, amphibious warfare was inevitable; it was up to the marines to be part of it.

On a strategic level, Ellis proposed that in a war with Japan American amphibious forces would first have to mobilize, train, and equip in Hawaii before seizing the Marshall Islands as advance bases. Marines would then island hop from the Marshalls to the Carolines and Marianas, establishing more bases along the way to support the naval war against Japan itself.[24]

Ellis tried to organize the dizzying mountains of information relevant to amphibious operations against Japan: geography, character of the seas, weather, native populations (soporific, he wrote, with "mental indigestion" from the combined forced-feeding of Western missionary culture and Japanese influence) and their languages and economy, and prevalent native diseases. He judged that the Japanese would have first-rate materiel and training, and that they would have the edge in experience and time. But despite Japanese cunning and organizational skills, "[o]ur advantages over the enemy will be those generally common to the Nordic races over the Oriental—higher individual intelligence, physique, and endurance."[25]

The central section of the monograph described the landing operation in detail. Special Marine Corps training and preparation, Ellis argued, would be absolutely crucial for dealing with the formidable enemy defenses: "To effect a landing under the sea and shore conditions obtaining and in the face of enemy resistance requires careful training and preparation to say the least; and this along Marine lines. It is not enough that the troops be skilled infantry men or artillery men of high morale; they must be skilled water men and jungle men who know it can be done—Marines with Marine training."[26]

Ellis's description of the ship-to-shore movement served as the basis for amphibious planning throughout World War II. After making extensive reconnaissance by air and deciding on objectives, the landing force would disembark from transports into small landing boats. The boats would then form up and advance to the shore in waves, just like an infantry advance on land. After landing, the troops would remain in formation to reach their objectives. Ellis detailed landing formations, the composition and weapons of the landing force, the roles and conduct of aerial and naval gunfire support, as well as the structure of communications systems and the supervision of prisoners. In working out a sample case, Ellis anticipated almost exactly the size of the force later needed to invade Eniwetok during World War II.[27]

Ellis's "Advanced Base Operations" was also one of the first operational plans to recognize that landing operations would require special technology. While he paid relatively little attention to technological issues, Ellis argued that the nature of marine amphibious warfare demanded that any special equipment be rugged and simple. "Delicate or complicated materiel," he asserted, had no place in the Marine Corps.[28]

General Lejeune approved "Advanced Base Operations in Micronesia" on 13 July 1921, thus making it a cornerstone of Marine Corps planning for an Orange war.[29] Ellis was determined to continue the work. Recently hospitalized several times for depression stemming from alcoholism and kidney disease, Ellis was granted a ninety-day leave to visit Europe in the spring of 1921. The leave was a ruse. In reality, Ellis went to the Micronesian islands disguised as an American businessman to perform on-site reconnaissance.[30]

The intelligence mission was terribly planned. No American governmental or military officials in the region were alerted. Nor was Ellis prepared to portray his assumed identity, a guise that was easily penetrated by other travelers. He suffered several more mental breakdowns after reaching the western Pacific, including a lengthy stay at the naval hospital in Yokohama. Lejeune ordered Ellis home, but on 6 October 1922 he slipped out of the hospital, absent without leave.

Eluding both Japanese and American officials, Ellis moved among the tiny Marshall, Caroline, and Palau Islands, drinking heavily and getting into fights with local police. Japanese police, who identified him as a spy but were apparently unaware that he was a military officer, followed him constantly. Several of the people who came to know him testified later that by the spring of 1923 Ellis's drinking had become severe and violent. He died, drunk, on the morning of 12 May 1923. The exact cause of his death was never determined.

Among marines, the rumor circulated (and is still fervently believed by some) that the Japanese had poisoned Ellis. The situation was complicated by the fact that the Navy officer sent to retrieve Ellis's remains was ordered to take the opportunity to do some on-the-spot intelligence gathering. Although he succeeded in recovering Ellis's cremated remains, he returned glassy-eyed, ashen, and unable to communicate beyond incoherent mutterings. The Navy doctor who examined him reported that he appeared to have been drugged. The mystery was immortalized when the officer and his wife were killed two weeks later in an earthquake that devastated Yokohama in September, 1923. Ellis's remains were recovered and buried in his hometown of Pratt, Kansas.

Lejeune had harnessed Ellis's imagination to produce a blueprint for amphibious warfare as envisioned by marines. The assault from the sea was to become the Corps's true mission, and "Advanced Base Operations" laid out the technical details of how that mission might best be accomplished. But for all his technical acumen, Ellis had not appreciated the technological demands of the new warfare. After his death, Lejeune still needed to make the amphibious assault a technological reality.

Chapter 7

Technology and Training

In hindsight, it is easy to imagine that the technology for amphibious operations consisted of easy-to-design, straightforward machines. After all, the amphibious assault might be regarded as little more than an unusually hazardous ferrying job. Diesel-engine boats chugged their way to the beach, and gravity-powered bow ramps clanked down onto the sand, disgorging marines to meet their destinies. Winches hauled the ramps back up, and the boats backed off to return to the staging area for another load.

This is, of course, an extremely narrow understanding of what technology is and how it works. The boat ride to the beach is only one element in the amphibious landing, comprising neither the beginning nor the end of the military operation, and certainly not exhausting technology's role in the endeavor. Before any marines climb down the cargo nets into the landing craft, for example, naval vessels that are specially equipped for antishore (rather than antiship) bombardment pound the landing beaches in an effort to destroy enemy defenses and drive off any surviving defenders. Before the naval bombardment, aerial bombardment or commando raids requiring an entirely new set of technologies may be in order. Then, after the marines hit the beaches, yet another host of machines and objects—including rifles, hand grenades, radios, wire cutters, and combat rations—come into play.

And this only includes the technological hardware. What we would today properly regard as the necessary software includes all of the training and techniques for the operation. This means, among other things, teaching coxswains how to avoid traffic jams during the approach to the beaches, marines how to keep their rifles dry, and quartermasters how to load the transports so that supplies came off in the order needed.

In short, amphibious operations require a technological system that relies less on individual machines or technological objects than on large and complex sets of hardware and software that have to cooperate synchronously and whose creations stretch over great distances and time-frames.

Historian of technology Thomas Hughes originated the useful metaphor of the reverse salient in technological development.[1] In combat, pockets of enemy resistance can cause an expanding front to advance unevenly, and particularly forceful resistance can create a reverse salient—a concave bulge that needs to be eliminated before the front can advance securely. Hughes likens the development of technological systems to the uneven expansion of a military front. The insightful engineer, like the skilled general, is quick to recognize reverse salients and devise ways to destroy them. For historians of technology, the reverse salient image illuminates how engineers and managers identified critical problems and tried to solve them. Specifically, it reveals the nature of the goals of the innovation. In a military operation, whether any particular unit is running "ahead" of the front or lagging "behind," the front line can be gauged simply by its distance from the geographic objective. In technological matters, where the map is more ambiguous, the identification of critical problems—technical or political—exposes the nature and definition of the objective. Two elements of that technological system that became "reverse salients" in Thomas Hughes's sense were the landing craft themselves and marine training. The engineering of both of these served the Corps's bureaucratic needs and also bore the stamp of the marines' institutional culture.

Landing Craft R&D

The purely technical demands of the landing craft envisioned by marines were surprisingly troublesome. The boats would have to possess relatively high speed, seaworthiness, great maneuverability, excellent surf-riding characteristics, and the ability to land on the beach and retract with ease. To survive enemy fire, they would have to be extraordinarily rugged, perhaps armored. And, since many landing boats would be necessary for sizable operations, they also had to be economical and able to be quickly produced in large quantities.

This list of requirements presented a daunting challenge in naval engineering and architecture. The most difficult task by far was to design a hull that would exhibit the desired beaching characteristics in surf. Most Pacific atolls have shorelines that are continuously pounded by heavy surf that makes landing and retracting extremely difficult. This could result in rudders and propellers being driven deep into the sand, often too far from the beach to land fully loaded marines. In addition, the roiled silt could clog water-cooled engines, and the quickly retreating water could leave boats broached and stranded.

The obvious solution was a shallow-draft boat—a flat-keel design with some shielding of the rudder and propeller. Hulls with drafts down to about one foot were not unknown, but boat designers had always wrestled with the trade-off in performance. For example, the shallowest design of all—a raft—has a draft approaching zero. However, it obviously lacks the hydrodynamic qualities necessary for good handling underway. Most of the successful shallow-draft boats, which had been designed for service on the relatively calm water of rivers, performed poorly in open seas and especially in surf. The flat keel also inhibited the hull's ability to slice through the water, thus increasing the engine power necessary to drive the boat at a desired speed.

The drawbacks of shallow-draft design were exacerbated by the hydrodynamic complexity of the beaching problem. The state of naval architecture after World War I allowed designers to draw ocean-going ships' hulls with fairly high confidence because the interaction between hull and water was easily modeled both on paper and using towing tests in a model basin. The situation for designing landing boats was entirely different, however. Introducing sand and beach into the interaction between hull and water presented a problem that was essentially impossible to solve a priori. The only reliable method of determining a new boat's beaching characteristics was to build it and test it in the water.

For most of the 1920s the primary research and development agency for marine landing craft was the Navy's Bureau of Construction and Repair (BuCon), which had been responsible for the design and maintenance of all of the Navy's ships since the late nineteenth century. Technical issues regarding propulsion fell to the Bureau of Engineering (BuEng).

When the Navy needed designs for new ships or refits, naval architects at BuCon would produce the drawings, often with the help of scale model tests conducted at their Experimental Model Basin at the Washington Navy Yard. As with the Navy's other technical bureaus, the chief of BuCon reported directly to the chief of naval operations and the secretary of the Navy. In 1940 BuCon and BuEng were merged into the Bureau of Ships (BuShips).[2]

Since BuCon housed the Navy's experts in naval architecture, it was only logical to assign them the job of designing landing craft for the marines. Ironically, however, BuCon's expertise in naval architecture often became an obstacle for landing-craft development. Since the early twentieth century, naval architects had successfully focused their attention on the intricacies of the behavior of large ships in the water, particularly scaling down fluid mechanics so that a new design could be accurately tested in a model tank. By the 1920s this work had vastly improved the Navy's ability to design the hulls and spaces for capital ships, but had contributed almost nothing to enhance their ability to design small boats. Naval architects at the time paid almost no attention to small craft.[3]

But why was knowledge of large ships not equally useful for small-boat design? Could the same mathematical models be scaled down? No, because the enormous differences in sizes and weights made the fluid dynamics for boats much different from that for ships. One example: Running at ten knots, a three-hundred-foot ship weighing six thousand tons will experience ten times the resistance of a fifty-foot boat weighing fifteen tons. Even worse, about 80 percent of the ship's resistance will stem from friction, and only about 20 percent from wave formation. For the small boat, that ratio will be exactly reversed.[4] Trying to predict the behavior of a small boat by scaling down the model for a large ship simply does not work. While the design of large ships had become a mature branch of engineering by the early twentieth century, the design of small boats remained a craft.

The situation for landing-craft design was even more difficult. Since most formally trained naval architects specialized in ship design, they had been taught to regard a beached vessel as something to be avoided. When one of their designs landed on a beach, it was usually the end of a very bad day. So, for much of this story, the officers and designers at BuCon were simply out of their element.

Early Attempts: Beetles, Barges, and Lighters

In 1922 General Lejeune provided BuCon with the general characteristics of a boat for landing marines on a hostile shore. The bureau in turn drew plans for a fifty-foot landing barge capable of carrying 125 men. Construction began at the Norfolk Navy Yard after Lejeune and the CNO approved the plans. The resulting boat was built of riveted steel, weighed forty-six thousand pounds, and had a top speed of nine knots. It was fitted with metal air tanks to increase buoyancy and encased in a smooth metal shell that provided armor protection above and a smooth beaching surface below. The troops disembarked from the steel belly via a large bow hatch. The boat, officially named Troop Barge A, was universally referred to by all concerned as the "Beetle Boat."[5]

The Beetle Boat's first service test came at the Culebra landing exercises in the winter of 1924. The Culebra exercises, conducted at the island of that name off Puerto Rico, were, for the most part, a disaster, and demonstrated that an enormous amount of work had to done before amphibious operations would be militarily viable. The Beetle Boat itself performed relatively well, landing men and machines with ease. The majority of the exercise, however, took place in smooth water, and the Beetle Boat's behavior in heavier seas left a great deal to be desired because it tended to roll perilously and violently pound the crests of incoming waves.[6]

The evaluating board made many suggestions for improvement, including finlike bilge keels fitted along the bottom to increase seaworthiness by damping the roll.[7] The revisions were incorporated into the designs for a second fifty-foot troop lighter in February, 1926. At the same time, BuCon suggested plans for an open forty-foot boat to land subsequent waves of troops (the enclosing armor thought necessary only for the first wave), as well as a fifty-foot powerless lighter for landing artillery. The new boats were generally called types A, B, and C, respectively, and all had a draft of less than three feet. After getting approval from Commandant Lejeune, BuCon closely supervised the building of these boats at Norfolk.

The A-, B-, and C-boats exhibited several new features that characterized landing-craft development for the next decade. These included specially designed housings to protect the rudder and propeller, even at some expense in propeller efficiency, and heavily filtered engine-circulating systems to keep out sand and mud. The Bureau of Construction and Repair also

Marines get their feet wet emerging from the "Beetle Boat" in a 1924 landing exercise.
Photograph courtesy of the National Archives and Records Administration

tested the designs at the Washington Navy Yard's model basin to determine the effective horsepower needed to drive the hulls at different speeds.[8]

The A- and C-boats were completed in July, 1926, and naval and marine officers conducted preliminary tests at Hampton Roads, Virginia, the next month. The board quickly received a lesson in the dangers of using riveted steel to build boats of this type. While it was being loaded, the artillery lighter took on a slight list and appeared to ship water. Upon being towed away from the pier by the A-boat as planned, it looked very sluggish and unstable, and sideswiped the pier on the way out. The starboard list grew and, about a hundred yards out, the boat capsized, dumping the artillery piece, tractor, and equipment overboard. One Navy observer dryly reported, "This concluded the tests of the artillery lighter."[9] After it was hauled out of the water, the lighter was found to have popped a rivet, allowing one of the tanks to fill with water. All subsequent metal landing craft were welded rather then riveted.

The A-boat, in comparison, appeared to be a total success. Although it only made about eight knots fully loaded, it handled very well and easily landed and unloaded its 120 marines. The board was pleasantly surprised to find that the boat also retracted from the beach much better than expected. General Lejeune, delighted by the potential economy of this "feature," strongly recommended that all future landing-craft models incorporate every possible trait to facilitate getting back off the beach quickly under their own power.[10]

Engineers at BuCon, although pleased with the A-boat's performance, reminded the marines that the trial had only been preliminary, and that a much more rigorous battery of tests was needed before any such boats could be approved. In particular, BuCon wanted to see rough-water tests with various loads.

As the A-boat underwent further revisions and testing, BuCon completed the forty-foot B-boat and tried to incorporate features gleaned from earlier tests. In compliance with General Lejeune's request to make the boat retractable, the B-boat was equipped with a stern winch and anchor that could be used to break it free from the sand and allow it to return to sea. A forty-five-foot arc-welded artillery lighter was similarly fitted.

But the work went very slowly. The Navy's austere budgets in the late 1920s left little room for experimentation with something so undramatic

Clambering over the bow of the Navy-designed A-boat landing craft during a landing exercise in the 1930s. Photograph courtesy of the Marine Corps University Research Archives, Quantico, Va.

as landing barges. Moreover, the marines' attention and manpower was often drawn to the on-going operations in Nicaragua, and some tests were delayed because of a dearth of marines to conduct them.[11]

Even more stifling was a growing uncertainty over precisely what kind of landing craft the marines wanted. Major Ellis's study of operations in Micronesia had done a spectacular job of outlining the strategic issues of amphibious war but had not gone into any detail on the specific technical characteristics of the hardware required. Further tests of the A-boat, B-boat, and the new artillery lighter indicated that the fifty-foot A-boat was clearly the most promising of the lot. However, by the early 1930s the marines' thinking had changed. Marine theorists working out the specific procedures for amphibious assaults were gradually convincing themselves that the first wave of an invasion force should approach the beach in smaller boats that would provide more difficult targets for enemy shore batteries. After five years of testing, the marines decided that their most promising landing craft was just too big.

"Marines with Marine Training"

Landing craft comprised only one part of the technological system that the marines needed to make the amphibious-assault mission a reality. The software for the system was just as important as the hardware. For the marines, this meant training the officers and men who would operate the machinery—in fact, become part of it—during the amphibious assault.

The marines held their first substantial postwar landing exercise in the Caribbean. From December, 1923, to February, 1924, a thirty-three-hundred-man marine force worked out a series of landing problems at Culebra and the Panama Canal Zone. The results were discouraging at best. Although one attacking force was ruled victorious over Army defenders, most of the exercises were disastrous. In spite of the use of some newly designed landing equipment, both the boats and the boat handlers proved to be woefully inadequate. According to Brig. Gen. Eli K. Cole, commander of the Marine Expeditionary Force, "Chaos reigned. The boat officers had not been informed of the designated landing beaches. There was no order maintained among the boats carrying the landing party . . . to the landing beaches. Certain boats became lost for a time and landings were made on beaches which had not been designated for units."[12]

The ship-to-shore movement was not the only problem. The simulated naval gunfire support would have caused almost no damage to the artillery positions on the reverse slope overlooking the landing beach. Logistical planning was also dismal. Although the landing force set up the post exchange within a few hours, no food came ashore until the second day, and medical supplies ended up at the bottom of the transport hold, completely inaccessible until nine days later.[13]

Another set of exercises was held in April, 1925, in Hawaii. These landings were smaller than the previous year's, but much better organized. Although the landings went more smoothly, they again reinforced the need for better landing boats. American intervention in China and Nicaragua diverted marines from exercises the following year, and the 1925 landings turned out to be the last until the mid-1930s.

Still, the exercises showed that seizing advance bases from an enemy was probably possible, and thus played into Lejeune's bureaucratic struggle to claim the advance-base mission for the Marine Corps. Lejeune and his allies at Marine Corps headquarters realized early on that their most serious competitor was the U.S. Army. If anyone could steal the amphibious mission from the marines, it was the Army. To defend themselves, marine advance-base activists skillfully tapped into the ancient rivalry between the Army and the Navy. Amphibious operations must only be performed by marines, they argued, because the landing force and the Navy would have to work as an intimate team, and because the land-locked Army simply could not be trusted to serve the interests of their seagoing brothers in arms. As readers of the *Marine Corps Gazette* learned in 1923,

> In order that the authority of control in combined operations may be fully established and not open to question, it is necessary that both belong to the same department, be indoctrinated with the same ideas and principles, and operate under the same rules and regulations. As the operation of seizing advance bases and of holding them, at least in the initial stages, is entirely and obviously an operation undertaken for the serving of the interests of the navy, it is apparent that if one control be established, such control should rest in the navy itself. For this reason, the forces designated for the advance base operations should be a part of the naval service, insuring unified control, with greatly increased prospects of success.

The marines are the logical solution of the problem presented for the personnel of the advance base forces.[14]

Cultivating the Army-Navy rivalry yielded fruit in 1925, when a new controversy between the two services over responsibility for coast defense led the Navy to reexamine the Marine Corps's role. Lejeune urged the General Board to make the reassessment a comprehensive statement of Marine Corps duties, particularly the marines' sole responsibility for the initial seizure and defense of advance bases.[15]

The Navy concurred and took the marines' case to the Joint Army-Navy Board. In 1927 the Joint Board sorted out the peacetime and wartime responsibilities of all the services, and then delineated them in an unclassified pamphlet titled *Joint Action of the Army and Navy.* In it, the marines kept their traditional missions (including serving as infantry with the Army), but received sole rights to the amphibious mission. *Joint Action* assigned to the Marine Corps "[l]and operations in support of the fleet for the initial seizure and defense of advance bases and for such limited auxiliary land operations as are essential to the prosecution of the naval campaign."[16]

At the same time that marines were battling to secure the advance-base mission on paper, they also began systematically to indoctrinate the rank and file in the Corps's new purpose in life. Most of this educational work was done in the sleepy town of Quantico, Virginia, some fifty miles south of Washington on the Potomac River. The Marine Corps Schools (MCS) were established there during World War I, but classes met only intermittently until the early 1920s.[17] The primary school was the Field Officers' Course, designed for up-and-coming officers who appeared destined for positions of high rank.[18]

The Field Officers' Course ran from September to June, and its curriculum in the early 1920s reflected the Corps's traditional jobs, especially its recent service in World War I. Almost all of the coursework was patterned after the classes taught at the Army's Infantry School at Fort Benning, Georgia, and its Command and General Staff School at Fort Leavenworth, Kansas. The overwhelming focus was on traditional land warfare, and the tactics texts were books, pamphlets, and mimeograph copies taken from the Army schools.[19]

General Lejeune gradually added the MCS to his amphibious warfare arsenal. He successively appointed two advance-base advocates to serve as MCS commandant: Col. Ben Fuller in 1922, and Col. Robert Dunlap in 1924. After the 1925 landing exercises Lejeune directed Dunlap to expand the MCS's curriculum devoted to landing operations to include classes on Pacific strategy, embarking and loading troops and supplies, hydrography and meteorology, tactical principles for securing a beachhead, landing sites, naval gunfire, beach and shore parties, landing boats, and night landings.[20] During the 1924–25 academic year, amphibious operations occupied 2 hours out of the roughly 1,000 hours of class time. In 1926–27, the number increased to 49 hours; in 1927–28, over 100 hours; and by 1930–31, MCS students were spending 216 hours—more than one-fifth of their coursework—on landing operations. By that time the coursework also included analyses of the British landings at Gallipoli, the British raid on Zeebrugge, and German landings on Russian islands in the Baltic.[21] Despite the loss of personnel diverted to expeditionary duty in Nicaragua and China from 1928 to 1930, the MCS was fast becoming the center of doctrine and indoctrination for amphibious operations. Between 1920 and 1930, 198 marine officers passed through the Field Officers' Course.[22]

Threats and Growth

Despite its growing success at the MCS, the amphibious mission was stumbling on the bureaucratic front, largely because of personnel cutbacks during the depression-ridden Hoover administration. Between 1929 and 1932 the Corps's authorized complement dropped from 17,586 to 15,355, making it increasingly difficult for Lejeune's eventual successor, Ben Fuller, to divert more men to the Advanced Base Force.[23] In 1932 General Fuller gravely reported that it was "impossible for the corps to carry out its primary mission of supporting the United States Fleet by maintaining a force in readiness to operate with the fleet. . . . The Marine Corps is not prepared to perform its allotted task in the event of a national emergency."[24]

More troubles were coming. In another territorial threat, the Army Air Corps in 1930–31 sought to absorb marine aviation, which, like the Air Corps, was responsible for close air support of ground operations. Once again the commandant took the challenge as an opportunity to reestablish the Corps's position within the Navy. The General Board, after again reexamining the Marine Corps's mission, recommended to Navy Secretary Charles Francis Adams that the Corps once again be enlarged. It further recommended that it be "organized to provide the forces for the execution of its war-time missions: primarily, assisting the fleet in the seizure and initial defense of advanced bases."[25]

Fuller well knew that the Corps's fortunes would rise and fall with its usefulness to the Navy. "The need of a Marine Corps," he warned, "will cease to exist when the necessity of the Corps as a branch of the Naval Service ceases to exist."[26] At Quantico, MCS instructors taught their students to honor their bureaucratic parent:

> We are just as proud of our record, and sing with pride that part of our Marine Hymn—"From the Halls of Montezuma to the Shores of Tripoli, We Fight Our Country's Battles on the Land as on the Sea."
>
> But who took us to the land where we fought? Who took us across the sea? Upon whom did the government place the initial responsibility for the enforcement of its determined policy? The NAVY. The Navy has been our father and mother, tutored us during our childhood days, afforded opportunities for us to learn by experience, watched and guarded our growth to manhood, and demanded of our nation that we be allowed to grow strong and sufficient to perform the tasks which she has assigned to us. Do not weaken that demand.[27]

Throughout the Corps, marines cultivated strong ties to high-ranking naval officers. They were particularly successful at the Navy's doctrinal headquarters, the Naval War College. The college's president, Rear Adm. Harris Laning, lobbied the CNO's office hard to increase the Navy's attention to amphibious operations, particularly in the area of landing force equipment. The ranking marine at the college, Col. Richard M. Cutts, reported back to marine headquarters that Laning had become a staunch ally and that his conversion to the cause was "not a surface penetration."[28]

This coalition building may have preserved the Corps's existence in 1932–33, when it faced its most serious bureaucratic threat of the interwar years. For fiscal year 1933, the Hoover administration recommended a reduction in marine strength of nearly 25 percent from its 1931 level. The administration proposed no reduction in the Army and only a 5.6 percent cut in the Navy for the same period.[29] At the same time, a rumor began circulating in Washington that the president was about to sign an executive order drafted by General MacArthur, the Army chief of staff, that would transfer the Marine Corps from the Navy to the Army.

Herbert Hoover had developed a deep resentment of the Marine Corps by 1932, particularly after several embarrassing public disputes with Maj. Gen. Smedley Butler. After Butler retired he became a vociferous Hoover critic and leader of the Bonus Army march on Washington. To Hoover, the marines appeared a prime target in the relentless pressure to economize. Likewise, the relationship between the marines and the Army had not improved since the squabbling over Belleau Wood. The discord had worsened, in fact, with the marines' ever-closer ties to the Navy.

A parade of supporters publicly came to the Marine Corps's defense, including many members of Congress, notably the Naval Affairs Committee chairmen in both the House and Senate, and a stream of high-ranking Navy officials, including the CNO and the Navy secretary. In January, 1933, the much-feared executive order evaporated in heated White House meetings, and the House Naval Affairs Committee restored the marines to their 1931 strength of eighteen thousand.[30]

This latest hostile take-over threat coincided with two other events that greatly enhanced the prospects of the amphibious-assault mission. First, 1933–34 saw large numbers of marines come home from China, Nicaragua, and Haiti. The influx of personnel returning from expeditionary duty provided the manpower necessary to strengthen the amphibious forces. In fact, Marine Corps headquarters had to assign these men quickly to justify their hard-won personnel levels.

Second, the former assistant secretary of the Navy in charge of Marine Corps affairs during World War I became president of the United States. Franklin Roosevelt fondly recalled his successful effort to restore the globe and anchor to the uniforms of marines serving in the AEF. The Corps later stumbled into an even better connection to the first family. One night over dinner, Roosevelt's son James turned to the president's Marine Corps aide and mentioned that he was interested in a reserve commission. The president thought it was a "grand idea," but since the Army aide was also at the dinner table, the marine officer quickly dropped the subject. Shortly thereafter, James Roosevelt, having had no prior military experience, was commissioned a lieutenant colonel in the Marine Corps Reserve. Subsequently, Marine Corps headquarters made sure that Lieutenant Colonel Roosevelt (privately dubbed "Son James" by marine leaders) observed every landing exercise, participated in maneuvers, and camped with the troops. One of Roosevelt's Marine Corps handlers happily informed the commandant that Son James was getting a "forced feeding" of amphibious adventure and loving it. "[M]uch to our gratification," he reported, "[James Roosevelt] seems to be assimilating a remarkable amount of the food. I impressed everybody with the importance of arousing his interest and all hands have put their shoulders to the wheel."[31] In return, the Marine Corps got an ever-present booster with unlimited access to the president.

It did not need one. Franklin Roosevelt (like his eventual counterpart, Winston Churchill), was a former Navy official who took from World War I the lesson that the stalemate of trench warfare ignored the many clever ways of waging war offered by modern technology. Roosevelt, who was particularly captivated by the amphibious assault, frequently asked his naval and marine attachés for the latest reports on landing exercises and materiel development. He was especially interested in landing-craft design, and would personally inspect new prototypes and make suggestions for improvements.[32] General Fuller exulted that "the 'New Deal' seems to be working," and that the future looked much brighter with Roosevelt than "when the Engineer [Hoover] was hamstringing us."[33]

To Maj. Gen. John Russell, an old personal friend of the president's, the time was right to permanently remedy the personnel difficulty that had plagued the amphibious-landing mission since World War I. Russell, then serving as assistant commandant and soon to become commandant, argued that amphibious troops scattered within the marines' expeditionary forces were too vulnerable to assignments that drew them away from the Corps's true mission. He convinced General Fuller to let him begin the staff work to create a permanent amphibious force immune to extraneous demands. He suggested that the force be called something like the Fleet Base Defense Force or the Fleet Marine Force since the term "expeditionary force" was "too general in its meaning and wide in its significance to be appropriate for a force having as specific an aim as [amphibious operations]."[34] This new force would be directly controlled by the commander in chief of the U.S. Fleet while engaged in fleet operations or exercises. Russell's proposal met with rapid approval from the CNO, the U.S. Fleet commander, and the War Plans Division, and the Fleet Marine Force (FMF) became reality with the issuance of Navy General Order 241, on 7 December 1933.

The FMF grew slowly, from a strength of 2,000 (about one-tenth of total Marine Corps strength) in 1934 to about 4,500 in 1939. After war broke out in Europe, the complement rose to almost 10,000, and to over 22,000—the size of two full divisions—by early 1941.[35] Despite its slow increase in size, the FMF permitted—in fact required—the Corps to maintain a permanent force in readiness for amphibious operations. And while the U.S. Fleet commander held permanent authority over this force, he also was responsible for its training and readiness. The earlier turf fights over policies like *Joint Action*, although important, were abstract commitments on paper. The FMF, on the other hand, was a material commitment of ever-precious manpower.

On an institutional cultural level, too, Marine Corps headquarters was determined to "indoctrinate" the rank and file in the new order. Headquarters informed its officers that it was

> the unqualified duty of every Marine officer to keep the importance of this force in view at all times; to realize that the interests of the fleet (the Fleet Marine Force) are paramount; to inform himself thoroughly of the object and purpose of the Fleet Marine Force and its importance to the fleet; and, in his official and personal contacts both within and without the service, to support and assist this Headquarters in its settled policy of developing and strengthening the Fleet Marine Force. . . . You are requested to take steps to indoctrinate all Marine officers under your command accordingly.[36]

Headquarters also did its part to indoctrinate all officers by cycling as many officers as possible through the FMF, often immediately after a stint studying amphibious operations at the MCS. By 1940 the majority of active-duty officers had completed the amphibious warfare regimen, and many of the Corps's best officers were handpicked for the FMF.[37]

With the personnel now in place, the task remained to work out precisely what all those men were supposed to do.

Chapter 8
Doctrine and Fishing Boats

By the early 1930s the Marine Corps had done much of the political, intellectual, and technological spadework for making the amphibious assault its mission in life. The Navy had been convinced that amphibious operations were a necessary part of its Pacific strategy, and, more importantly, that the marines would be a much better bureaucratic partner in an island-hopping campaign than the Army. The Corps also developed a staunch ally in Franklin Roosevelt, who was increasingly captivated by the bold, exotic character of amphibious warfare. Tests of the landing-craft prototypes developed by BuCon had not been particularly successful, but they were promising enough to accommodate the optimistic hope that where the will led, technology would follow. Finally, the marines had begun indoctrinating themselves in the creed that the amphibious assault was their true calling, perfectly harmonious with the Corps's institutional identity as a warrior elite that was always "First to Fight." Leathernecks at the MCS at Quantico were told many times and in many ways that amphibious warfare was the reason for their existence.

But while the MCS curriculum was devoting more and more class hours to the amphibious assault, concrete doctrine had advanced little in the decade since Pete Ellis's "Advanced Base Operations in Micronesia" study had laid out the rudiments of amphibious landings in 1921. The Navy's 1920 *Landing Force Manual* had devoted seven pages (out of 760) to the subject, and the 1927 revision compressed this brief treatment to five pages.[1] In 1931 a small MCS committee assembled to write a landing operations manual had failed to get very far. Worst of all, the doctrinal materials the marines did have were still coming from U.S. Army textbooks.

If the marines wanted to make the advance-base mission their own, this would have to change. Almost literally, they would have to write the book on this new warfare, and then make sure that the globe and anchor was emblazoned on the cover.

Writing the Book

General Fuller visited Quantico in August, 1932, and met with the new MCS commandant, Brig. Gen. James C. Breckinridge, and his executive officer, Col. Ellis B. Miller, both amphibious warfare proponents. The three officers agreed that the MCS curriculum had "not hitherto placed sufficient emphasis upon the peculiar mission of the Corps."[2] Miller, a graduate of the Naval War College and both Army schools, was especially convinced that the MCS was simply not doing its job of infusing the institutional identity of the Marine Corps into the officers who passed through its doors.

Consequently, Miller composed a long, impassioned manifesto on how the MCS had thus far failed to serve the Corps's true interests and how emergency action was necessary. In particular, he argued that the institutional culture of the marines' bureaucratic nemesis, the U.S. Army, was still far too prevalent at Quantico.

The MCS, he argued, had been started from scratch after World War I, and was totally lacking in trained instructors or course materials. In order to get the schools up and running as quickly as possible, its administrators "took the line of least resistance and went to the Army School of the Line at Ft. Leavenworth" for the information and material they needed. In this way, Miller mourned, the MCS became "an Army School, hook, line, and sinker."[3] Despite periodic attempts to focus on the marines' peculiar mission (amphibious operations), "the constant and prolonged use of this Army material . . . has so saturated the entire Marine Corps Schools System that its foundation is still resting on army principles, army organization, and army thought."[4]

"Why teach them army?" he implored. "Why? Why? If fighting on land is a Marine's job then why not teach them Marine? . . . Must we always go to the Army to learn our job?"[5]

The time had come, Miller argued, for the marines to assert their cultural and intellectual independence from the Army. As far as the MCS was concerned, the key was to develop their own textbooks and teaching materials ("It's all a matter of text books. The Army Schools have them. We have not."[6]) After World War I, he noted, the Army Schools correctly recognized the uniqueness of the American soldier when they stopped relying on German military textbooks.

Certainly, [abandoning the German texts] could not have been conceived because the Germans did not know how to wage war. On the contrary the entire military world took their hats off to the German methods. But the American military experts determined that they must stand on their own feet; that an American soldier is different from a German soldier; that the development of American military organization, strategy, tactics and command must be based on our own policies and not the policy of some foreign state. . . .[A]nd so, since 1919, they have been developing American principles, American doctrine, American tactics, American organization, American equipment and plans for operations of the American Army based on American policy and American strategy.[7]

Now, the marines must do the same. "What I have said with regard to the [Army] Schools and the American Army," he argued, "can be applied to the Marine Corps Schools and the Marine Corps."[8] It was time to develop "Marine Corps Doctrine, organization, and equipment."[9]

To this end, Miller recommended radical action. He urged Breckinridge and Fuller to direct the MCS to devote the entire 1932–33 academic year to developing a new curriculum for the schools. The instructors and students would be merged into one large research group whose goal was to work out the details of Marine Corps doctrine (especially regarding the amphibious assault), Marine Corps organization, and Marine Corps equipment and armament. Their efforts would pay particular attention to coordinating with the marines' Navy patrons, and conversely rooting out much of the Army influence that lingered. The ultimate goal of the year would be to produce a textbook that could serve as the foundation for all future MCS instruction.[10]

The MCS commandant, General Breckinridge, was initially daunted by Miller's radical proposal. Although he believed that he and Miller "think strangely alike in these matters," Breckinridge had not expected to recast the schools so thoroughly so quickly.[11] Nevertheless, he became convinced that the time was right for this "radical departure."

We are in a state of change; and I feel that a point has been reached (now, at this very time) where the change must take a decided and radical turn. . . .

In a manner of speech we have arrived at a turn-table, upon which we shall place ourselves for the year 1932–1933. During this year we will reorient ourselves, and pick up the new track upon which we must travel for the future as far as we can see it.[12]

Breckinridge asked for and received "blanket approval in principle" for Miller's proposed conversion of the MCS curriculum in 1932–33.[13]

Traditional courses at the MCS were suspended while the faculty and students (some fifty officers) devoted themselves to writing the new textbook. They began by studying, in withering detail, one of the largest and best-documented examples of an amphibious assault from World War I: the disastrous British and Australian landings at Gallipoli. Each marine was issued a copy of the official British history of the Gallipoli operation, and the new Gallipoli course became the centerpiece of the year's study.[14]

This study of past landing operations, focusing on Gallipoli, consumed the entire year. In 1933 Breckinridge recommended to General Fuller that the MCS continue the radical experiment by suspending all classes entirely and devoting the next school year exclusively to writing a manual laying out the doctrine of the amphibious landing. Fuller agreed, and classes stopped in mid-November.[15]

The procedure for laying out the manual was deliberately designed to permit the broadest range of ideas. Instructors were directed to plan an entire amphibious assault operation and produce a chronological list of all staff and operational tasks from the initial conception of the mission to the actual landing. A committee of nine then studied all of these plans and synthesized them into a master list. Each member of this committee also submitted a list of his own. A committee of five then analyzed these summaries and drew up a rough outline for the manual.[16]

On 9 January 1934, some seventy officers, ranging from lieutenants to brigadier generals, assembled at Quantico to thrash out the manual's outline. The group also included four Navy officers and an Army lieutenant. The assembly heard reports on the major sections of the manual—command issues, naval gunfire and aerial support, ship-to-shore movement, securing the beachhead, and logistics—and gradually built a consensus on what should go into the manual.[17] At long last the marines at Quantico felt they were articulating a new form of warfare, in all its magnificent detail, that bore the Corps's stamp from beginning to end.

In the midst of this burst of military theorizing, however, the Corps's bureaucratic concerns bared themselves once again—and in a way that even the politically savvy officers at Quantico considered unseemly. At the very end of the January, 1934, conference, the Marine Corps headquarters representative asked to deliver a message from General Russell, the assistant commandant. Even the otherwise dry minutes of the meeting capture the tension of the moment.

> Major Barrett [the headquarters representative] asked if he might be allowed to deliver a message from General Russell, and stated that he was authorized by General Russell to present it at this conference. The following record of what Major Barrett said may not be correct, in view of the fact that the message as delivered was not clear to General Breckinridge, General Lyman [of the FMF], Colonel Miller, and, I believe, others; and when Major Barrett was asked to more broadly interpret this message he stated that he could do no more than present the message as given to him. This message, as I recall it, was to the effect that General Russell wanted a manual that would indicate to the Navy the broad general part that we should play in Landing Operations so that the Naval officer who would read this manual (and it should be short in order to get him to read it) would realize the necessity for preparation and training and the things that the Navy should provide us in way of boats, beach parties, and equipment essential for the defense of a base; that General Russell was especially interested in training and defense of bases, and that we should put that fact over to the Commander in Chief [of the U.S. Fleet].[18]

For John Russell, an amphibious warfare activist who soon replaced Fuller as Marine Corps commandant, the primary point of all this doctrinal analysis was to convince the *Navy* of the importance of equipment and training.

The suggestion that all of this doctrinal labor was really intended to impress their institutional patrons in the Navy infuriated the senior marines present.

General Breckinridge replied to Major Barrett: "We are painting the entire picture, and you can take out what you want to. I have no picture of what you have been painting. We will send the entire picture to Marcorps [headquarters] and any part that is not wanted can very easily be taken out."

Colonel Miller asked Major Barrett: "Who are we writing this manual for? As from your remarks I gather that we are writing it for the Navy. We thought this was to be a manual for Marine officers, indicating what and how they should operate in this type of operation."

Major Barrett replied that he told us exactly what General Russell said, and that he was not in a position to amplify or interpret General Russell's remarks.[19]

Undaunted by Russell's suggestion, or perhaps hopeful that they had misunderstood it, the meeting's participants divided the manual up into three primary sections: (1) tactics, including the landing and defense of the base, (2) staff functions, logistics, plans, and orders, and (3) training. Separate sections were also dedicated to aviation and naval activities such as gunfire support. These sections were then assigned to committees and subcommittees of the staff and students at the MCS, where the chapters were actually written. The first parts of the text were submitted to the MCS commandant in March, 1934, and the first draft was finished in June, and revised several times over the next year.

The *Tentative Manual for Landing Operations* became the exclusive point of departure for all amphibious warfare planning until after America's entry into World War II. It was widely distributed throughout the Navy and Marine Corps in 1935, and was later adopted as the Navy's *Fleet Training Publication No. 167: Landing Operations Doctrine.* The manual served as the basis for planning the invasion of Guadalcanal in August, 1942.

The *Tentative Manual* contained chapters entitled "Landing Operations, General"; "Task Organization"; "Landing Boats"; "Ship to Shore Movement"; "Naval Gunfire"; "Aviation"; "Communications"; "Field Artillery, Tanks, Chemicals, and Smoke"; and "Logistics".[20] According to the manual there were six essential elements to a successful amphibious operation.

First, since unity of command and coordination were vital, the landing force should be under the supreme authority of the senior Navy flag officer. Second, since the landing force would be extremely vulnerable during the trip to shore, fierce and effective naval gunfire support would be necessary to suppress enemy shore batteries. To do so, naval ordnance would have to be modified to attack targets on reverse slopes. Even more importantly, naval officers would have to be purged of the traditional wisdom, prevalent since the age of Nelson and reinforced at Gallipoli, that a ship's a fool to fight a fort. Third, aerial support would have to provide covering fire when the first boats hit the beaches, since the offshore bombardment would then have to stop. Fourth, the ship-to-shore movement must be in a tactical combat formation, and not treated as a ferrying operation. Given the small size of most Pacific islands, tactical surprise would be virtually unattainable, so the landing force would have to be ready to fight on the beach. The manual illustrated numerous landing formations, most of which closely followed traditional formations for squads of infantry in a ground assault. Fifth, securing the beachhead would require a sufficiently large landing zone to permit continued landings and maneuver, well-trained beach and shore parties, and good communications to direct traffic. Finally, well-organized logistics, sorely lacking at Gallipoli, would have to be arranged under the principle of combat loading: supplies must be accessible at the landing site in the order they would be needed in the assault. While this would usually result in less packing efficiency, it would prevent urgently needed ammunition and medical supplies from ending up at the bottom of the cargo holds.

The tenets of the manual became the subject of much further study and training, and they often required technological, as well as doctrinal, innovation. The central problem with adequate naval gunfire support, for example, was that traditional naval ordnance was unsuited to the task. The new marine doctrine, taken directly from World War I artillery tactics, called for gunfire support to lay down a high-trajectory barrage, a vertical sheet of fire that would suppress enemy shore batteries, even those on the opposite sides of slopes overlooking the beach. However, most naval ordnance and gunfire doctrine was designed to attack other ships, and hence consisted of high-velocity, low-trajectory, armor-piercing shells—a form of artillery almost useless in supporting an amphibious assault (though the *Tentative Manual* did note the "definite demoralizing effect" of direct, high-velocity fire).[21] Naval units training for amphibious-assault support thus experimented with lower muzzle velocities and higher trajectories, and high-explosive and fragmentation shells.[22]

It was clear that these sorts of technical concerns would require greater and more concentrated Marine Corps attention. Commandant Russell accordingly created a permanent Marine Corps Equipment Board in the summer of 1935 specifically for this purpose. With representatives from the commandant's office, the FMF, the MCS, the quartermaster's department, and the Operations and Training Division, the board met almost monthly until World War II.[23] The board dealt with the full spectrum of technical equipment for amphibious operations, including landing craft, field telephones, water purifiers, ammunition belts, machetes, sunglasses, combat rations, and canteen cups.[24]

Although written in the language of military technicians, the blood and guts vision of the amphibious assault permeates the *Tentative Manual*. The marines in the first landing waves, for example, should expect to be under enormously heavy fire from enemy shore batteries and aircraft. In response, the landing craft should be equipped with machine guns, mortars, and a one-pound deck gun, and the boat should hit the beach with guns blazing.

> Boats in the leading subwave should be prepared to put down a heavy volume of fire on the enemy defenses on or near the beach. This fire may not be accurate on specific targets but it can be sufficiently well directed and intense enough to have an important effect upon enemy troops near the shore which are most dangerous to the landing. . . .[F]ire delivered while actually moving forward in the assault, . . . while it cannot be considered accurate, has been found efficacious in keeping the enemy down. The fire from boat guns is assault fire delivered under extremely advantageous conditions and is of particular value during the period between the lifting of naval gunfire and the time troops are deployed on shore. After the boat grounds, opportunity may develop for well-directed fire on visible targets at short range.[25]

In discussing as mundane a point as the fact that the landing craft must have a shallow draft (in order to get as high onto the beach as possible), the *Tentative Manual* dispassionately noted that "Troops going over the side in water above their waists and wading ashore are under a severe handicap. They are unprotected by naval gunfire during this period, movement is slow, equipment is handled with difficulty, and the morale effect is bad. . . . Under such conditions, heavy casualties even against slight enemy opposition may be anticipated. Light draft boats are particularly desirable for the leading echelons."[26]

The *Tentative Manual* was a remarkable intellectual achievement. Ex nihilo, the marines at Quantico had envisioned a new military enterprise that they could claim as their own. In addition to convincing their Navy benefactors that the amphibious assault was a viable military operation, and one that can and should be performed exclusively by marines, the *Tentative Manual* outlined for the first time precisely how a technological system for amphibious warfare might actually work. But it was still only an outline. The next step in making the theory a reality was to create marines who knew what it felt like to storm a hostile shore.

FLEXing

The Marine Corps engineered the software for amphibious landings through a series of annual Fleet Landing Exercises (FLEXs) held between 1935 and 1941. Usually conducted on the small Puerto Rican island of Culebra, the exercises grew from small operations of fifteen hundred men and a handful of ships and boats to large maneuvers involving full divisions, battleships, and carrier air groups. The exercises tested various techniques of naval gunfire support, combat loading, and close air support, and although the results were rarely conclusive, marines and sailors at long last began getting the considerable amount of training necessary to make the mission feasible.[27]

The FLEXs also proved to be yet another bureaucratic battleground. Ellis Miller's crusade to purge the MCS of any Army trappings had an analogue in field exercises: to keep the Army out of the marines' FLEX training. After modest Army participation in FLEXs Three and Four, Gen. Malin Craig, MacArthur's successor as chief of staff, asked Adm. William Leahy, the CNO, to permit the Army to expand its role in the 1939 exercise by taking part in a joint Army-Navy planning staff.

As far as marines were concerned, the request was nothing more than another attempted takeover. After arguing that the Army was doing little more than stealing the publicity and fruits of Marine Corps labor, the commander of the First Marine Brigade appealed to the commandant to do everything possible to block further Army meddling.

[Army] Colonel Dannemiller (the pain in the neck) approached me on the subject . . . concerning the Army's functioning on the next maneuvers on an equality basis with the marines as far as command and staff work goes. It is all wrong to consider these maneuvers in the light of "Joint Exercises." They are purely "Naval Maneuvers" in which the Army has no place except possibly for instruction purposes and the Army should not be permitted to take from or slow down our training by being accepted on a basis of equality. I am really quite worried over the damage they may do us and would put nothing beyond them. . . . I hope I have seen the last of them.[28]

Marine Corps headquarters initiated a well-coordinated attack on the Army request, and the Navy needed little reason to be suspicious of Army motives. Leahy rejected the offer, limiting Army participation to its previous role as trainees only. The Army abruptly pulled out of the FLEX and did not participate again until 1941. The episode made the front page of the *New York Times,* which considered the incident "serious evidence of friction and inadequate cooperation between the two services."[29] But for marines, keeping the Army a junior partner in the amphibious assault business was a bureaucratic necessity.

Undaunted by the snub from their Navy brethren, the Army decided to have its own amphibious landing exercises anyway. After all, the Army had both the manuals and the men to organize the training operation without Navy support. What the Army did not have was Marine Corps materiel, especially landing craft. No matter. In the Army's 1939 landing exercise, a formation of trucks with large signs saying "LANDING CRAFT" on their sides rumbled across an open field, each carrying a "boat-load" of soldiers to a line of pennants marked "BEACH." The drivers were careful to maintain textbook amphibious assault formation. Upon "landing," the soldiers stormed the "beach" with a cheer. The trucks then "retracted" to the "staging area" "offshore."[30]

Cape May

While the fifty-foot A-boat had looked very promising during its trials in the early 1920s, marine planners a decade later saw major flaws. In their eyes, it now looked like a large, slow, easy target. It also carried too many

Landing craft would also be expected to land arms and materiel. Not all landing tests were encouraging. Photograph courtesy of the Marine Corps University Research Archives, Quantico, Va.

eggs in one basket: Since each A-boat carried more than a hundred men, direct hits on even a few boats would likely break up an attack. The *Tentative Manual* also noted that even if most of the boats reached the beach, disgorging such a large volume of men and equipment on a narrow front would only make them more vulnerable to concentrated fire from machine guns and automatic rifles. Against a capable defender, securing the beachhead would be extremely difficult if not impossible.[31]

A Navy and Marine Corps board created to study the issue had come to this conclusion in 1931. Headed by Brig. Gen. Randolph C. Berkeley, the Experimental Landing Lighter Board concluded that the fifty-foot A-boat did indeed have "an important place in landings against opposition, but, NOT IN THE ASSAULT SUB-WAVES." Rather, it should be used in the later waves to land supplies and supporting troops. The initial landing force would have to be brought up in smaller landing craft, each carrying perhaps ten to twenty men prone. The proposed "X-boat" would allow for much greater flexibility in planning the landing formation. The boat's size and speed (a proposed twelve knots) would make it a much more difficult target for enemy defenses.[32] Here is a clear case where doctrinal considerations were shaping technical decisions. Berkeley went on to become one of the primary authors of the *Tentative Manual*.

The board had gotten a lead on just such a boat from its Coast Guard colleagues. Private fishermen along the New Jersey shore would return from far out at sea and face a tricky conclusion to the day's labor. The paucity of good inlets along the coast required them to land their boats, heavily laden with fish, through surf on the steep, sandy beaches. Their wooden boats—usually made by the fishermen themselves with whatever materials were at hand—had wide, flat bottoms and high, bluff bows. They were commonly known as sea skiffs.

Berkeley's board gave one sea skiff ("procured gratis" from the Coast Guard) a brief trial in 1931, and was pleased enough with the initial results to urge that BuCon design and build one as an X-boat prototype.[33] When the *Tentative Manual for Landing Operations* was written a few years later, one chapter focused on the design of landing boats and called for craft very much along the lines of Berkeley's X-boat proposal.[34] After consulting with BuCon's engineers, who specialized in the design of large ships rather than small landing boats, the marines decided to draw on the expertise of commercial sea-skiff builders. With a privately designed prototype in hand, BuCon itself could then make the final alterations necessary for a satisfactory landing boat. For the first time in this endeavor, the Navy and Marine Corps turned to private industry.

In the summer of 1935 BuCon requested bids from boatyards to build a prototype X-boat. Although the circular specifically mentioned the sea skiff's promise, it was deliberately vague. The bureau wanted to give designers considerable leeway in how they met the stated requirements, and thus encourage different and innovative designs. The specifications called for a boat that could carry eighteen men; that was seaworthy in heavy weather; that measured no more than thirty feet long and weighed less than ten thousand pounds; that could run at fifteen miles per hour in the open sea; that had a draft "as shallow as practicable"; and, most importantly, had the "ability to land through surf in anything less than storm conditions and remain upright when grounded" and then "get off the beach under its own power."[35]

From the developers' standpoint, however, the waters were dangerous. The burden of development costs still lay with the contractor, who could see little reason to gamble so much time and capital on what could become a lottery. One well-established boatyard contacted by the Navy declined to submit a bid and explained, "[W]e do not believe that it would be safe to enter into a definite contract for the construction of such a boat when so many elements are involved and the possibility of falling short of some one requirement is so obvious."[36] Moreover, even if the boat did prove generally satisfactory, there was no guarantee the Navy would buy it in quantity.

Despite those risks, BuCon received bids from eleven builders before the bidding closed in November. Four were deemed promising—all from small boat companies along the New York and New Jersey shores: Red Bank, Bay Head, Greenport, and Freeport. The Red Bank, Bay Head, and Freeport boats were sea-skiff designs. The Greenport was a "sea sled," a boat with an inverted-V keel that had proven very stable and fast.

The contracts with all four companies were signed in February and March, 1936. A marine noncommissioned officer, dispatched to each of the boatyards to oversee construction on site, submitted weekly progress reports directly to Marine Corps headquarters. Throughout the building period these awkwardly written reports from marine corporals and sergeants made their way up to the desk of the Marine Corps commandant.[37]

As the boats were being designed, Navy engineers pressured the small-boat builders to stretch their technical limits, often by reminding them of the prospect of large government contracts for the winner. When the Bay Head boatyard balked at installing a new type of cooling system, the Navy gently noted: "Your attention is again invited to the fact that four different experimental boats are being purchased for a competitive demonstration of the merits of each individual design and it is probable that future orders of larger numbers will be awarded to the successful boat builder. It is therefore to the advantage of both the contractor and the government to incorporate in their design such features as tend to improve the performance of the boats."[38]

Marine officers periodically toured the boatyards, trying in vain to keep the builders on schedule. The delays were no doubt exacerbated by the continuous stream of criticism from marine inspectors who made suggestions on everything from engine design to the shape of the wooden skegs used to protect the propeller while beached. All of the prototypes came in late. The last, the Greenport design, missed the deadline by more than two months.[39]

By order of the Marine Corps Commandant, a special board to test the boats convened at Cape May in early August. It consisted of four Navy officers, four Marine Corps officers, and observers and technical assistants from the Coast Guard, the Bureau of Construction and Repair, and the Bureau of Engineering.

The fate of the Cape May boat builders spectacularly illustrates how the military services' relationship with private contractors in the 1930s differed profoundly from that relationship today. Unbeknownst to any of the Cape May boatyards, the evaluation board was not directed to put the boats through competitive trials and select a winner. Rather, it was to weigh the "desirable and undesirable characteristics of each boat tested," and to use these to make recommendations on the "general type, design features, and specifications . . . *for further construction.*"[40] Even before the tests began, the board's job was essentially one of distillation. Instead of choosing one of the existing boats, it was to ferret out the characteristics of an ideal new boat.

The tests ran until 6 October, and covered every one of the boats' features: ruggedness, height, freeboard, draft, seaworthiness, engines, speed, and so on, with special attention given to beaching and retracting characteristics. Although the sea skiffs performed well overall and had particularly good beaching and retracting capabilities, every boat was found lacking in one characteristic or another. The Red Bank boat's freeboard was too high, the Bay Head boat's twin engines were too fuel hungry, and the Freeport boat's propeller housing was not rugged enough. The board concluded that while "none of the boats tested are without certain objectionable features," the New Jersey sea-skiff design showed considerable promise, and recommended that BuCon immediately begin designing and building a new boat that embodied the most desirable characteristics of the Cape May boats.[41]

The board was understandably concerned that the builders of the Cape May boats would be unable to produce landing craft in the huge quantities necessary in the event of war.[42] However, an even more pressing issue centered on the royalties the Navy might have to pay to manufacture privately patented designs. The Greenport boat quickly fell out of the running, for example, when the Navy discovered that it was "covered by patents which would complicate its production in quantity."[43] At best, the Navy and Marine Corps had hoped to obtain a prototype that they could produce in quantity, unburdened either by royalties or large purchasing commitments to the designer. The entire research and development cost to the military would thus be covered by the cost of one prototype, in this case, around $6,300—much less than the approximately $35,000 it cost to produce the A-boat.[44] In a sense, the Cape May boatyards were used, without their knowledge, as a development branch for an already existing boat-building establishment comprised of the Navy yards and their large private contractors.

The board members emerged from the Cape May trials with two convictions. First, they felt that they had learned enough from the exercise to enable the Navy bureaus to design a boat of their own, and second, that quantity production should rest with their own Navy yards or one of their familiar contractors. It was not until January of the following year that the Cape May boat builders got the bad news. After repeated inquiries to the Navy regarding the status of the landing-boat project, the Red Bank Yacht Works finally received a curt notice:

[T]he Bureau of Construction and Repair has, as a result of recommendations of the Trial Board for landing boats, prepared a design of a sea skiff following the recommendations of the Board. It is the present intention of this Department to build one of these boats in a Navy Yard and give it complete trials before asking for bids on any additional boat.

The Department greatly appreciated your cooperation in its attempt to develop a sea skiff type of surf boat.[45]

The Bureau Boat

After the Cape May tests the Navy created two boards to coordinate landing boat development. The first was responsible for overseeing the design of the craft, and resided within the Navy Department staff. The second was responsible for overseeing tests of the boats, and was attached to the Fleet. Both boards' first order of business was to evaluate the new craft being designed by BuCon to embody the best features of the Cape May sea skiffs. To the Fleet Boat Board, the proposed copy looked a little too faithful to the original. Upon inspection of the plans, the Fleet Board noted that "[t]he proposed landing boat is essentially the same as the RED BANK boat in dimensions and underwater body. . . . It is the opinion of the Board that very little would be gained by the construction of a landing boat so similar in design to one now undergoing tests."[46]

Furthermore, the board noted that these relatively small boats, roughly thirty feet in length, would likely have trouble landing in a running sea. When testing the Cape May boats in FLEX 3, "[t]here were times ... when scheduled landings had to be canceled because of the sea and yet the conditions that prevented the landings might well be expected on any Pacific island."[47] The board suggested that BuCon build a slightly larger boat, about thirty-six feet long, whose greater seaworthiness would permit landings in heavier surf but would still be small enough to avoid the doctrinal objections to the fifty-foot A-boat. The additional space could be used to mount one or more machine guns for covering fire. At the same time, this larger boat, with some design variations from the sea skiff, would provide a greater contrast to the Cape May boats than BuCon's proposed distillation.[48]

The Fleet Board therefore submitted a new design for a thirty-six-foot landing boat. Like the BuCon design, it benefited greatly from the experience of the Cape May trials, but it also incorporated some new design features, notably a very sharp sheer (to increase buoyancy) and a double-ended design (the pointed stern would better enable the boat to retract from the beach stern seaward).[49]

There was a serious problem, though, with any design of a landing boat longer than thirty feet. Getting the troops onto the beach was only part of the problem. Getting them to the staging area was another. The marines hoped to convert old destroyers into transports for this purpose with as little alteration as possible. However, the ships came with boat davits that could handle only thirty-footers, which was why the Cape May boats had been limited to thirty feet. The Fleet Board's proposed thirty-six-foot boat was therefore deemed unacceptable.

The boat davit problem now seems ludicrous, especially in light of the acrimonious debate it would later cause with another boat designer, Andrew Jackson Higgins. But the restriction reveals once again the overwhelming pressure to economize. In this instance, both doctrine and technology were beholden to budgets.

Developing suitable landing craft had clearly become the reverse salient of the amphibious warfare system by the late 1930s. With the *Tenta-*

tive Manual, the marines had articulated a bureaucratically useful and militarily feasible mission for the Corps, and the Fleet Landing Exercises were beginning to produce marines who had the software necessary to make the hardware work. But the marines still needed a way to get to the beach.

Chapter 9

Eureka

While the Navy was trying to extract a cheap landing-craft prototype from the Cape May boatyards, the marines were once again engaged on the bureaucratic front. The 1927 edition of *Joint Action of the Army and Navy* had officially acknowledged Marine Corps ownership of the amphibious assault. After celebrating that political conquest, the marines then made sure that the standard procedures for amphibious operations (as outlined in the *Tentative Manual for Landing Operations*) were pure Marine Corps from beginning to end. By the middle 1930s, they had staked their institutional existence on the advance-base mission.

Confusion over *Joint Action*

Then, without warning or explanation, the 1935 edition of *Joint Action* appeared. All mention of the marines' mission of seizing advance bases had mysteriously disappeared, and, worst of all, the job was listed as an Army responsibility.

Precisely how this revision happened is unclear. It may very well have been little more than an extended typographical error. It also ended up being of little material consequence, since the Joint Army and Navy Board quickly issued a correction that restored all of the Marine Corps's roles. However, the marine leaders' immediate panic over the apparent revision once again revealed the fundamental importance of the advance-base mission to the Corps's institutional well-being. When General Russell, the Marine Corps commandant, read the 1935 edition, he immediately objected to the CNO. His first memo was frantic: "[T]he undersigned wishes to further protest the relinquishment by the Navy and the allotment to the Army of those functions of National Defense peculiarly applicable to the Marine Corps. I refer to the functions of protecting national interests in disturbed countries and the seizure and defense of advanced bases. The relinquishment by the navy of these functions will seriously endanger the Marine Corps as an establishment of the National Defense and will limit its future to the status of a police force."[1]

A week later, after verbal assurances that the revision had been merely an oversight, Russell recorded one more objection before asking for a retraction: "In the seizure and temporary defense of advanced bases, the Marine Corps can, it is believed, make its most valuable contribution to a naval campaign. The Marine Corps considers this function its primary mission. . . . Considering the important purpose of this publication [*Joint Action*], the failure to provide specifically, for this as a naval function, may react seriously to the disadvantage of the Marine Corps."[2]

Russell sent along his suggestions for the correction to *Joint Action*, and they were quickly approved verbatim by both the CNO and the Joint Board.

This latest bureaucratic threat heightened the Marine Corps's need to move the amphibious landing out of the realm of theory and onto the beach. The lack of a suitable landing craft was now becoming debilitating, and the reverse salient had to be eliminated.

Unfortunately, the focused effort of the Cape May trials had yielded little. The Bureau of Construction and Repair's attempt to glean the best features of the Cape May boats and produce one that the Navy could call its own had produced a thirty-foot copy that was no better than any of the originals. Tests of the Bureau Boat (also known as the Philadelphia Boat because it was built at the Philadelphia Navy Yard) during FLEX 4 had shown it to be no better than adequate.

Even the Bureau Boat's designers were not enthusiastic about it. The chief of BuCon, Rear Adm. William G. DuBose, was an academically trained naval architect who had a long-standing interest in landing craft for the Marine Corps and an appreciation for the Navy's lack of expertise in designing them. He had been involved in the design and testing of the A-, B-, and C-boats back in the 1920s, and had always been on the lookout for other boat designs that could serve the marines' advance-base needs.[3] In 1938 DuBose confided, "The Bureau is not, by any means, sold on the 'Philadelphia' type boat."[4] The search would continue.

Two new prototypes were in the offing. After consulting with Admiral Leahy, the CNO, BuCon contracted with Welin Davit and Boat Corporation for a twenty-eight-foot metal boat that would be much cheaper and easier to produce than the wooden boats previously tried. Even more promising was another design from a New Orleans boat builder, and DuBose was hopeful: "Just today, we issued a requisition to purchase a Higgins boat, delivery at Norfolk. This boat has received very favorable reports on all qualities except that rough weather reports are lacking. The Boat will be standard but if the type is promising we can adapt it to Naval use. It is fast and, according to reports, stops at no obstruction."[5]

Higgins

Andrew Jackson Higgins was a New Orleans businessman who was reputed to have made and lost three fortunes in the lumber business before becoming a professional boat builder. Born in Nebraska in 1886, Higgins was a barrel-chested man with sharp blue eyes and a ruddy complexion who proudly claimed to abide by the axiom that a man should live so that he can look any other man in the eye and tell him to go to hell.[6]

Higgins's fondness for profanity, bourbon, and fisticuffs accompanied a supreme fondness for technical innovation. He had taken up boat building and design as a hobby in his youth and eventually turned the hobby into a business when he expanded his lumber interests into the production of small boats. Higgins settled in New Orleans in 1910 and specialized in shallow-draft workboats for trappers, loggers, oil drillers, and eventually, according to persistent rumor, both bootleggers and their Coast Guard pursuers who needed the boats to ply the cluttered waters of the bayou.[7]

Like most successful boat designers of his era, Higgins was a self-taught craftsman. He never finished high school, and his only formal training in the field of boat design consisted of a correspondence course in naval architecture. Nevertheless, Higgins was a skillful innovator who recognized the value of technical expertise. Higgins Industries, founded in 1930, regularly employed large numbers of engineers from New Orleans's technical schools, as well as stray inventors who Higgins thought showed promise. He housed most of them in New Orleans mansions bought or leased for the purpose. Higgins referred to his engineers as "my geniuses."[8]

By the early 1930s Higgins and his geniuses had produced a remarkable shallow-draft design. The boat had a recessed, semitunnel stern that protected the rudder and propeller, enabling the screw to turn in shallow and even weed-choked water. The boat also had a pram or "spoonbill" bow. Made from a solid block of pine and reinforced with glued wooden plugs, the rounded bow effectively absorbed the shock of running high onto riverbanks without damage.[9]

The primary problem with Higgins's early shallow-draft boats was that the recessed propeller would cause tremendous cavitation, leaving the screw turning in froth much more than solid water. Higgins estimated that the shallow draft was costing the boat about 40 percent of its engine power, and he enrolled in the naval architecture correspondence course specifically to try, unsuccessfully, to find a solution to this problem.[10]

Higgins worked on the problem for several years, and he finally hit upon a solution around 1936. Several stories, most supplied by Higgins himself, later circulated to explain how he made the design change. One story had it that he had been inspired by the shape of the underside of the blue whale. Another alleged that a foreman's oversight accidentally caused the aft hull of one of Higgins's boats to become misshapen in a particularly fortuitous way during production.[11] As in most craft endeavors, it is now probably impossible to know precisely where the design came from, beyond the cut-and-try curiosity and constant tinkering of Higgins and his workers.

Regardless of its origins, the design change was simple and effective. A V-shaped keel amidships and a reverse curve aft turned out to have exactly the desired hydrodynamic characteristics: Objects and froth near the bow and amidships tended to be pushed to the side while solid water was drawn directly into the tunnel toward the screw. The propeller thus bit into water rather than froth, and the increase in efficiency was enough to drive the boat at an impressive twenty knots. The unusual aft hull contour also happened to channel a rail of water directly under the keel, giving the boat an extremely tight turning radius. Delighted with the design, Higgins dubbed it the *Eureka*.[12]

Higgins had approached the Navy on several occasions since 1934 to promote his designs, and BuCon responded in October, 1935, by specifically inviting him to submit a prototype for the Cape May trials. To BuCon's disappointment, Higgins declined.[13] Why Higgins decided not to enter the competition is not clear. However, he may have (correctly) suspected that the enterprise was not likely to bring much financial reward.

In any case, after the Navy and Marine Corps conducted their tests of the Cape May boats and decided to build their own through BuCon, Higgins apparently became concerned that he had missed his chance, and started bombarding the Navy with letters advertising his boats.[14] By this point, however, BuCon's landing craft budget allowed for no further outside purchases, and, more importantly, the bureau saw no reason to investigate other models in any detail until its own Bureau Boat could be evaluated. Not surprisingly, the Navy showed little interest in actually procuring a Higgins boat during this period.

The bureau was curious, however. Despite the Departmental Boat Board's opinion that the *Eureka* was far too heavy for service as a landing boat, BuCon engineers requested information on the Higgins boat from their Coast Guard colleagues, who had performed detailed trials to determine if it was suitable for beach station supply operations or service as a fast rescue or crash boat.[15]

The initial Coast Guard report described the *Eureka* as an engineering marvel with performance characteristics that had to be seen to be believed: "The performance and behavior of the 31-foot *Eureka* model shallow draft boat is so unusual . . . that explanations at some length are necessary to picture the results of the observations made. Such photographs as could be taken under the circumstances, accompany this report and will serve to convey action which otherwise could not properly be described."[16]

The boat was incredibly maneuverable. Its turning radius was shorter than the length of the hull because when making a full turn it essentially revolved around a point slightly aft of amidships. Furthermore, its seaworthiness and maneuverability were excellent in both forward and reverse.

Because the Coast Guard was interested in it primarily as a rescue or crash boat, the *Eureka* was tested for its ability to handle obstructions in the water. It was run in shallow water, over sandbars, and then repeatedly run at full speed up a seaplane ramp on Lake Ponchartrain. It retracted each time without difficulty. The boat was then run up an inclined concrete seawall so far that about two-thirds of the hull was out of the water, and again retracted without problem.

The obstacle test continued with a log jumping demonstration in the Mississippi River.

The river at the time of the tests was high and filled with numerous floating logs, stumps and debris. It is difficult to describe the unusual and remarkable performance of this boat in accomplishing and fulfilling the claims of the builder. At least a dozen large logs were run over, in the course of these tests, some as large as three feet in diameter and 25 feet long in addition to numerous smaller stumps, some of the logs or stumps having limbs and snags projecting. The boat was run at full speed against these obstructions, sometimes at right angles and on other occasions, practically in line with the boat and except for a slight thud or two, the impact of hitting the obstruction is not noticeable and apparently no damage is involved.[17]

The *Eureka* proved similarly able in a test negotiating water so choked with hyacinth and weed that it would have rendered "a normal boat helpless."

All of this must have sparked considerable interest among the sailors and marines, but several obstacles prevented procuring a boat from Higgins. First, the *Eureka* had been designed and tested as a riverboat, and there was no hard data on how well it would handle in open or heavy seas. The Coast Guard test tried to address this issue in a limited way by running the boat in the wake of passing ferries and tugboats on the Mississippi, but this was obviously inconclusive. Second, the Bureau Boat was still being built, and until its results were in, further purchases looked premature. Finally, there was the nagging issue of paying royalties for private designs.

By January, 1938, however, the Bureau Boat had undergone some preliminary tests and it did not look as promising as originally hoped. Commander Ralph S. McDowell, the BuCon officer in charge of landing-craft development, wrote to Higgins and invited him to visit the Navy Department at his convenience to discuss the *Eureka*. Higgins and his chief designer caught the next train to Washington.[18] Commander Roswell B. Daggett, another BuCon officer working on the landing-boat project, was particularly intrigued by Higgins's creation. Daggett advised his superiors that Higgins "impressed me as having something worthwhile looking into for crash and landing boats. I suggest we either arrange for a demonstration or purchase one."[19] As luck would have it, a naval vessel would be in port at New Orleans in early March, and an officer on board was detailed to meet with Higgins.

Andrew Higgins's Eureka *riding up and retracting from a steep seawall near New Orleans.*
Photograph courtesy of the National Archives and Records Administration

Higgins immediately sensed his opportunity. He wrote to BuCon saying that he was grateful that he would at last have the opportunity to demonstrate his boat to the Navy. However, besides some minor concern over the shortness of the inspection trip (two days might not allow rough weather tests, for example), Higgins felt obliged to warn the Navy of a new development:

> We wish to advise your Department that we recently had a call from two men unquestionably connected with the Russian Navy. . . .We deducted from the interest they showed, and from the tests they requested us to make, that they are figuring on giving us an order for a large number of these boats, for use under shallow draft conditions, as well as for high speed operation.
>
> We understand that this order would come to us as a commercial order, but we feel it proper that we should advise your Department of this prospective business.[20]

Higgins was later able to caution, probably with greater veracity, that the British were also interested in his *Eureka*.

Raising the specter of foreign purchases was only one of Higgins's sales techniques. Higgins also enlisted the formidable talents of George Rappleyea as his advertising director and publicity agent.[21] Rappleyea was a master of public spectacle. A decade earlier, while sipping lemon phosphates in a corner drugstore, he had convinced John T. Scopes to put their sleepy town of Dayton, Tennessee, "on the map" by deliberately breaking the state law prohibiting the teaching of evolution. Somehow, Rappleyea managed to remain relatively anonymous in the ensuing "Monkey Trial."[22] For Higgins, he hired a full-time filmmaker to produce a cinematic demonstration of the wonders of the *Eureka*. He then arranged to show the film to anyone in the Navy or Marine Corps willing to see it, always whetting the appetite with prescreening notices worthy of Hollywood:

> I know that you and other officials of the Marine Corps will certainly obtain a thrill in seeing these remarkable moving pictures of a boat performing feats of landing and navigation that have never been performed before.
>
> You will see 27 foot and 33 foot *Eureka's* climbing to the top of ten foot concrete sea walls and with barely a foot or two of its stern left in the water sliding gracefully back into its natural element; you will see these boats play leap frog with floating mahogany logs and other menaces to navigation; you will see them climbing canal banks several feet in height and in every instance they slip back into the water as easy as they climb the embankment. You will see these boats running up shallow, narrow drainage ditches with merely eight or nine inches of muck; you will see them in a ditch too narrow for them to turn around in which they do turn around by running up on the embankment and without even reversing the motor are able to thus reverse their direction; you will see them running across fields of water lilies so thick that a person could almost walk on them.[23]

The film showed to standing-room-only crowds of Marine Corps officers.

These hard-sell techniques, including an offer to build a prototype for less than cost, and a very favorable report from the Navy observer in New Orleans convinced the Navy and Marine Corps that Higgins had something promising.[24] In the spring of 1938 BuCon contracted him to build one *Eureka* modified for service as a thirty-foot landing boat. The demonstrations on Lake Ponchartrain and the banks of the Mississippi River had been impressive, but the Navy needed to see how the boat would perform in real surf.

Higgins built the boat in under two weeks, all the while keeping BuCon apprised through a flurry of letters, blueprints, and telephone calls, particularly to McDowell. Higgins was pleased with the final result. His primary concern was that the unusual behavior of his boat near the beach might be perplexing to sailors accustomed to more conventional surf boats, and he arranged to have his own coxswain conduct the test landings. Higgins was particularly careful, however, not to offend his potential customer: "We trust you will accept this . . . in the spirit intended. We know that the Navy Department and other Government service have most competent men, but . . . we have found that 'old heads' or experienced heads, that are in a rut, more or less, in the handling of conventional type craft, are not too quick to appreciate what can be done with the *EUREKA* boat."[25]

With Higgins's man at the helm, the *Eureka* performed wonderfully, riding the surf without problem and able to land and retract without even using a stern anchor. Higgins's experienced coxswain played a crucial role in the boat's excellent performance, carefully starting his run by "riding a wave surf board fashion" and then accelerating gently to position just behind the preceding wave. This maneuver kept plenty of water under the screw all the way up to the shallow beach. The testing board concluded that it was "the best of the experimental landing boats thus far tested."[26]

The testing board had one serious reservation: the Higgins boat was made of wood. While this probably made the *Eureka* structurally more resilient, it raised other problems. Wooden boats were more susceptible to deterioration in storage than metal boats, and they were more vulnerable to gunfire. But, most importantly, they were considerably harder to produce in quantity, requiring the labor of expensive, skilled craftsmen. Metal boats, while somewhat more susceptible to damage during beaching, could be stamped out on an assembly line.[27]

This concern over the merits of wood versus metal construction was heightened by the thirty-foot metal boat designed by BuCon and built by Welin. While its surf characteristics were not quite as good as the *Eureka*'s, the Welin was far cheaper (about $4,000, compared to about $7,000 for each *Eureka*), it was not patented, and it was made of metal.[28]

Thus began a protracted debate over whether landing craft should be made of wood or metal. The officers of BuCon and the Fleet Boat Board leaned toward metal boats largely for production reasons. While Higgins was able to make *Eureka* boats out of metal, he repeatedly expressed his preference for wood. Wood, he argued, held the hull contours better and was simply more rugged.[29] Although he did not point it out, Higgins also had prevailing interests in the lumber industry.

For the most part, the marines sided with Higgins. The hardy simplicity of wood seemed much more in keeping with the spirit of the Corps than the modern flashiness of metal. Technology historian Eric Schatzberg has argued that aircraft designers during the 1920s and 1930s forsook wood in favor of metal less for technical reasons and more because metal harmonized better with a futuristic "progress ideology" prevalent in that industry.[30] To a great extent, precisely the opposite dynamic worked within the Marine Corps. Marine discussions of landing boat design during this period almost always focused on two characteristics: simplicity and ruggedness. One study at Quantico declared that the proper Marine Corps landing craft, best made of factory-shaped plywood, "belies any suspicion of frailty."[31] Wooden boats might be tough and even primitive, but that was what the Marine Corps was all about.

The marines also preferred wood because Andy Higgins preferred wood, and Higgins was rapidly becoming a Marine Corps darling. His reputation as a hard-drinking, hot-tempered, often foul-mouthed brawler easily endeared him to the marines. Brigadier General Holland M. Smith, at the time the chief of the Marine Corps general staff's Operations and Training Division and who later commanded all marine forces in the Pacific, became one of Higgins early partisans. After the war, Smith fondly described Higgins as "a fighting Irishman" and the "scourge of the Washington bureaucrats," whose boat designs "did more to help win the war in the Pacific than any other single piece of equipment."[32] The marines loved him. The affection was mutual, as Higgins eventually insisted on dealing almost exclusively with marines rather than the Navy officers on the landing boat boards and at BuCon.[33]

With these issues of cost, quantity production, and materials unresolved, the Navy was unable to reach a final decision on a standard boat design. Since training marines and boat crews remained of paramount importance, the Navy ordered four more *Eureka*—two each of metal and wood—and three more Welin boats in time for FLEX 5 in January, 1939.[34]

As Higgins built these additional boats, he kept his clients at BuCon apprised of all manner of technical concerns, sending long, discursive letters (sometimes several per day) on the benefits of various cooling systems, stern shapes, building materials, and methods for reducing weight. Higgins also learned the benefits of conducting his own performance tests, often with the spare-time help of Army engineers and Coast Guard officers in the New Orleans area. He performed these trials almost continuously, and never failed to pass on the results to his Navy clients. The tests provided Higgins both with basic technical knowledge and greater authority to direct development. Armed with the results of these quasi-official evaluations, Higgins was able to substantiate his sundry technical claims and propose new avenues of investigation. A few years earlier, the Cape May boat builders had only been able to admit their inexperience when pressured by the Navy to go with new, experimental designs. Now it was Higgins who was bombarding the Navy with all sorts of innovations, including a revolutionary cooling system designed by his "geniuses" that did a much better job of preventing sand and silt from clogging the engine. Navy engineers and designers were often struggling to keep pace.[35]

Fleet Landing Exercise 5, like its predecessors, was primarily a training exercise that also provided an opportunity to evaluate new technologies and techniques. To train as many marines as possible in the complications of a landing, the exercise employed every serviceable landing craft built to date: all of the wood and metal Bureau Boats, Higgins's *Eureka* boats, and even the venerable Cape May sea skiffs. While FLEX 5 provided marines and sailors with the amphibious training they so desperately needed, it revealed little that was new regarding landing craft. Both the *Eureka* and Welin boats performed well. Higgins's boats were more maneuverable, but the Welin remained cheaper and seemingly easier to produce. Its performance shortcomings seemed minor enough that there was hope that further development might perfect it. The Navy and Marine Corps concluded that, for the time being, both boats should still be considered standard.[36]

The inability to commit to one type again raised the question of development and procurement policy. The Marine Corps five-year plan adopted in 1936 had called for on-going development plus the procurement of twenty boats a year. Yet by early 1939 the entire U.S. amphibious fleet numbered fewer than twenty landing craft, including the obsolescent Cape May and Philadelphia boats. Commander James Ware, head of the Fleet Boat Board, believed the stagnant economy dictated that the experimental program should continue, with no large-scale procurement unless an actual emergency arose. Technical improvements were always forthcoming, and the boats could be built on relatively short notice.[37]

This was the greatest question surrounding Higgins's *Eureka*. The wooden boat was the best yet seen, but it simply did not seem possible to produce it quickly and in quantity at a reasonable cost. To be sure, Higgins had produced his prototypes for the Navy with astonishing speed, taking only weeks where the navy yards had taken months or more. He had displayed a remarkable gift for acquiring the necessary materials and incorporating technical innovations on short notice. But these were single, sporadic orders for no more than a few boats at a time. A war emergency would require production of thousands.

Moreover, Higgins had taken out a patent on the *Eureka* design just as FLEX 5 was getting underway. Although he promised that "It will not be our purpose to take any monetary advantage of this protection," it ensured his control over all peacetime production of the *Eureka*.[38] For the time being, only Higgins Industries, and not the navy yards or any of the Navy's contractors, could build Higgins boats.[39]

Production Engineering

By 1940, however, Higgins had proven to the Navy that he was equal to the task of quantity production. He and his sons gained permission from the city of New Orleans to commandeer a side street and set up an outdoor assembly line. By adapting Henry Ford's experimental production line to fabricate Eagle boats during World War I, Higgins established a small but extremely efficient pilot plant for mass-producing wooden boats. It proved to be one of the first successful methods for assembly-line production of wooden boats.[40]

Also by 1940, international tensions and the eventual declaration of a national emergency had resulted in a dramatic rise in appropriations for naval construction. The Navy let its first contracts that summer calling for quantity production of landing boats—a total of sixty-four craft. But since the naval and marine officers on the boat boards were still unable to make an unequivocal decision between the Welin and *Eureka* designs, the contracts were for thirty-two of each.[41]

A few months later, the issue was finally decided in Higgins's favor—not because of any new test results or improvements in the boats themselves, but because another question regarding amphibious operations had been resolved. Ever since the 1936 training exercises, the Navy had used converted destroyers as transports to get marines and materiel to the staging area for the landing. As noted earlier, the thirty-foot davits on these destroyers had imposed a length restriction on landing craft. However, in the fall of 1940 BuCon received authorization and appropriations to begin converting large merchant ships into Marine Corps transports, complete with larger, thirty-six-foot davits.

The Fleet Boat Board and Higgins both had long argued that thirty-six-foot landing boats would be far superior to thirty-footers in terms of both performance and carrying capacity. Higgins had originally designed the *Eureka* as a thirty-six-foot boat and had grudgingly scaled it down to thirty feet to fit the davit limitation. "To hell with designing a boat to fit the davits!" he had thundered at the Navy. "Why don't you design davits to fit a proper sized boat?"[42] He still had many on hand for demonstration immediately after the Navy received money for the larger transports.

The thirty-six-foot *Eureka* was quickly evaluated in late September, 1940, by Boat Board officers from the Marine Corps and the newly consolidated Bureau of Ships (BuShips). This larger Higgins boat turned out to be the best of all. It retained all of its predecessor's superior handling and beaching characteristics while increasing by half the number of marines or amount of cargo that could be put on the beach and allowing the same speed without an increase in horsepower. The Department Boat Board immediately recommended that it be considered standard and procured in quantity. The CNO and the secretary of the Navy approved the board's recommendation the next day and instructed BuShips to contract with Higgins for 335 of the thirty-six-foot *Eureka* boats.[43]

One final revision to Higgins's *Eureka* came from an unlikely source. All of the landing craft tested until 1941 had a solid bow, forcing marines to climb over the bow or sides to disembark. Attempts to speed the unloading process had accomplished little. A 1939 experiment with an outboard step, for example, proved worse then useless because marines tended to pause on top of the gunwale to try to look or feel for the step, thus becoming high, stationary targets at precisely the moment they were most vulnerable. They actually unloaded faster without any step at all.[44]

In 1937, however, 1st Lt. Victor H. Krulak had observed a Japanese landing operation in China and taken photographs of Japanese landing craft.[45] Krulak was captivated by many of the features of the Japanese designs, especially a hinged bow ramp that allowed troops and materiel to disembark extremely rapidly upon hitting the beach. Upon his return from China in 1939 Krulak made a scale model of the ramped Japanese landing boat and showed it to anyone who would listen.[46] In March, 1941, Krulak showed Higgins some of the photographs he had taken of Japanese landing craft and asked if the *Eureka* could be fitted with a bow ramp. Higgins was instantly fond of the idea, which proved to be a relatively minor engineering task. He made several prototypes by simply cutting off the front ends of some of his boats and replacing them with hinged metal ramps. Upon beaching, the ramp was released and fell open. After the troops or cargo were off-loaded a simple cable and winch hauled it back up before the boat retracted.[47] Higgins's ramped *Eureka* eventually was designated Landing Craft Vehicle, Personnel (LCVP), and quickly became the workhorse in amphibious operations.

Higgins's influence with the Navy and Marine Corps gradually extended beyond his technical expertise regarding his boat. Because of its special characteristics, the *Eureka* made unusual demands upon otherwise well-trained Navy boat crews. For example, most boat operators would automatically cut power if a boat ran aground atop a sandbar. A *Eureka*, by contrast, would clear the bar easily—but only if operated at full throttle.[48] As of 1941, the overwhelming concentration of expertise for operating, maintaining, and repairing *Eureka* boats was at Higgins's New Orleans plant. Consequently, at the request of the Navy and Marine Corps, Higgins established a Boat Operators and Marine Engine Maintenance School at Higgins Industries in July, 1941.[49] The school grew from two weeks of lectures to six weeks of lectures and hands-on training, and served as the model for five other Navy-operated schools around the country.[50] Higgins thus provided both the hardware and software for this low-tech system.

Moreover, technical guidance gradually evolved into doctrinal recommendations, as Higgins's input on how to operate his boat blurred into suggestions on how the boat should be used. As he and his engineers observed Navy and Marine Corps exercises and conducted more tests of their own, Higgins felt increasingly confident in advising his clients on various landing formations, the configuration of boat crews, methods of handling logistics, and the constitution and function of the shore party.[51] Although these ideas were seldom revolutionary or directly counter to prevailing amphibious doctrine, they became a new source of military theory as the line between technology and doctrine faded.

Results

The effect of military patronage on Higgins Industries was colossal. Even before Pearl Harbor the Navy had begun ordering *Eureka* boats by the thousands, resulting in multimillion-dollar contracts for Higgins. When the United States entered the war, the orders became so large that Higgins eventually geared his assembly line up for round-the-clock production, employing some eighty thousand people. Early in the war he received some of the largest government contracts to date, not only for his landing craft, but also for Liberty ships and, later, airplanes. The Liberty-ship contract, though canceled due to a shortage of steel, had amounted to $385 million. The contract for cargo planes was for $200 million.[52] From a relatively small boat builder with capitalization of a few million dollars, Higgins Industries became a defense contractor with an annual volume in the hundreds of millions of dollars.

Higgins was not the only beneficiary of his relationship with the Navy and Marine Corps: The LCVP was a mainstay in every major landing operation in the Pacific during World War II.

The Marines Corps's success in World War II enormously enhanced its prestige in the American military establishment, and marines ever since have been regarded as a rough-and-ready force with the unique ability to deploy rapidly to hostile shores, slogging their way up the beach under enemy fire if necessary. Upon hearing of the flag raising on Mount Suribachi on Iwo Jima, the first words out of Navy Secretary James Forrestal's mouth were, "This means there will be a Marine Corps for the next 500 years."[53]

Chapter 10
Victory: Military,
Bureaucratic, and Cultural

By the time the bombs fell on the fleet at Pearl Harbor, both the Army Air Corps and the Marine Corps had remade themselves. Military leaders like Hap Arnold, Carl Spaatz, John Lejeune, and Benjamin Fuller had worked strenuously to manage the convergence and interaction of bureaucratic needs, institutional self-images, and strategic concerns to reshape their services along new cultural and doctrinal lines. Before the United States entered World War II, airmen and marines had already embraced, articulated, and engineered high-tech strategic bombing and low-tech amphibious warfare. In a very real sense, they were wagering their institutional futures in the bargain.

The gamble paid off in World War II.

The Fortunes of War

The wartime experiences of the Army Air Forces and the Marine Corps have filled the pages of countless volumes, ranging from academic analyses to personal memoirs.[1] World War II became the ultimate test of the political, cultural, and technological viability of strategic bombing and amphibious operations.

Bombing the Cities
The Army Air Corps and GHQ Air Force were merged into the Army Air Forces (AAF) in the summer of 1941. Under the command of Gen. Hap

Arnold and his lieutenants Maj. Gen. Carl Spaatz and Brig. Gen. Ira Eaker, the AAF deployed to Europe to make the ACTS's theorizing a military reality. The B-17s and B-24s began arriving in England in significant numbers in the summer of 1942, and the rest of that year was spent on relatively low-risk bombing missions against targets in France. In early 1943, the AAF and the RAF's Bomber Command launched the Combined Bomber Offensive, which was designed to destroy the Nazi war machine by bombing industrial targets deep inside Germany.

Striking from bases in East Anglia and the Mediterranean, the AAF followed a bombardment war plan drawn directly from ACTS doctrine. While the British followed Bomber Command's tenets of bombing entire cities with incendiaries under the cover of darkness, American B-17 and B-24 crews, armed mostly with demolition bombs and Norden bombsights, attacked individual factories and rail centers during the day. Their targets were Germany's choke-point industries, at least in the minds of AAF planners: ball-bearing plants, oil refineries, and aircraft factories.

The wartime experience held two primary surprises for the bomber proponents. First, the mantra that "the bomber will always get through" turned out to be a very expensive shibboleth. By the fall of 1943 unescorted raids on Schweinfurt, Stuttgart, and Regensburg had resulted in such staggering losses—ranging from 10 to 20 percent per raid—that bombing operations against targets in Germany were suspended until long-range fighter escorts could be engineered. The bill for purging Claire Chennault and other fighter proponents from the ACTS in the 1930s had come due. Ironically, the high-tech bomber offensive was eventually saved by a low-tech device: the external drop tank. Disposable fuel tanks, slung beneath the belly or wings of a fighter, allowed the fighters to escort bombers deep into Germany.[2] Large-scale bombing raids against the Third Reich resumed in the spring of 1944.

Second, the military effect of the bombing campaign was, and continues to be, difficult to assess. One thing is certain: the bombing did not cause the hysteria and collapse of civilian morale that Douhet and Mitchell had predicted in the 1920s. "[T]he 'panic' that was expected to spread through a city or even a nation as bombs began to fall has turned out to be a myth," lamented Alexander de Seversky in 1943.[3] After the war the Strategic Bombing Survey could only conclude that while bombing may have lowered morale, "its effect upon behavior was less decisive."[4]

The high-tech delivery system comes together—heavy bomber, bombardier, and Norden bombsight on bombing run to target. Photograph courtesy of the National Archives and Records Administration

Bombing's material effect on Germany's industry has also been a point of controversy. Attacks on the German oil industry almost certainly crippled the German war effort by hampering panzer and Luftwaffe operations and training and disrupting the chemical industry's attempts to produce artificial nitrates and rubber.[5] Similarly, the belated decision to target the German war machine's transportation system in mid-1944 crippled logistical operations. But other choke-point industries, like ball-bearing and aircraft factories, turned out to be unexpectedly resilient. German industrial production in these areas remained high, and the output of fighters for the Luftwaffe actually rose throughout the Combined Bomber Offensive.[6]

Hitting the Beaches

The Marine Corps's war in the Pacific closely resembled the war outlined in War Plan Orange, Pete Ellis's study of Micronesia, and the Marine Corps School's *Tentative Manual for Landing Operations.* After initial Japanese successes in the western Pacific, the marines hopped islands back to the Phil-

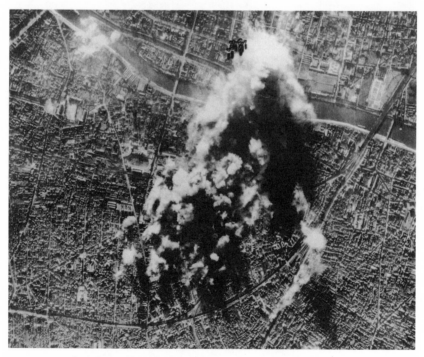

An American daylight precision bombing raid against German-occupied France, 1943.
Photograph courtesy of the National Archives and Records Administration

ippines and to the doorstep of Japan itself, seizing advance naval and air bases along the way. The first landings were relatively small operations on islands in the South Pacific to secure Australia, New Zealand, and New Guinea. The most prominent was the landing on Guadalcanal, an operation that was literally planned out of the *Tentative Manual.* By late 1943 the offensive turned north and west to the Gilbert Islands (with landings at Tarawa and Makin), and then to the Marshall and Caroline Islands (with landings at Kwajalein and Eniwetok). By mid-1944 the offensive had reached north to the Marianas (Saipan, Tinian, and Guam), some fifteen hundred miles from Tokyo.

As American forces began threatening to retake the Philippines and seize islands like Iwo Jima (only five hundred miles from Tokyo), Japanese resistance intensified. Japanese forces defending Peleliu in September retreated into caves, tunnels, and pillboxes. Marines and soldiers ended up crawling from one entrenchment to the next, attacking with grenades, flamethrowers, and demolition equipment, suffering six thousand casualties and taking few prisoners in the process.

The scene was repeated twice more in the last, largest, and bloodiest landings of the war. On 19 February 1945 a landing force of 70,000, almost all marines, embarked for Iwo Jima. The beach took four days to secure, at a cost of more than 3,000 American casualties. Fighting in the caves and tunnels on the rest of the island lasted for almost a month, resulting in 26,000 more American casualties. Almost none of the 21,000 Japanese defenders survived. In April, a 183,000-man force landed on Okinawa. The fighting there lasted for two months, with 19,000 Marines, 65,600 soldiers, and 10,000 sailors killed or wounded. The Japanese suffered 110,000 casualties, almost all dead. The use of atomic bombs ended the war less than two months later. In all, 669,000 men and women served in the Marine Corps during the war, amounting to less than 5 percent of all U.S. forces. More than 19,700 were killed and 67,200 wounded, amounting to more than 10 percent of all U.S. casualties.[7]

For the marines, the tumult of war brought surprises as well. The pressure to produce landing craft in huge quantities quickly erupted into a public battle between Andrew Higgins and BuShips, particularly over the design of tank lighters. Higgins, characteristically uncompromising, was convinced that the best way to transport tanks to the beach was aboard modified *Eureka* boats. The Bureau of Ships on the other hand, particu-

Storming down the ramp of a Higgins boat, American troops hit a beach in New Guinea during World War II. Photograph courtesy of the National Archives and Record Administration

larly Comdr. Roswell Daggett, became inexplicably attached to a BuCon tank-lighter design. The disagreement came to a head in the spring and summer of 1942. Higgins emerged victorious again, and BuShips was humbled at the hands of Sen. Harry Truman's investigation of the industrial mobilization.[8]

The largest departure from interwar planning was bureaucratic: The expansion of the Pacific war necessitated the conversion of Army divisions into amphibious forces. By war's end, eighteen different Army divisions had participated in twenty-six landings, while the Marine Corps's six divisions had made only fifteen.[9] Nevertheless, the surface war in the Pacific remained primarily naval and marine. In 1942 the U.S. Joint Chiefs of Staff had divided the world, awarding primary strategic authority to the Army in Europe and to the Navy in the Pacific. So, although the army's Gen. Douglas MacArthur and Adm. Chester W. Nimitz occasionally had their differences, Navy and Marine Corps planning dominated in the Pacific theater of operations.

Despite these twists, it is remarkable how well ACTS and MCS theorists in the 1930s anticipated the general shape of World War II operations. However, if this makes them look like prophets, it is important to recognize the degree to which their prophecies were self-fulfilling. The Air Corps's bomber advocates and marine amphibious-assault proponents were effective political and military activists who shaped their institutions almost exclusively for those forms of warfare. By the time war came, the Air Corps and Marine Corps were prepared to do little else.

New Technological Frontiers

The Air Corps and Marine Corps quests for better technology continued throughout the war. As had been the case between the wars, their technological choices were constrained by bureaucratic and cultural pressures. The airmen continued to clamor for bigger, more advanced bombers. When it first flew in September, 1942, Boeing's B-29 "Superfortress" was truly a state-of-the-art aircraft. Its wings were forty feet longer than the B-17's and could carry the colossus—along with two thousand pounds of

The price of success: Marine Corps casualties at Tarawa. Photograph courtesy of the National Archives and Records Administration

bombs—more than five thousand miles. Its compartments were pressurized, allowing the eleven-man crew to breathe and work more comfortably at higher altitudes. The airplane's defensive machine guns were remote-controlled, permitting a single gunner to fire several guns simultaneously. B-29s arrived in the Pacific in large numbers in the spring of 1944. They waged the fire-bombing campaign against Japan's cities through the summer of 1945, before two B-29s ended the war with the ultra-high-technology bombing raids against Hiroshima and Nagasaki.[10] By then even larger bombers, like the six-engine B-36, were in development.

The atomic bombs that ended the war were the ultimate high-tech explosives and epitomized the science-fiction imagery of strategic bombing. The futuristic vision instantly came to mind for the crew of the *Enola Gay* after they dropped the uranium bomb on Hiroshima. Watching the mushroom cloud rise, copilot Robert Lewis recalled, "We were struck dumb at the sight. It far exceeded all our expectations. Even though we expected something terrific, the actual sight caused all of us to feel that we were Buck Rogers 25th Century Warriors."[11]

The marines continued their development of landing craft, especially for landing vehicles. Many of these were modified Higgins boats, but some were larger vessels like the Landing Ship, Tank (LST). When the landings at Tarawa revealed that Higgins's *Eureka* could be easily stranded on coral reefs, the marines turned to the Landing Vehicle, Tracked (LVT), also known as the "Alligator," a tracked amphibian developed by Donald Roebling. During the war the marines also investigated the prospect of building landing craft out of plastic.[12]

Another technical innovation was brought on when much of the fighting moved off the beaches in the latter stages of the war. The most brutal and costly part of the campaigns against Peleliu, Iwo Jima, and Okinawa consisted not of the landing but of the inland fighting. Here again the marines turned to a technology that fit the Corps's cultural image: the flamethrower. On Okinawa especially, marines neutralized Japanese forces holding out in well-defended caves using a technique they referred to as "blowtorch and corkscrew," in which they attacked the cave's defenders with flame and then sealed the entrance with explosive.[13]

Winning

World War II secured victory for the Air Corps and Marine Corps, not only over Germany and Japan, but over their institutional threats as well. Although the Combined Bomber Offensive was at best a mixed success, no one after the war could deny that strategic bombing was an entirely new form of military art, as independent from the older services as the Army was from the Navy. After the Air Force gained its independence in 1947, it continued to justify its existence by emphasizing the importance of bombing. In the 1950s the Air Force's bombing tradition earned it a controlling majority of America's burgeoning nuclear force. While the trauma of Vietnam revealed further weaknesses in bombing doctrine, the Air Force remained committed to its vision of a sudden, decapitating strike from the blue in the 1970s and 1980s, now manifested in stealth aircraft and smart bombs. The display of precision bombing in the Persian Gulf War, and more recently in Serbia, is only the latest chapter in a story begun in the 1920s.

The Marine Corps has likewise been bureaucratically secure since World War II. While the marines, like the rest of the defense establishment, have enjoyed and suffered the fluctuations of American military spending, there have been no serious threats to the Marine Corps's existence since 1945. Moreover, the National Security Act of 1947 laid down a new charter for the Corps, complete with an explicit recognition of its responsibility for amphibious operations. It is now a point of law that "It is the duty of the Marine Corps to develop . . . those phases of amphibious operations which pertain to the tactics, technique, and equipment employed by landing forces."[14] Since World War II the Marine Corps has enjoyed a reputation as a rough-and-ready but efficient and elite fighting force that is always ready to storm ashore when needed.

Lessons

Culling universal truths from specific cases is always difficult, even dangerous. Nevertheless, this study of the Air Corps and Marine Corps during the interwar years illustrates several facets of the broader interaction between technology, culture, and the military in the American context.

Contingency

The first is by now obvious to the point of being mundane, but bears repeating nonetheless: None of the technologies developed by the Air Corps or Marine Corps during this period were in any way natural, necessary, or inevitable. There was no internal logic emanating from the technology itself to drive Air Corps and Marine Corps leaders into the technological choices they made during the 1920s and 1930s. Rather, the development of these technologies was contingent upon the specific desires of military and industrial decision makers and the specific environments in which they worked.

The same is true for the military doctrines of strategic bombing and amphibious warfare. These two forms of warfare, and the technologies that made them possible, served the various and specific needs of the Air Corps and the Marine Corps—strategic, political, and cultural—that obtained during the interwar years in America. Under different circumstances, both military services might have made very different choices, and thereby cast themselves into a very different future.

Consider, for example, the degree to which the institutional structures of the Air Corps and Marine Corps shaped their decisions. What sorts of directions might the Air Corps have taken had it not been working to gain its independence from the Army during the period? How might the Marine Corps have behaved were it not trying to reinforce its place within the Navy as a preemptive response to any hostile takeover attempts by the Army? Had the Norden bombsight not belonged to the Navy, would the Air Corps have pushed so hard for the upgraded bombsight from Sperry? Imagining these alternative paths illuminates the contingent nature of the paths actually taken.

Institutional culture played as profound a role as organizational structure in these stories. The airmen's institutional self-image as futuristic and gallant knights of the sky shaped the vision of strategic bombing they articulated and embraced. Daylight precision bombing grew out of this high-tech culture. Similarly, the Marine Corps's vision of itself as a rough and simple warrior breed shaped its vision of amphibious warfare and its attendant hardware. In different cultural environments, things could have gone differently. Within certain bounds, the Air Corps could have gone low-tech. While airplanes themselves were necessarily high-tech, strategic bombing was not. By giving up on the extremely difficult technical requirement of daylight precision bombing, Air Corps theorists could have greatly simplified their technological needs. While area bombing, especially at night, can hardly be described as easy, it is certainly simpler from a purely technical point of view. Likewise, the Marine Corps could have gone high- (or at least higher-) tech. Rather than opting to take that eternal ride from the transport to the beach in slow, simple landing craft, the marines could have investigated the prospect of using helicopters or hydrofoils. Both were cutting-edge technologies in the 1930s that might have made the assault from the sea much safer. However, these options would have been much more difficult and expensive to engineer, giving marines solid reasons to be suspicious of them during a time of austere federal budgets. But this is merely another way of saying that such a high-tech approach would have been out of keeping with Marine Corps culture.

That the airmen and especially the marines turned to technology in the first place also reflects the attitudes of 1920s America more broadly. It was a decade of intense technological optimism in America. Marvels like the radio, telephone, automobile, and airplane created a widespread perception that anything was possible from the combination of technology and Yankee ingenuity. In that environment, it may have been obvious to Air Corps and Marine Corps leaders to look for technological solutions, both high and low, to their problems. In a different time or place, those same people might have made very different decisions.

Moreover, even within their time and place, they had other choices. The ACTS theorists began their deliberations with Mitchell's idea of conducting terror-bombing raids on cities. Had they pursued that idea they most likely would have taken different technological paths. Highly precise optical bombsights designed to put demolition bombs on target would have been less important, and perhaps incendiary or even poison-gas munitions would have been more so. In addition to amphibious operations, the marines considered making small wars the Corps's purpose in life. Their expeditions to Haiti, Nicaragua, and China during the early years of the twentieth century made this prospect completely plausible. Had they chosen that mission instead, and planned for a future of unconventional wars in generally nonindustrialized nations, they might have spent more of their research efforts on small arms, jungle or wilderness fighting, or even a 1920s version of counterterrorism. They certainly would not have spent so much on landing craft for amphibious operations.

Finally, the contingent nature of these technological developments is further underlined by the alternate technological paths taken by other military forces during this same period. The other major military powers in the decades prior to World War II all developed or transformed their air, sea, and ground forces during this period, too. But they did so in ways that responded to their own situations and desires during those decades. In general terms, the British focused on a fighter defense for their island and the terror bombing of enemy cities. The Germans devoted most of their airpower to ground-attack aviation, and conducted only sporadic research into long-range strategic bombing. The Soviet Union did likewise.[15] Japan, a small island nation in a very large ocean, put most of its resources into its surface navy and naval aviation. Expecting little in the way of forceful resistance to their initial wave of Pacific conquest, the Japanese did not make the amphibious landing under enemy fire a large part of their military doctrine. The paths that these nations took were understandably very different from one another, and from the paths taken by the U.S. Army Air Corps and U.S. Marine Corps during that same period.

Technological Determinism

This study of technological and military development during the interwar years also impinges on an old theme in the history of technology known as technological determinism. The fundamental idea is straightforward enough: Technology has come to play such a large role in shaping historical developments that it makes sense to treat it as an actor, even the dominant actor, in historical narratives. Technologically deterministic stories enjoy a compelling simplicity. The development of the magnetic compass in the West led to European maritime exploration and colonization. Johannes Gutenberg's development of the printing press begat much wider reading of the Bible and paved the way for the Reformation. Eli Whitney's cotton gin reinvigorated the economics of slavery in the United States and ultimately precipitated the sectional crisis that led to Civil War. The development of nuclear weapons transformed the abstract ideological tension between the United States and the Soviet Union into a long, twilight struggle that threatened civilization itself.

However compelling, such stories also suffer from a host of difficulties.[16] Of particular relevance for this study of the interwar period is that technologically deterministic narratives imply that technology develops of its own accord, insulated from the messy forces of history that drive other events. The autonomous technology then presumably works its will upon the world. In contrast, the cases of strategic bombing and amphibious operations demonstrate that technology evolved amidst other historical developments—political, bureaucratic, strategic, and diplomatic—and in similarly complex and convoluted ways. Rather than a unidirectional dynamic from technology to history, the interaction between strategic military needs, technological possibilities, bureaucratic pressures, and institutional culture was complex and ran in many directions along many different axes. The strategic and bureaucratic environments during the 1920s and 1930s left the Air Corps and Marine Corps open to innovation. Their institutional self-perceptions and the technological possibilities of the age converged to make precision bombing and amphibious operations particularly attractive to them. As airmen and marines articulated the doctrines for those new forms of warfare, they then shaped further technological developments. Yet, they often found themselves bound by political, strategic, and technological constraints. This was a complex interaction of forces in which history drove technology as much as the reverse.

A Seamless Web

The complex and multidirectional interaction between technology, culture, politics, and society has led many technology historians to question whether it is even possible to distinguish technological issues from political, social, or economic ones, and to talk instead about a "seamless web."[17] Technology, politics, economics, and society thus blend together to form an intricate network, and questions or controversies that may have seemed purely technical in nature are revealed to be much more complex and heterogeneous.

This examination of the Air Corps and Marine Corps during the interwar years largely supports this metaphor. Here, too, the distinctions between technology, politics, and culture were blurry. The Marine Corps's devotion to Higgins's *Eureka* and the Air Corps's tensions over the Norden bombsight were jointly technical, strategic, political, and cultural. At times it seems pointless, if not impossible, to distinguish these forces from one another, to untangle the threads of a web that is seamless.

But not always. The one difficulty with the seamless web metaphor is that, taken to its logical extreme, the web becomes a vast, amorphous, homogeneous haze, and can obscure the dynamics that it hopes to capture. Ultimately, it can lead to the opaque and mundane observation that everything is related to everything else. The examples of strategic bombing and amphibious operations indicate that while it may be impossible to draw sharp lines between these forces, it is still useful to think about an interaction of concerns and agendas that were predominantly political, or predominantly economic, or predominantly technical. It is still useful to regard the Navy's development of War Plan Orange as predominantly political, diplomatic, and military, and less technical. Likewise, it makes sense to think about the addition of the bow ramp to Higgins's landing craft as predominantly technical and tactical. While the boundaries of these forces are necessarily fuzzy, we may still get a clearer picture of their interaction by treating it as a convergence of imperfectly identifiable forces. They may invariably become entangled in a weblike network, but even the most complex web is made of individual threads.

Stress and Innovation

Finally, this examination of technology and the military between the world wars indicates that times and sites of stress should be very fruitful points for scholars to observe the interaction between technology, policy, and culture. In a Darwinian sense, such times are extremely conducive to innovation, and the cases of the airmen and marines demonstrate that relatively coherent innovation can take a multitude of forms simultaneously. The evolutions of strategic bombing and amphibious operations were simultaneously technological, military, and cultural transformations.

Other periods of stress should show similar dynamics. The period immediately after World War II, for example, saw similar changes. The development of the atomic bomb was as much a technological surprise for most within the U.S. military as it was for the Japanese. It forced a painful and contentious rethinking of all of these same issues for all branches of the American military: strategic missions, technological capabilities, and institutional identity. The Air Force, for example, born in the midst of these tensions, had to come to grips with a technology that put to shame any earlier Buck Rogers flights of the imagination. It also threatened the notion of precision bombing and even (when mounted on long-range missiles) the central primacy of the airplane and pilot. In the late 1940s and early 1950s, the Air Force and the other armed services had to recreate themselves yet again.

Another obvious period and place of such tension is the early post–Cold War period (the time of this writing). At the beginning of the twenty-first century, the United States finds itself demobilizing after fifty continuous years of war and anticipation of war. With the Cold War over, the military finds itself once again under a familiar postwar stress—budgets are cut, personnel levels drop, and defense industries suffer. Once again, military agencies will either adapt or perish. The Department of Defense certainly recognizes the danger: By 1998 there had been no fewer than four comprehensive government studies of the roles and missions of the U.S. military since the end of the Cold War.[18]

History does not predict the future. Nevertheless, much that was true during the 1920s and 1930s is true again today. As foreign policy concerns continue to exert bureaucratic pressure on military institutions, those institutions will continue to embrace technology-based military doctrines in ways that are both constrained and empowered by their institutional cultures. In the process they will probably create new forms of warfare and new technologies that will one day be stunningly obvious. Recall that bombers and landing craft once represented bold and drastic leaps of imagination.

So, to return to a question raised in the preface to this book: Can entire technological systems bear the imprint of the institutional identities that created them? Judging by the examples of Air Corps strategic bombing and Marine Corps amphibious operations examined here, the real question is: How can they not?

Notes

Chapter 1. Culture, Technology, and Institutions

1. Martin Campbell-Kelly and William Aspray, *Computer: A History of the Information Machine*, 271–73; Robert X. Cringely, *Accidental Empires: How the Boys of Silicon Valley Make Their Millions, Battle Foreign Competition, and Still Can't Get a Date*, 194–95.
2. For a discussion of the effect of the return to normalcy on the U.S. military, see Allan R. Millett and Peter Maslowski, *For the Common Defense: A Military History of the United States of America*, 361–67.
3. Like political scientist Barry Posen, I am using the term *military doctrine* to refer to the operational paradigm within which officers plan and conduct military operations. Doctrine determines what kinds of forces a military agency employs and how it employs them; it reflects the judgment of officers on what is and is not militarily possible and necessary. See Barry R. Posen, *The Sources of Military Doctrine: France, Britain, and Germany between the World Wars*, 13–15.
4. It is crucial to realize that low-tech is not "no-tech"; neither, as we shall see, is it "easy-tech." Low technology is distinguished from high technology only in that it is relatively inexpensive and does not rely on cutting edge scientific and engineering knowledge. Despite the popular American fascination with military high technology, low-tech is at least as important to winning wars. For a look at the importance of the combat ration, the duffel bag, and the five-gallon jerry can (among other low-tech creations), see Irving B. Holley, "Technology and Strategy: A Historical Overview," in *Technology, Strategy and National Security*, ed. Franklin D. Margiotta and Ralph Sanders, 15–41.
5. Daniel J. Kevles, "R&D and the Arms Race: An Analytical Look," in *Science, Technology, and the Military*, ed. Everett Mendelsohn, Merritt Roe Smith, and Peter Weingart, 477; Herbert York, *Race to Oblivion: A Participant's View of the Arms Race*, 176; Robert W. Seidel, "From Glow to Flow: A History of Military Laser Research and Development," *Historical Studies in the Physical and Biological Sciences* 18, pt. 1 (1987): 111–13; Paul Forman, "Behind Quantum Electronics: National Security as Basis for Physical Research in the United States, 1940–1960," *Historical Studies in the Physical and Biological Sciences* 18, pt. 1 (1987): 149–55.

6. Harvey Brooks, "The Military Innovation System and the Qualitative Arms Race," in *Arms, Defense Policy, and Arms Control*, ed. Franklin A. Long and George W. Rathgens, 92; quoted in Kevles, "R&D and the Arms Race," 469.

7. Herbert Sherman, "The Role of the Military Laboratory in Electronics Research and Development," *Transactions of the Institute of Radio Engineers Professional Group on Engineering Management*, PGEM-1 (Feb., 1954): 34.

Chapter 2. The Bombers' Vision

1. Joseph J. Corn, *The Winged Gospel: America's Romance with Aviation, 1900–1950*, 11.

2. George H. Quester, *Deterrence Before Hiroshima: The Airpower Background of Modern Strategy*, 44; James P. Tate, "The Army and Its Air Corps: A Study of the Evolution of Army Policy Towards Aviation, 1919–1941" (Ph.D. diss., Indiana University, 1976), 3. For an example of the conversion from tons to pounds, see Robert Frank Futrell, *Ideas, Concepts, Doctrine: A History of Basic Thinking in the United States Air Force, 1907–1964*, 1:25.

3. Irving B. Holley, *Ideas and Weapons: Exploitation of the Aerial Weapon by the United States during World War I; A Study in the Relationship of Technological Advance, Military Doctrine, and the Development of New Weapons*, 37; David Eugene Johnson, "Fast Tanks and Heavy Bombers: The United States Army and the Development of Armor and Aviation Doctrines and Technologies, 1917 to 1945" (Ph.D. diss., Duke University, 1990), 75.

4. Corn, *The Winged Gospel*, 31.

5. Leighton Brewer, *Riders of the Sky*. For biography on Brewer, see *The National Cyclopedia of American Biography*, 55:233.

6. Brewer, *Riders of the Sky*, 7.

7. Ibid., 23; Corn, *The Winged Gospel*, 11.

8. Brewer, *Riders of the Sky*, 23–24.

9. Ibid., 26.

10. House Committee on Military Affairs, *Hearings, Aeronautics in the Army*, 63d Cong., 1st sess., 1913, 77, 83; Johnson, "Fast Tanks and Heavy Bombers," 63.

11. William Mitchell, *Memoirs of World War I: From Start to Finish of Our Greatest War*, 59. Most of these memoirs appeared in the 1920s in *Liberty Weekly* magazine.

12. William Mitchell, *Winged Defense: The Development and Possibilities of Modern Air Power—Economic and Military*, 8.

13. Ibid., 97–119.

14. H. H. Arnold, *Global Mission*, 106; Tate, "Army and Its Air Corps," 26–28.

15. Carl Spaatz (Major, USAAS) to Gerald Garard, 29 Jan. 1926, Carl A. Spaatz Papers, Box 4, Manuscripts Division, Library of Congress (hereafter Spaatz Papers).

16. Johnson, "Fast Tanks and Heavy Bombers," 184–89.

17. House Select Committee of Inquiry in Operations of the United States Air Services, *Hearings*, 68th Cong., 1st sess., 1925, 292.

18. Ibid., 1673–76, 1682–84.

19. Editorial, "An Indiscreet General," *New York Times*, 14 Feb. 1925.

20. Johnson, "Fast Tanks and Heavy Bombers," 191; Alfred F. Hurley, *Billy Mitchell: Crusader for Air Power*, 97–98.

21. Quoted in Hurley, *Billy Mitchell*, 101.

22. Carl A. Spaatz Oral History, U.S. Air Force Historical Research Center, Maxwell Air Force Base, Ala., 1965, quoted in Johnson, "Fast Tanks and Heavy Bombers," 196.

23. Tate, "Army and Its Air Corps," 53–54.

24. Thomas H. Greer, *The Development of Air Doctrine in the Army Air Arm, 1917–1941*, 28.

25. Johnson, "Fast Tanks and Heavy Bombers," 194.

26. Tate, "The Army and Its Air Corps," 68–72.

27. Mitchell, *Winged Defense*, xv–xviii.

28. Mitchell, *Memoirs*, 3–4.

29. For an efficient discussion of European airpower theorists, especially Giulio Douhet, Hugh Trenchard, B. H. Liddell Hart, and J. F. C. Fuller, see Michael S. Sherry, *The Rise of American Air Power: The Creation of Armageddon*, 23–29.

30. Mitchell, *Memoirs*, 105–107.

31. Greer, *Development of Air Doctrine*, 49.

32. Arnold, *Global Mission*, 157–58.

33. Robert T. Finney, *History of the Air Corps Tactical School, 1920–1940*. Although the official name of the school changed over the years, I refer to it throughout as the Air Corps Tactical School (ACTS).

34. Ibid., 7.

35. William Mitchell, "Tactical Application of Military Aeronautics," 5 Feb. 1920, quoted in Greer, *Development of Air Doctrine*, 37.

36. "Fundamental Conceptions of the Air Service," quoted in Johnson, "Fast Tanks and Heavy Bombers," 205–207.

37. Air Service Tactical School, *Bombardment* text, 1926, quoted in Johnson, "Fast Tanks and Heavy Bombers," 108. See also Greer, *Development of Air Doctrine*, 41.

38. Max Hastings, "The Bomber as the Weapon of Choice" (paper presented at the National Air and Space Museum Symposium on the Legacy of Strategic Bombing, Washington, D.C., 11 Jan. 1990).

39. Maj. Oscar Westover to Maj. Gen. Mason Patrick, chief, Air Service, 14 July 1925, quoted in Johnson, "Fast Tanks and Heavy Bombers," 210.

40. Finney, *History of the Air Corps Tactical School*, 31.

41. Air Corps Tactical School, *Bombardment* text, 1930–1931, quoted in Johnson, "Fast Tanks and Heavy Bombers," 212. Emphases in original.

42. Finney, *History of the Air Corps Tactical School*, 31.

Chapter 3. The Bombers' Technology

1. Martin P. Claussen, *Materiel Research and Development in the Army Air Arm,
   1914–1945,* Air Historical Studies no. 50, 14–17.
2. Although the agency's name changed during the 1920s, I will refer to it as the
   Materiel Division throughout.
3. Claussen, *Materiel Research and Development,* 42.
4. Brig. Gen. Benjamin Foulois, chief of Training and Operations, to Chief of Air
   Corps, 7 Jan. 1929, Record Group (RG) 18, Entry 166, File 400.112C, Box 806,
   National Archives, Washington, D.C. (hereafter NA).
5. Benjamin S. Kelsey, *The Dragon's Teeth? The Creation of United States Air Power
   for World War II,* 43–44.
6. Claussen, *Materiel Research and Development,* 41.
7. H. H. Windsor Jr., president, *Popular Mechanics* magazine, to F. Trubee Davison
   (assistant secretary of war), 13 Sept. 1929; Maj. L. W. McIntosh to Chief, Materiel Liaison Section, 19 Sept. 1929, RG 18, Entry 166, File 400.112C, Box
   806, NA.
8. There exists a considerable literature on the creation and administrative operation of NACA. See Roger E. Bilstein, *Orders of Magnitude: A History of the
   NACA and NASA, 1915–1990;* Alex Roland, *Model Research: The National Advisory Committee for Aeronautics, 1915–1958;* and Norriss S. Heatherington,
   "The National Advisory Committee for Aeronautics: A Forerunner of Federal
   Governmental Support for Scientific Research," *Minerva* 28 (spring, 1990):
   59–80.
9. See RG 18, Entry 166, File 334.8, "NACA," Box 546, NA; and Roland, *Model
   Research,* 431–35.
10. Capt. D. F. Stace, Materiel Liaison Section, to Brig. Gen. H. H. Arnold, 10 Feb.
    1936, RG 18, Entry 166, File 334.8, Box 545, NA.
11. See RG 18, Entry 166, File 400.112A, Boxes 806–807, and File 334.8, Box 545,
    NA.
12. Maj. Gen. Mason Patrick, chief, Air Service, to Secretary of War, 16 Dec. 1925
    [penciled note at top reads, "Prepared by JFV—sent forward by Gen. Patrick"];
    "Report of Special Committee on Proposed Consolidation of the National Ad-
    visory Committee for Aeronautics with the Bureau of Standards," 15 Dec.
    1932; Brig. Gen. Oscar Westover, acting chief, Air Corps, to Rep. Clifton A.
    Woodrum, 12 Jan. 1933; Secretary of War Hurley to Senator Hale, 31 Jan.
    1933, all in File 334.8, Box 546, ibid.
13. Kelsey, *Dragon's Teeth?,* 92–93.
14. Col. L. W. McIntosh, chief, Engineering Division, to Office of the Chief of Air
    Service, 21 Feb. 1924, RG 18, Entry 167, File 452.1, Box 21, NA.
15. Glenn L. Martin to Department of State, 15 Mar. 1934, File 452.1, Box 22, ibid.
16. Maj. Gen. Benjamin Foulois, chief, Air Corps, to The Adjutant General, 4 Apr.
    1934, Box 21, Benjamin D. Foulois Papers, Manuscripts Division, Library of

Congress (hereafter Foulois Papers); this document is also in RG 18, Entry 167, File 452.1, Box 22, NA.

17. Foulois to Adjutant General, 4 Apr. 1934. The phrases "Though I am loathe to recommend it," and "and to keep these facilities available for national emergency" were stricken from the final version of the letter.

18. Robert Gross, treasurer, Lockheed Aircraft Corporation, to Secretary of War, 28 June 1934; Capt. Ray G. Harris to Chief of Inspection Branch, Wright Field, Ohio, 22 Nov. 1934; and Chief of Air Corps to Chief of Materiel Division, 12 Dec. 1934, all in RG 18, Entry 167, File 452.1, Box 22, NA.

19. Richard P. Hallion, "Philanthropy and Flight: Guggenheim Support of Aeronautics, 1925–1930," *Aerospace Historian* 28 (spring, 1981): 11.

20. Ibid., 12–13.

21. Capt. A. F. Hegenberger to Maj. Gen. Benjamin Foulois, chief, Air Corps, 24 June 1934, Box 23, Foulois Papers.

22. Claussen, *Materiel Research and Development*, 46–47.

23. Even as a colonel, Arnold sometimes complained that his technical suggestions were not receiving sufficient attention. See Lt. Col. H. H. Arnold to Brig. Gen. H. C. Pratt, chief, Materiel Division, 24 Oct. 1933, Box 6, Spaatz Papers.

24. Kelsey, *Dragon's Teeth?*, 72.

25. Ibid., 85.

26. Ibid., 83–84.

27. Chief of Air Corps to Adjutant General, 12 Mar. 1929, "Funds spent for 'Research and Development' and Limited Rearmament, fiscal years 1920– 1929 inclusive," RG 18, Entry 167, File 400.112, Folder "Test, development, research of supplies, equipment, 1923–1935," NA. All-purpose developments consisted of work on aerodynamics, propellers, power plants, armament, materials, aircraft equipment, and work contracted to NACA.

28. Jean H. DuBuque and Robert F. Gleckner, *The Development of the Heavy Bomber, 1918–1944*, Air Historical Studies no. 6, 61–62; Merle C. Olmsted, "The Martin Bomber: First of the U.S. Heavies," *Aerospace Historian* 20 (fall, 1973): 150–54.

29. Earl H. Tilford Jr., "The Barling Bomber," *Aerospace Historian* 26, no. 2 (summer, 1979): 92. Most of this account of the Barling bomber comes from Tilford.

30. House Committee on Appropriations in Charge of War Department Appropriation Bill for 1923, *Hearings*, 67th Cong., 2nd sess., 1923, 898.

31. Tilford, "Barling Bomber," 95–96.

32. House Committee on Appropriations in Charge of War Department Appropriation Bill for 1925, *Hearings*, 68th Cong., 1st sess., 1925, 926.

33. Ibid.

34. Arnold, *Global Mission*, 128–29.

35. Lloyd S. Jones, *U.S. Bombers: B1–B70*, 11–15.

36. DuBuque and Gleckner, *Development of the Heavy Bomber*, 66–67.

37. Haywood S. Hansell, "The Keystone Bombers: Unhonored and Unloved," *Air Force Magazine*, Sept., 1977, 130–36.

38. Maj. Hugh J. Knerr, president, Bombardment Board, to Chief of Materiel Division, 7 Feb. 1928, RG 18, Entry 166, File 471.6, Box 1143, NA. A great deal of military staff work between the wars was done by ad hoc boards of officers; the board system prevailed in every sector of the army and navy.

39. Office of the Chief of the Air Corps to Chief of Training and Operations, 21 Dec. 1928, Box 23, Foulois Papers.

40. Brig. Gen. W. E. Gillmore, chief, Materiel Division, to Chief of Air Corps, 22 Nov. 1928, RG 342, File 371.63, RD 3416, Box 1282, Sarah Clark Collection, Washington National Records Center, Suitland, Md. (Hereafter Clark Collection.)

41. H. B. Inglis, "Report on Bombsight Development since the Armistice" (Dayton, Ohio: Air Service Engineering Division, 8 Jan. 1926), 3-4. Copy in file "Bombsights, USA #3," File number S2009401, National Air and Space Museum Archives and Branch Library, Smithsonian Institution, Washington, D.C. (Hereafter NASMA and BL.)

42. Brig. Gen. W. S. Pierce, assistant chief of Ordnance, to Chief of Air Service, 4 Jan. 1921, RG 18, Entry 166, File 471.6, Box 1143, NA.

43. More than 90 percent of skilled pilots were over five degrees off of vertical line terminating at the target (Inglis, "Report on Bombsight Development," 5).

Chapter 4. Political Opportunities and Daylight Precision

1. Col. Oscar Westover, assistant chief, Air Corps, to Maj. Gen. Benjamin Foulois, chief, Air Corps, 10 Nov. 1933, RG 18, Entry 167, File 452.1, Box 21, NA.

2. John F. Shiner, *Foulois and the U.S. Army Air Corps*, 167.

3. The army-navy fight over coast defense is described in DuBuque and Gleckner, *Development of the Heavy Bomber*, 130–44; Wesley Frank Craven and James Lea Cate, eds., *The Army Air Forces in World War II*, vol. 1, *Early Plans and Operations: January 1939 to August 1942*, 61–63; and Greer, *Development of Air Doctrine*, 31–33, 67–69.

4. "Large Fleet of Aircraft Carriers Needed to Defend Coast, Says Admiral Moffett," *Los Angeles Examiner*, 24 Aug. 1930, quoted by Maj. Carl Spaatz in "Airplane Carriers Impotent against Shore-Based Aircraft," 29 Aug. 1930, Box 5, Spaatz Papers.

5. Spaatz, "Airplane Carriers Impotent."

6. Maj. Carl Spaatz to Office of the Assistant Secretary of War, 29 Aug. 1930, Box 5, Spaatz Papers.

7. DuBuque and Gleckner, *Development of the Heavy Bomber*, 134.

8. Craven and Cate, eds., *Army Air Forces in World War II*, 1:62.

9. Westover to Foulois, 10 Nov. 1933.

10. Ibid.

11. The best source on the airmail fiasco is Shiner, *Foulois*, 125–49; most of the following comes from Shiner.

12. Benjamin D. Foulois and C.V. Glines, *From the Wright Brothers to the Astronauts: The Memoirs of Major General Benjamin D. Foulois*, 238.

13. Shiner, *Foulois*, 131.

14. Foulois and Glines, *From the Wright Brothers to the Astronauts*, 255.

15. Ibid., 253–56.

16. Quoted in Tate, "The Army and its Air Corps," 169.

17. Shiner, *Foulois*, 198; and Johnson, "Fast Tanks and Heavy Bombers," 408.

18. Quoted in Shiner, *Foulois*, 199.

19. Ibid., 203–204.

20. Johnson, "Fast Tanks and Heavy Bombers," 413; Shiner, *Foulois*, 207; and Greer, *Development of Air Doctrine*, 73.

21. Brig. Gen. Frank Andrews, "The GHQ Air Force," n.d. [1935], File "GHQ Air Force Directives," Box 9, Frank Andrews Papers, Manuscripts Division, Library of Congress.

22. Ibid.

23. 1st Lt. H. L. George, "Lecture Given at the Marine Corps School, 'Bombardment Aviation,'" n.d., [1932?], quoted in Johnson, "Fast Tanks and Heavy Bombers," 397.

24. Finney, *History of the Air Corps Tactical School*, 32.

25. Kenneth N. Walker to Assistant Commandant, ACTS, 24 Sept. 1932, quoted in Johnson, "Fast Tanks and Heavy Bombers," 398.

26. ACTS Air Force lecture, 1932–1933, quoted in Finney, *History of the Air Corps Tactical School*, 32.

27. ACTS bombardment text, 1933, quoted in Johnson, "Fast Tanks and Heavy Bombers," 399.

28. Futrell, *Ideas, Concepts, and Doctrine*, 1:IV. Futrell dedicated his book to Walker, who died in 1943, and used the axiom as an epigram for the book.

29. Finney, *History of the Air Corps Tactical School*, 56–69.

30. Claire L. Chennault, ACTS Pursuit lecture, "The Role of Defensive Pursuit, Part II: Interceptions," 1933, quoted in Johnson, "Fast Tanks and Heavy Bombers," 400–401.

31. Mark Clodfelter, "Pinpoint Devastation: American Air Campaign Planning before Pearl Harbor," *Journal of Military History* 58, no. 1 (Jan., 1994): 84.

32. Air Force Tactical School, "The Air Force," Apr., 1930, File 248.101-1, USAF Collection, Air Force Historical Research Agency, Maxwell Air Force Base, Ala. (hereafter USAF Collection), 5.

33. Muir S. Fairchild, text of ACTS lecture, "National Economic Structures, 5 Apr. 1938, 3–5, Air Force Historical Research Agency, File 248.2019A-19, quoted in Clodfelter, "Pinpoint Devastation," 85.

34. Maj. Gen. Haywood S. Hansell Jr., "The Development of the U.S. Concept of Bombardment Operations," lecture at the Air War College, Maxwell Air Force Base, Ala., 19 Sept. 1951, quoted in Greer, *Development of Air Doctrine*, 80–81.

35. ACTS, "Study of New York City," 1935, File 249.211-28, pts. 1–11, USAF Collection.

36. Hansell, "Development of the U.S. Concept of Bombardment Operations," quoted in Greer, *Development of Air Doctrine*, 81.

37. Laurence S. Kuter Oral History, U.S. Air Force Historical Research Center, Maxwell Air Force Base, Ala., 111, quoted in Johnson, "Fast Tanks and Heavy Bombers," 434.

38. Johnson, "Fast Tanks and Heavy Bombers," 435.

39. Quoted in ibid., 430.

40. Hansell, "Development of the United States Concept of Bombardment Operations," quoted in Greer, *Development of Air Doctrine*, 60; Johnson, "Fast Tanks and Heavy Bombers," 433.

41. Lt. Col. A. H. Gilkeson to Commanding General, 2d Wing, 28 Mar. 1936, quoted in Futrell, *Ideas, Concepts, Doctrine*, 1:77.

42. Finney, *History of the Air Corps Tactical School*, 34.

Chapter 5. A High-Tech Delivery System

1. See Eric Schatzberg, "Ideology and Technical Choice: The Decline of the Wooden Airplane in the United States, 1920–1945," *Technology and Culture* 35 (Jan., 1994): 34–69.

2. Chief of Air Corps to Materiel Division, 12 Dec. 1930, RG 18, Entry 167, File 452.1, Box 22, NA.

3. Brig. Gen. Benjamin Foulois, acting chief, Air Corps, to Assistant Secretary of War, 12 Oct. 1931, File 452.1, Box 21, ibid.

4. DuBuque and Gleckner, *Development of the Heavy Bomber*, 70.

5. "Proceedings of a Board of Officers Appointed to Consider the Suitability of the B-907 Airplane for Procurement and to Consider Any Other Matters Concerning Bombardment Aviation Equipment," Nov., 1932, RG 18, Entry 167, Box 21, NA.

6. Col. Oscar Westover, acting chief, Air Corps, 13 Dec. 1933, File 452.1, Box 21, ibid.; Maurer Maurer, *Aviation in the U.S. Army, 1919–1939*, 352.

7. Maurer, *Aviation in the U.S. Army*, 353–54.

8. "Secret Equipment Projects," n.d. [1933?], Box 23, Foulois Papers.

9. DuBuque and Gleckner, *Development of the Heavy Bomber*, 14–15.

10. Robin Cross, *The Bombers: The Illustrated Story of Offensive Strategy and Tactics in the Twentieth Century*, 76.

11. Maj. Carl Spaatz to Col. Hap Arnold, 5 Feb. 1935, Box 7, Spaatz Papers.

12. Erik Nelson, Boeing, to Lt. Col. Carl Spaatz, 8 Nov. 1935, Box 7, Spaatz Papers.

13. Michael J. H. Taylor, *Boeing* (London: Jane's, 1982), 118; DuBuque and Gleckner, *Development of the Heavy Bomber*, 83–84.

14. Maurer, *Aviation in the U.S. Army*, 358-359; Georges G. Bouché, "Grandpappy: The XB-15," *Aerospace Historian* 26, no. 3 (fall, 1979): 175–76.

15. Brig. Gen. John H. Hughes, assistant chief of staff (ACofS) for Operations and Training, to Maj. Gen. R. E. Callan, ACofS for Supply, 22 Jan. 1934, RG 18, Entry 167, File 452.1, Box 22, NA.

16. Maj. Gen. Hugh A. Drum, deputy chief of staff, to Maj. Gen. R. E. Callan, 29 Jan. 1934, ibid.

17. Curtis E. LeMay and Bill Yenne, *Superfortress: The B-29 and American Air Power*, 18.

18. Cross, *Bombers*, 76; Taylor, *Boeing*, 108.

19. Wellwood E. Beall, "Design Analysis of the Boeing B-17 Flying Fortress," *Aviation* 44, no. 1 (Jan., 1945): 123–24.

20. Ibid., 135.

21. Ibid., 121–23.

22. "Boeing Test Bomber, Model 299," *Air Corps Newsletter* 18 (15 July 1935): 18.

23. DuBuque and Gleckner, *Development of the Heavy Bomber*, 16.

24. Taylor, *Boeing*, 108.

25. DuBuque and Gleckner, *Development of the Heavy Bomber*, 16–17, 75; Taylor, *Boeing*, 108.

26. Maurer, *Aviation in the U.S. Army*, 354; LeMay and Yenne, *Superfortress*, 20.

27. Maurer, *Aviation in the U.S. Army*, 354; DuBuque and Gleckner, *Development of the Heavy Bomber*, 16–17.

28. DuBuque and Gleckner, *Development of the Heavy Bomber*, 21–22.

29. Maurer, *Aviation in the U.S. Army*, 360.

30. Ibid., 360–61.

31. Ibid., 361.

32. Taylor, *Boeing*, 109.

33. Cross, *Bombers*, 77; Taylor, *Boeing*, 109.

34. "Flying Fortresses on Exhibition at Golden Gate Fair," *Air Corps Newsletter* 22 (1 Mar. 1939): 9; "Much Viewed Bomber Resumes Normal Role," *Air Corps Newsletter* 22 (15 Nov. 1939): 19.

35. Maurer, *Aviation in the U.S. Army*, 355.

36. Ibid., 356.

37. Walter R. Close, "The B-18—A Reminiscence," *Aerospace Historian* 29, no. 2 (summer, 1982): 92.

38. Jones, *U.S. Bombers*, 51.

39. Close, "The B-18," 92.

40. DuBuque and Gleckner, *Development of the Heavy Bomber*, 127.

41. A useful comparison is again that of the British version of strategic bombing, which made no real (or even rhetorical) effort to target individual buildings or sets of buildings. Bomber Command generally targeted entire cities. Consequently, strategic bombing meant something very different to the British, and British technology differed accordingly.

42. Stephen R. McFarland, *America's Pursuit of Precision Bombing, 1910–1945*, 16–17.
43. F. A. Lindemann, "The Chief Causes of Error in Bomb Dropping from Aeroplanes," National Advisory Committee on Aeronautics Report T-1059, Jan. 1918, File: "Military Armament, Bombsights, Foreign, British #2," #S2009700, NASMA and BL.
44. The best study of Sperry is Thomas P. Hughes, *Elmer Sperry: Inventor and Engineer.*
45. Ibid., 173–200.
46. See Estoppey File, RG 342, File 371.63, RD2644, Box 2323, Clark Collection; and McFarland, *America's Pursuit,* 30–32.
47. Brig. Gen. William E. Gillmore, chief, Materiel Division, to Chief of Air Corps, 19 Jan. 1928, RG 18, Entry 166, File 471.6, Box 1143, NA.
48. Ibid., 14 Dec. 1926.
49. Ibid., 21 Feb. 1928.
50. Gillmore to Chief of Air Corps, 14 Dec. 1926, 19 Jan. 1928, and 21 Feb. 1928.
51. Ibid., 22 Nov. 1928, RG 342, File 371.63, RD 3416, Box 1282, Clark Collection.
52. Ibid., 19 Jan. 1928.
53. "Comparative Tests of Bombsights," 3 Feb. 1932, and "Progress of C-4 Bombsight Tests," 23 Dec. 1932, RG 342, File 371.63, RD 3222, Box 531, Clark Collection.
54. Robert Vance Brown, "The Navy's Mark 15 (Norden) Bomb Sight: Its Development and Procurement, 1920–1945," Office of the General Counsel, U.S. Navy, Apr., 1946, 22–25; copy in Navy Department Library, Naval Historical Center, Washington Navy Yard. See also McFarland, *America's Pursuit,* 49.
55. McFarland, *America's Pursuit,* 49–51.
56. Quoted in ibid., 38.
57. Brown, "The Navy's Mark 15," 51.
58. Ibid., 66.
59. McFarland, *America's Pursuit,* 54–55.
60. 2d Lt. A. J. Kerwin Malone to Chief of Air Corps, 14 June 1929; and Chief of Air Corps to Chief of Navy Bureau of Aeronautics, 5 Sept. 1931, both in RG 18, Entry 166, File 471.6, Box 1143, NA.
61. Lt. Col. R. T. Kirtland to Chief of Materiel Division, 27 Nov. 1931; and Chief of Air Corps to Chief of Materiel Division, 8 Mar. 1932, both in ibid.
62. Brown, "The Navy's Mark 15," 78–84.
63. Loyd Searle, "The Bombsight War: Norden vs. Sperry," IEEE *Spectrum* 26, no. 9 (Sept., 1989): 60; Norden Bombsight Patent, U.S. Patent Office, no. 2,428,678, 7 Oct. 1947.
64. "Handbook of Instructions for Bombsight Type M-9," Army Air Forces, 5 June 1945, call number 168.69-30, Center for Air Force History, Bolling Air Force Base, Washington, D.C. (hereafter CAFH), 53–62; "Precision Bombing," Office of the Chief of Naval Operations, June 1944, File: "Bombsight, Norden," NASMA and BL, 25–32.

65. Brown, "The Navy's Mark 15," 89. McFarland points out that such accuracy was never reproduced in combat, and suggests that some engineers taking the "revolving door" between the navy and Norden may have shaded the data to ensure the Mark XV's adoption by the navy (McFarland, *America's Pursuit*, 71–72).

66. Brown, "The Navy's Mark 15," 111–24.

67. Searle, "Bombsight War," 63.

68. McFarland, *America's Pursuit*, 119–25.

69. Sperry Gyroscope to Chief of Materiel Division, 11 Dec. 1933, and Sperry Gyroscope to Chief of Air Corps, 5 Apr. 1934, both in RG 18, Entry 166, File 471.6, Box 1143, NA.

70. Searle, "Bombsight War," 61.

71. Brig. Gen. F. M. Andrews, commanding GHQ Air Force, to Chief of Air Corps, 21 Jan. 1936, and "Case History of the Norden Bombsight" (Wright Field, Ohio: Historical Office, Air Technical Service Command, Jan., 1945), CAFH, Bolling Air Force Base, document 13.

72. Col. R. E. Jarmon, Materiel Division, "Recent Visit to the C. L. Norden Company," 29 Dec. 1943; "Case History of the Norden Bombsight" (Wright Field, Ohio: Historical Office, Air Technical Service Command, Jan., 1945), CAFH, Bolling Air Force Base, document 176.

73. Chief of Air Corps to Chief of Materiel Division, 20 Jan. 1936, RG 18, Army Air Forces General Correspondence, 1917–1938, File 471.6, Box 1143, NA.

74. "Development of Bombing Equipment," Historical Office, Air Service Technical Command, Wright Field, Ohio, 1945, CAFH, 59–62. Searle argues that the Sperry *did* perform as well as the Norden. However, based on contemporaneous documents, this opinion was clearly not widespread in the Air Corps during the 1930s and into World War II (Searle, "Bombsight War," 62–64).

75. "Development of Bombing Equipment," 70–71; McFarland, *America's Pursuit*, 144–45.

76. At that time the Norden was declared the Air Corps's only standard bombsight, and all remaining contracts with Sperry for the S-1 were canceled ("Development of Bombing Equipment," 71–73).

77. Brown, "The Navy's Mark 15," 320–21.

78. Searle, "Bombsight War," 64.

79. The Adjutant General to Commanding General, GHQ Air Force, 29 June 1936, RG 18, Entry 166, File 334.7, Box 532, NA.

80. Office of the Chief of Air Corps, Personnel Order no. 152, 29 June 1936, ibid.

81. "Balanced Air Corps Program," 5 Aug. 1936, RG 407, Records of the Air Advocate General, 1926–1939, File 580, Bulky, NA. Arnold proposed a force that included approximately thirty-five bombardment squadrons and twenty pursuit squadrons.

82. "Five Year Program for the Air Corps," War Department General Staff, 3 Mar. 1938, File 580, Box 2738, ibid.

83. Ibid.

84. "Directive to the War Plans Division in re Balanced Air Corps Program," War Department General Staff, 5 Feb. 1937, ibid.

85. Greer, *Development of Air Doctrine*, 97–99.

86. The Adjutant General to Chief of Air Corps, 26 Aug. 1938, RG 407, Records of the Air Advocate General, 1926–1939, File 580, Box 2738, NA.

87. Brig. Gen. H. H. Arnold, acting chief, Air Corps, to the Chief of Staff, 17 Aug. 1938, ibid.

88. "Air Corps Program and Directive," War Department General Staff, 26 Sept. 1938, ibid.

89. "Air Corps Program and Directive," 26 Sept. 1938.

90. Johnson, "Fast Tanks and Heavy Bombers," 438–40.

91. Ibid., 440; Arnold, *Global Mission*, 177–78; Sherry, *Rise of American Air Power*, 79.

92. Arnold, *Global Mission*, 177.

93. John Morton Blum, *From the Morganthau Diaries: Years of Urgency, 1938–1941*, 48–49.

94. Johnson, "Fast Tanks and Heavy Bombers," 442.

95. Arnold, *Global Mission*, 177.

96. Ibid., 179.

97. Even the Air Corps's official history reveals the bureaucratic importance of strategic bombing. The official Air Force history of World War II, a generally heroic account of the struggle against Germany and Japan, contains a chapter on the Air Corps between the wars that identifies three "paramount trends of the period" and lists them in this order: "the effort to establish an independent air force; the development of a doctrine of strategic bombardment; and the search for a heavy bomber by which that doctrine could be applied." (Craven and Cate, eds., *Army Air Forces in World War II*, 1:17).

Chapter 6. Political Pressure on a Warrior Elite

1. "Our Gallant Marines Drive 2½ Miles; Storm Two Towns, Capture 300 Prisoners," *New York Times*, 8 June 1918.

2. Robert Lindsay, *This High Name: Public Relations and the U.S. Marine Corps*, 31–33; Allan R. Millett, *Semper Fidelis: The History of the United States Marine Corps*, 294, 302–303; Edwin H. Simmons, "The U.S. Marines and Europe," Edwin H. Simmons Papers, Folder 24, Personal Papers Collection, Marine Corps Historical Center, Washington Navy Yard, Washington, D.C.

3. Eugene Alvarez, "Marines in the Movies," *Marine Corps Gazette* 11 (Nov., 1985): 86–95.

4. Millett, *Semper Fidelis*, 318.

5. Expenditures on the Marine Corps plummeted from about $76 million for fiscal year 1918–1919 to about $25 million for fiscal year 1922–1923. See *Annual Reports of the Navy Department for the Fiscal Year 1923*, 588.

6. Millett, *Semper Fidelis,* 138–44.

7. John H. Russell, "A Plea for a Mission and Doctrine," *Marine Corps Gazette* 1, no. 2 (1916): 111–12.

8. Millett, *Semper Fidelis,* 282–84.

9. John A. Lejeune, "The Mobile Defense of Advance Bases by the Marine Corps," *Marine Corps Gazette* 1, no. 1 (Mar., 1916): 1–2.

10. Quoted in Millett, *Semper Fidelis,* 285.

11. Louis Morton, "War Plan ORANGE: Evolution of a Strategy," *World Politics* 11, no. 2 (Jan., 1959): 222–23.

12. Rear Adm. Albert Gleaves, commander in chief, Asiatic Fleet, to Secretary of the Navy, 8 Sept. 1920, RG 127, Entry 39D, Box 2, NA.

13. Quoted in Morton, "War Plan ORANGE," 225.

14. Adm. Robert E. Coontz, chief of naval operations (CNO), to Maj. Gen. George Barnett, commandant, USMC, 28 Jan. 1920, RG 127, Entry 39D, Box 3, NA.

15. Capt. W. S. Pye in the *U.S. Naval Institute Proceedings,* 1926, quoted in Russell F. Weigley, *The American Way of War: A History of United States Military Strategy and Policy,* 256–57.

16. Coontz to Barnett, 28 Jan. 1920.

17. Millett, *Semper Fidelis,* 322–23.

18. Merrill L. Bartlett, *Lejeune: A Marine's Life, 1867–1942,* 154–55; Lindsay, *This High Name,* 37–39.

19. Millett, *Semper Fidelis,* 325; Bartlett, *Lejeune,* 193–94.

20. Lejeune, "Mobile Defense of Advance Bases," 1. Emphases in original.

21. Lindsay, *This High Name,* 23–35.

22. John J. Reber, "Pete Ellis: Amphibious Warfare Prophet," *U.S. Naval Institute Proceedings* 103 (Nov., 1977), 53–64; Millett, *Semper Fidelis,* 284–85, 325–26.

23. Maj. Earl H. Ellis, "Advanced Base Operations in Micronesia," 1921, File 165, Historical Amphibious File, Breckinridge Library, Quantico, Va. (hereafter Breckinridge Library), 1–2. Emphasis in original. Ellis's study was recently reissued by the Marine Corps as Fleet Marine Force Reference Publication 12-46 (1992).

24. Ibid., 12.

25. Ibid., 11.

26. Ibid., 14.

27. Jeter A. Isely and Philip A. Crowl, *The U.S. Marines and Amphibious War: Its Theory and Its Practice in the Pacific,* 26.

28. Ellis, "Advanced Base Operations," 62–63.

29. Approval, dated 23 July 1921, in File 165, Historical Amphibious File, Breckinridge Library.

30. Much of the following material on Ellis's ill-fated intelligence mission to Micronesia is from Reber, "Pete Ellis," 53–64.

Chapter 7. Technology and Training

1. See Thomas P. Hughes, *American Genesis: A Century of Invention and Technological Enthusiasm*, 71–74; and "The Evolution of Large Technological Systems," in *The Social Construction of Technological Systems*, ed. Wiebe E. Bijker, Thomas P. Hughes, and Trevor Pinch, 51–82.

2. The University of Pittsburgh Historical Staff at the Office of Naval Research, "The History of United States Naval Research and Development in World War II," Navy Department Library, Washington Navy Yard, Washington, D.C. (hereafter NDL), 1:73–76, 148–57.

3. For example, two widely used texts in naval architecture, *Manual of Ship Construction* by MIT professor George C. Manning, and *Theoretical Naval Architecture* by Edward L. Attwood and Herbert S. Pengelly, make no mention of the design of small boats.

4. Douglas H. C. Phillips-Birt, *The Naval Architecture of Small Craft*, XI–XII.

5. 2d Lt. Wilson B. Trundle to Brig. Gen. Eli Cole, 3 Mar. 1924, RG 127, Entry 39C, Box 7, NA.

6. Ibid.

7. Comdr. H. S. Howard, BuCon, to Chief Constructor, 28 July 1928, RG 19, Entry 115, File S82-3, Box 4214, NA.

8. J. D. Beuret, BuCon, to CNO via BuEng and Marine Corps Commandant, 16 Mar. 1926; and BuCon to Construction Officer, Washington Navy Yard, 24 Apr. 1926, both in RG 19, Entry 115, File S82-3, Box 4214, NA.

9. Lt. Comdr. Harry W. Hill, Report on tests of 50' Troop and Artillery Lighters, July 1926, RG 127, Entry 39D, Box 4, NA.

10. Maj. Gen. John A. Lejeune, commandant, USMC, to BuCon, 18 Aug. 1926, ibid.

11. Rear Adm. George H. Rock, chief, BuCon, to Capt. Henry Williams, 27 June 1928, RG 19, Entry 115, File S82-3, Box 4214, NA.

12. Quoted in Isely and Crowl, *U.S. Marines and Amphibious War*, 31.

13. Ibid., 31.

14. Rufus H. Lane, "The Mission and Doctrine of the Marine Corps," *Marine Corps Gazette* 8, no. 1 (1923): 10.

15. Millett, *Semper Fidelis*, 328.

16. Quoted in A. T. Mason, "Special Monograph on Amphibious Warfare," Dec., 1949, NDL, 7–8; Millett, *Semper Fidelis*, 328; Isely and Crowl, *U.S. Marines and Amphibious War*, 28.

17. Anthony A. Frances, "History of the Marine Corps Schools," Dec., 1945, Breckinridge Library, 24–29.

18. Donald F. Bittner, *Curriculum Evolution: Marine Corps Command and Staff College, 1920–1988*, 1.

19. Bittner, *Curriculum Evolution*, 8–9; Frances, "History of the Marine Corps Schools," 30.

20. Kenneth J. Clifford, *Progress and Purpose: A Developmental History of the United States Marine Corps, 1900–1970*, 37–38.
21. Bittner, *Curriculum Evolution*, 17–18; Clifford, *Progress and Purpose*, 37–38; and Mason, "Special Monograph," 9.
22. Bittner, *Curriculum Evolution*, 13.
23. Maj. Gen. Wendell C. Neville served as commandant from 1929 to 1930; Maj. Gen. Fuller was commandant from 1930 to 1934.
24. "Report of the Major General Commandant of the United States Marine Corps," *Annual Reports of the Navy Department for the Fiscal Year 1932*, 1163, quoted in Millett, *Semper Fidelis*, 329.
25. General Board to Secretary of the Navy, 10 Aug. 1932, quoted in Millett, *Semper Fidelis*, 330.
26. Ben H. Fuller, "Mission of the Marine Corps," *Marine Corps Gazette* 15, no. 3 (1930): 8.
27. Col. Ellis B. Miller, "The Marine Corps in Support of the Fleet," Marine Corps Schools, 1 June 1933, File 40, Historical Amphibious File, Breckinridge Library.
28. Rear Adm. Harris Laning, president, Naval War College, to Capt. S. W. Bryant, Office of the CNO, 24 Oct. 1932; and Col. R. M. Cutts to Col. E. B. Miller, 29 Oct. 1932, both in File 133, ibid.
29. Most of this material on the 1933 takeover attempt is from R. D. Heinl, "The Cat with More than Nine Lives," *U.S. Naval Institute Proceedings* 80, no. 6 (June, 1954): 668–69.
30. Ibid., 668.
31. Col. J. C. Fegan to Maj. Gen. Louis McCarty Little, 2 Aug. 1936, Folder 20, Louis McCarty Little Papers (hereafter Little Papers); Maj. Gen. Thomas Holcomb, commandant, USMC, to Brig. Gen. Richard P. Williams, 2 Mar. 1938; Williams to Holcomb, 6 Mar. 1938; and Holcomb to Brig. Gen. Douglas C. McDougal, 17 Mar. 1938, all in Box 14, Thomas Holcomb Papers (hereafter Holcomb Papers). Both collections are in the Personal Papers Collection, Marine Corps Historical Center, Washington Navy Yard, Washington, D.C. See also Millett, *Semper Fidelis*, 335.
32. Capt. Paul H. Bastedo, naval aide to the president, to SecNav, 2 Aug. 1937, RG 19, Entry 115, File S82-3, Box 4220, NA; Brig. Gen. Richard P. Williams to Maj. Gen. Thomas Holcomb, commandant, USMC, 1 Mar. 1939, Box 26, Holcomb Papers.
33. Maj. Gen. Ben Fuller, commandant, USMC, to Maj. Gen. Louis McCarty Little, 14 Mar. 1933, Folder 8, Little Papers.
34. Maj. Gen. John H. Russell to Adm. William V. Pratt, CNO, 17 Aug. 1933, Box 3, Folder 2, John H. Russell Papers, Personal Papers Collection, Marine Corps Historical Center, Washington Navy Yard, Washington, D.C. (hereafter Russell Papers).
35. Mason, "Special Monograph," 58.

36. Maj. Gen. John H. Russell to Maj. Gen. Louis McCarty Little, 5 Dec. 1933, Folder 9, Little Papers.

37. Mason, "Special Monograph," 63; Frances, "History of the Marine Corps Schools," 47.

Chapter 8. Doctrine and Fishing Boats

1. Isely and Crowl, *U.S. Marines and Amphibious War,* 35.

2. Col. Ellis B. Miller to Brig. Gen. James C. Breckinridge, commandant of Marine Corps Schools, 15 Aug. 1932, File 274, Historical Amphibious File, Breckinridge Library.

3. Ibid., paras. 3, 5, and 6.

4. Ibid., para. 7.

5. Ibid., para. 8.

6. Ibid.

7. Ibid., para. 11.

8. Ibid., para. 13.

9. Ibid., para. 31.

10. Ibid., paras. 30 and 31.

11. Brig. Gen. James C. Breckinridge to Maj. Gen. Ben H. Fuller, commandant, USMC, 18 Aug. 1932, File 274, Historical Amphibious File, Breckinridge Library.

12. Ibid.

13. Ibid.

14. Clifford, *Progress and Purpose,* 45.

15. Frances, "History of the Marine Corps Schools," 47–48.

16. This procedure is outlined in "Proceedings for Conference Held at the Marine Corps Schools, Quantico Virginia, on Tuesday, Jan. 9, 1934, for the purpose of discussing, approving, or commenting on the various headings and sub-headings of the tentative Landing Operations Manual, prepared by the Marine Corps Schools, and what it should include," File 41, Historical Amphibious File, Breckinridge Library.

17. Ibid.

18. Ibid.

19. Ibid.

20. Marine Corps Schools, "Tentative Manual for Landing Operations," 1935, copy in Breckinridge Library.

21. Ibid., 152.

22. Lt. Comdr. David L. Nutter, "Gunfire Support in Fleet Landing Exercises," Report Prepared by Direction of Rear Adm. A. W. Johnson, commanding Atlantic Squadron, Sept., 1939, File 73, Historical Amphibious File, Breckinridge Library.

23. Maj. Gen. John H. Russell, commandant, USMC, Marine Corps Order no. 87, 3

June 1935; Brig. Gen. F. L. Bradman, president, Marine Corps Equipment Board, to Maj. Gen. Thomas Holcomb, commandant, USMC, 9 Aug. 1938, both in RG 127, Entry 18, File 1540, Box 76, NA.

24. Maj. A. E. Creesy, secretary, Marine Corps Equipment Board, to Maj. Gen. Louis McCarty Little, 19 Apr. 1937, Folder 22, Little Papers; Brig. Gen. Frederic L. Bradman, president, Marine Corps Equipment Board, to Maj. Gen. Thomas Holcomb, commandant, USMC, 9 Aug. 1938, RG 127, Entry 18, File 1540, Box 76, NA; Brig. Gen. Emile P. Moses, president, Marine Corps Equipment Board, to Maj. Gen. Thomas Holcomb, commandant, USMC, 8 Oct. 1940, RG 127, Entry 39D, File 1540, Box 12, NA.

25. *Tentative Manual*, 70–71.

26. Ibid., 71.

27. Lt. Col. B. W. Gally, "A History of U.S. Fleet Landing Exercises," Report Prepared by Direction of Rear Adm. A. W. Johnson, commanding Atlantic Squadron, Sept., 1939. Historical Amphibious File, File 73, Breckinridge Library.

28. Brig. Gen. Richard P. Williams to Maj. Gen. Thomas Holcomb, commandant, USMC, 6 Mar. 1938, Box 14, Holcomb Papers.

29. "Army Quits War Game with Navy; Landing Exercise 'Not Worth Cost'," *New York Times*, 1 Jan. 1939.

30. Commander-in-Chief, U.S. Fleet, "A History of the Amphibious Training Command, U.S. Atlantic Fleet and Its Antecedent the Amphibious Force, U.S. Atlantic Fleet," vol. 145a, "U.S. Naval Administrative Histories of World War II," I–8.

31. *Tentative Manual*, 68–69.

32. Brig. Gen. Randolph C. Berkeley to Maj. Gen. Ben H. Fuller, commandant, USMC, 26 Jan. 1931, Experimental Landing Lighters Board Report, 8–10, RG 127, Entry 39D, Box 6, NA. Emphasis in original.

33. Ibid.

34. *Tentative Manual*, 69–70.

35. Navy Department Board to Conduct Comparative Trials of Special Landing Boats, "Report on Special Landing Boats," 12 Nov. 1936, RG 127, Entry 39D, Box 11, NA, 3–4.

36. A. P. Richardson, president, Mantoloking Boat and Engine Company, Inc., Mantoloking, N.J., to BuEng, 2 Nov. 1935, RG 19, Entry 115, File S82-3, Box 4220, NA.

37. These reports are in RG 127, Entry 39D, Box 10, NA.

38. BuEng to Hubert S. Johnson, Inc., 17 Mar. 1936, RG 127, Entry 39D, Box 10, NA. The Bay Head representative replied: "Quite frankly, this concern has had no experience of any kind with this type of cooling system. . . . While we desire to co-operate to the fullest extent with your Department, . . . we cannot conscientiously recommend the use of such a system. However, we shall be only too glad to assist, if within our power, but responsibility for its operation, cannot rest with us."

39. Ibid.

40. Maj. Gen. Louis McCarty Little, acting commandant, USMC, to Comdr. Otto M. Forster, 15 July 1936, RG 127, Entry 39D, Box 10, NA. Emphasis added.

41. Board to Conduct Comparative Trials of Special Landing Boats, "Original Report on Special Landing Boats," 12 Nov. 1936, RG 127, Entry 39D, Box 10, NA, 27–28 (hereafter Cape May Board Report).

42. 1st Lt. C. P. Van Ness, "The Development and Procurement of Special Landing Boats for the Marine Corps," 1937, File 124, Historical Amphibious File, Breckinridge Library, 8.

43. Cape May Board Report, 23.

44. Ibid., 24; Commandant of Norfolk Navy Yard to Chiefs of BuCon and BuEng, 17 Aug. 1932, RG 19, Entry 115, File S82-3, Box 4214, NA.

45. BuCon to Pierre A. Proal, Red Bank Yacht Works, 25 Jan. 1937, File S82-3, Box 4220, ibid.

46. Comdr. James G. Ware, Landing Boat Development Board, U.S. Fleet, to Chief of BuCon, 26 Mar. 1937, ibid.

47. Ibid.

48. Ibid.

49. A boat's sheer is the degree to which the bow and stern lines curve up from the keel when viewed from the side. A double-ended boat has a rounded or pointed stern, as opposed to the traditional square stern.

Chapter 9. *Eureka*

1. Maj. Gen. John H. Russell, commandant, USMC, to CNO, 1 May 1936, RG 127, Entry 39C, Box 7, NA.

2. Ibid., 11 May 1936, File 38, Historical Amphibious File, Breckinridge Library.

3. For example, DuBose, upon hearing about a device by Elco that could be used to hitch two boats together side-by-side with a platform to carry heavy loads, quickly wrote to the company to see if the rig might be useful during amphibious landings. Although it came to naught, it was hardly due to a lack of interest on DuBose's part. See Capt. William G. DuBose, assistant chief, BuCon, to Elco Works, Bayonne, N.J., Aug., 1936, RG 19, Entry 115, File S82-3, Box 4220, NA.

4. Rear Adm. William G. DuBose, chief, BuCon, to Rear Adm. A. W. Johnson, 30 Mar. 1938, File S82-3, Box 4221, ibid.

5. Ibid.

6. Gilbert Burck, "Mr. Higgins and his Wonderful Boats," *Life*, 16 Aug. 1943, 100–101.

7. Ibid., 108; Jerry E. Strahan, *Andrew Jackson Higgins and the Boats that Won World War II*, 5–11.

8. Burck, "Mr. Higgins," 102, 105.

9. Ibid., 106; Strahan, *Andrew Jackson Higgins*, 22.

10. Strahan, *Andrew Jackson Higgins*, 11.

11. Ibid., 23; Burck, "Mr. Higgins," 108.

12. Strahan, *Andrew Jackson Higgins*, 23; Burck, "Mr. Higgins," 108.

13. Higgins's invitation to the Cape May trials later became a point of considerable controversy after he developed a contentious relationship with BuCon and its successor, the Bureau of Ships (BuShips), during World War II. Higgins and others suggested that he had never been notified of the Cape May competition (see Strahan, *Andrew Jackson Higgins*, 29), but this is almost certainly not the case. Navy documents clearly record the invitation to Higgins and his explicit reply declining to submit a bid. See Capt. William G. DuBose, assistant chief, BuCon, to Higgins Industries, New Orleans, Louisiana, 21 Oct. 1936, RG 19, Entry 115, File S82-3, Box 4220, NA; and Capt. H. Williams, assistant chief, BuCon, to Commandant, Eighth Naval District, 26 July 1937, RG 19, Confidential Correspondence, 1925–1940, File S82-3, Box 152, NA.

14. Andrew J. Higgins to Rear Adm., H. V. Butler, commandant, Eighth Naval District, 1 July 1937, RG 19, Confidential Correspondence, 1925–1940, File S82-3, Box 152, NA.

15. The *Eureka*'s weight was given as sixty-eight thousand pounds, far in excess of the hoisting capacity for the transports. The Bureau Boats, in contrast, generally weighed in at about thirteen thousand pounds. This weight figure, supplied by Higgins, is mysterious since later versions weighed only about as much as the Bureau Boat. See Department Continuing Boat Board for Development of Landing Boats to Chief of BuCon, Chief of BuEng, and CNO, 30 Apr. 1937, RG 19, Entry 115, File S82-3, Box 4220, NA.

16. Al Hansen, USCG naval architect, to Engineer-in-Chief, USCG, 23 May 1937, ibid.

17. Hansen to Engineer-in-Chief, 23 May 1937.

18. Frank O. Hough, Verle E. Ludwig, and Henry I. Shaw Jr., *Pearl Harbor to Guadalcanal*, vol. I, *History of U.S. Marine Corps Operations in World War II*, 26–27.

19. Comdr. Roswell B. Daggett to Capt. H. Williams, assistant chief, BuCon, 9 Feb. 1938; Capt. H. Williams, assistant chief, BuCon, to A. J. Higgins, 9 Feb. 1938, RG 19, Entry 115, File S82-3, Box 4221, NA.

20. A. J. Higgins to Capt. H. Williams, assistant chief, BuCon, 14 Feb. 1938, ibid.

21. Strahan, *Andrew Jackson Higgins*, 51.

22. Frederick Lewis Allen, *Only Yesterday*, 168.

23. George Rappleyea (Higgins Industries) to Maj. John Kaluf, Marine Corps Equipment Board, 10 Mar. 1939, Historical Amphibious File, File 54, Breckinridge Library.

24. Hough et al., *History of U.S. Marine Corps Operations*, 1:27.

25. A. J. Higgins to Comdr. Ralph S. McDowell, 20 May 1938, RG 19, Entry 115, File S82-3, Box 4221, NA.

26. Lt. Comdr. George H. Bahm to Chief of Naval Operations, 7 June 1938, ibid.

27. Ibid.

28. Fleet Landing Boat Development Board, 13 May 1938, RG 19, Confidential Correspondence, 1925–1940, File S82-3, Box 152, NA.

29. A. J. Higgins to Chief, BuCon, 21 July 1938 and 12 Aug. 1938, RG 19, Entry 115, File S82-3, Box 4221, NA.

30. Schatzberg, "Ideology and Technical Choice," 34–69.

31. 1st Lt. Victor H. Krulak, "The Design and Procurement of Suitable Landing Boats," May 1940, File 123, Historical Amphibious File, Breckinridge Library.

32. Holland M. Smith and Percy Finch, *Coral and Brass*, 72, 90–91.

33. Ibid., 93. Higgins particularly liked to communicate through Holland Smith, Smith's aide Victor Krulak, and Brig. Gen. Emile Moses and Col. John Kaluf of the Marine Corps Equipment Board, all of whom became die-hard Higgins supporters.

34. Department Landing Boat Board to CNO, 21 June 1938, RG 19, Confidential Correspondence, 1925–1940, File S82-3, Box 152, NA.

35. These letters between Higgins and BuCon and BuEng are in RG 19, Entry 115, File S82-3, Box 4221, NA. Note particularly the 25 June, 9 Aug., and 12 Aug. 1938 letters from Higgins.

36. Fleet Landing Boat Development Board to Chief, BuCon, 6 Apr. 1939, RG 127, Entry 39C, Box 7, NA.

37. Comdr. R. B. Daggett to Chief Constructor, 13 Feb. 1939, ibid.

38. A. J. Higgins to Chief, BuCon, 6 Feb. 1939, RG 19, Entry 115, File S82-3, Box 4221, NA.

39. Chiefs of BuCon and BuEng to Commandants of Naval Districts, 8 May 1940, RG 19, Entry 1266, File S82-3, Box 1532, Washington National Records Center, Suitland, Md. (Hereafter WNRC.)

40. Burck, "Mr. Higgins," 101.

41. Departmental Boat Board to CNO, 18 May 1940, RG 19, Entry 1266, File S82-3, Box 1533, WNRC. Also BuShips to Commandant, 5th Naval District, 8 July 1940, cited in Hough et al., *History of U.S. Marine Corps Operations*, 1:28.

42. Smith and Finch, *Coral and Brass*, 91.

43. CNO to Chief, BuShips, 23 Sept. 1940, RG 80, General Correspondence, 1940–1942, File S82-3, Box 249, NA.

44. Brig. Gen. Emile P. Moses, president, Marine Corps Equipment Board, to Maj. Gen. Thomas Holcomb, commandant, 9 June 1939, RG 19, Confidential Correspondence, 1925–1940, File S82-3, Box 152, NA.

45. 1st Lt. Victor H. Krulak, "Report on Japanese Assault Landing Operations, Shanghai Area 1937," 1937, File 51, Historical Amphibious File, Breckinridge Library.

46. Victor H. Krulak, *First to Fight: An Inside View of the U.S. Marine Corps*, 91.

47. Ibid., 94.

48. Strahan, *Andrew Jackson Higgins*, 89.

49. "Are We Ready III—additional data on Landing Boats and Lighters," 16 Sept. 1941, RG 127, Entry 39D, Box 15, NA.

50. Strahan, *Andrew Jackson Higgins*, 128–33.

51. Higgins Industries, "Report on Landing Exercises on Onslo Beach and Vicinity," 3 Nov. 1941, Historical Amphibious File, File III, Breckinridge Library.

52. "Andy Higgins Dies; Built Boats in War," *New York Times*, 2 Aug. 1952.

53. Millett, *Semper Fidelis*, 266.

Chapter 10. Victory: Military, Bureaucratic, and Cultural

1. There are many treatments of the Air Forces in World War II. The official history is Craven and Cate, eds., *Army Air Forces in World War II*, 7 vols. Among the better recent studies are McFarland, *America's Pursuit*; Ronald Schaffer, *Wings of Judgment: American Bombing in World War II*; and Sherry, *Rise of American Air Power*. Also useful is the voluminous *U.S. Strategic Bombing Survey*, produced by a presidential commission formed in early 1945 to conduct a bomb damage analysis of the Combined Bomber Offensive. The thirty-one principal reports were edited by David MacIsaac and republished in ten volumes in 1976 as *The United States Strategic Bombing Survey*.

   The marines' official history of the war is the *History of U.S. Marine Corps Operations in World War II*, 5 vols. Other useful treatments are chapters 13 and 14 of Millett, *Semper Fidelis*; Ronald H. Spector, *Eagle Against the Sun: The American War with Japan*; and Craig M. Cameron, *American Samurai: Myth, Imagination, and the Conduct of Battle in the First Marine Division, 1941–1951*. Prominent combat narratives include William Manchester's *Goodbye, Darkness: A Memoir of the Pacific War*, and E. B. Sledge's *With the Old Breed at Peleliu and Okinawa*.

2. Holley, "Technology and Strategy," 21–23.

3. Alexander P. de Seversky, *Victory through Air Power*, 145–46.

4. *U.S. Strategic Bombing Survey*, "Over-all Report (European War)," vol. I, 99.

5. Ibid., "Summary Report (European War)," vol. I, 8–9.

6. Ibid., 5–7.

7. Millett, *Semper Fidelis*, 431–39.

8. Strahan, *Andrew Jackson Higgins*, 102–107.

9. Millett, *Semper Fidelis*, 439.

10. Cross, *Bombers*, 173–81.

11. Quoted in J. Samuel Walker, *Prompt and Utter Destruction: Truman and the Use of Atomic Bombs against Japan*, 77.

12. Chief of BuShips to Inspector of Naval Materiel, Los Angeles District, 15 Nov. 1941, RG 19, Entry 1266, File S82-3, Box 1503, WNRC.

13. Cameron, *American Samurai*, 178–81.

14. National Security Act of 1947, Section 206, para. (c).

15. These overviews of British, German, and Soviet aviation during the interwar years come from Lee Kennett, *A History of Strategic Bombing*, 72–88.

16. Merritt Roe Smith and Leo Marx, eds., *Does Technology Drive History?*, is a col-

lection of essays that analyze the history of the idea of technological determinism, the many definitions of technological determinism, the difficulties with technologically deterministic stories, and why such stories remain analytically compelling. The magnetic compass, printing press, and cotton gin examples were identified (and critiqued) by Smith and Marx in their introduction to the volume (see page x).

17. The term *seamless web* originated with Thomas Hughes and has since been employed by Donald MacKenzie, Trevor Pinch, Wiebe Bijker, John Law, Paul Edwards, and others. See Thomas P. Hughes, "The Seamless Web: Technology, Science, etcetera, etcetera," *Social Studies of Science* 16 (1986): 281–92; Donald MacKenzie, *Inventing Accuracy: A Historical Sociology of Nuclear Missile Guidance*, 410–17; Bijker et al., eds., *Social Construction of Technological Systems;* and Paul N. Edwards, *The Closed World: Computers and the Politics of Discourse in Cold War America,* 33.

18. They are: the Base Force Review (1991), the Bottom-Up Review (1993), the Commission on Roles and Missions of the Armed Forces (1995), and the Quadrennial Defense Review (1997).

Bibliography

Archival Sources

Center for Air Force History, Bolling Air Force Base, Washington, D.C.

Historical Amphibious File, Breckinridge Library, Quantico, Virginia.

Manuscript Division, Library of Congress. Frank Maxwell Andrews Papers. Benjamin D. Foulois Papers. Carl Andrew Spaatz Papers.

Personal Papers Collection, Marine Corps Historical Center, Washington Navy Yard. Thomas Holcomb Papers. Louis McCarty Little Papers. John H. Russell Papers. Edwin H. Simmons Papers. Donald M. Weller Papers.

National Air and Space Museum Archives and Branch Library, Smithsonian Institution, Washington, D.C.

National Archives, Washington, D.C., and Washington National Records Center, Suitland, Md. RG 18, Office of the Chief of Air Corps: Entry 90, General Correspondence, 1919–1921. Entry 166, General Correspondence, 1917–1938. Entry 167, Security Classified Correspondence, 1918–1938. Entry 219, Security Classified Correspondence, Reports, and Maps Re Defense and Mobilization Plans, 1919–1935. Entry 290, General Correspondence, January, 1939–September, 1942. Entry 293, Security Classified Correspondence, January, 1939–September, 1942. RG 19, Bureau of Ships (Construction and Repair): Entry 115, General Correspondence, 1925–1940. [No Entry Number], Confidential Correspondence, 1925–1940. Entry 1266, General Correspondence, 1940–1945. RG 80, General Records of the Navy Department: [No Entry Number], General Correspondence, 1926–1940. [No Entry Number], General Correspondence, 1940–1942. RG 127, U.S. Marine Corps: Entry 18, General Correspondence, 1926–1942. Entry 39C, General Correspondence, Plans and Policies, War Plans Section, 1926–1942. Entry 39D, War Plans, Division of Plans and Policies, War Plans Section, 1915–1946. RG 342, Air Corps Sarah Clark Collection. RG 407, Office of the Adjutant General: File 580 (and Bulky), Air Corps.

Navy Department Library, Washington Navy Yard, Washington, D.C. "U.S. Naval Administrative Histories of World War II." Vol. 46, "U.S. Marine Corps." 1946. Vol. 70, "Bureau of Ordnance—Organization, Administration, and Special Functions." n.d. Vol. 73, "Bureau of Ordnance—Research and Development, Maintenance." n.d. Vol. 79, "Bureau of Ordnance—Fire Control (Except Radar) and Aviation Ordnance." n.d. Vol. 89, "History of the Bureau of Ships during

World War II." 1952. Vol. 131, "Bureau of Ordnance—The History of the Naval Ordnance Laboratory, 1918–1945." 1946. Vol. 134, "Naval Research Laboratory—War History of the Naval Research Laboratory." 1946. Vol. 145, "A History of the Amphibious Training Command, U.S. Atlantic Fleet and Its Antecedent, the Amphibious Force, U.S. Atlantic Fleet." n.d. Vol. 150, "History of the Amphibious Forces, U.S. Pacific Fleet," 1945. Mason, A. T. "Special Monograph on Amphibious Warfare." Dec., 1949. The University of Pittsburgh Historical Staff at the Office of Naval Research. "The History of United States Naval Research and Development in World War II." Vol. 1.

USAF Collection, Air Force Historical Research Agency, Maxwell Air Force Base, Alabama

Published Sources

Allen, Frederick Lewis. *Only Yesterday.* New York: Harper and Row, 1931.

Allison, David Kite. *New Eye for the Navy: The Origin of Radar at the Naval Research Laboratory.* Washington, D.C.: Naval Research Laboratory, 1981.

Alvarez, Eugene. "Marines in the Movies." *Marine Corps Gazette* 11 (November, 1985): 86–95.

"Andy Higgins Dies; Built Boats in War." *New York Times,* 2 August 1952.

Army Field Manual 100-5. *Operations.* Washington, D.C.: USGPO, 1986.

"Army Quits War Game with Navy; Landing Exercise 'Not Worth Cost'." *New York Times,* 1 January 1939.

Arnold, H. H. *Global Mission.* New York: Harper and Row, 1949.

Attwood, Edward L., and Herbert S. Pengelly. *Theoretical Naval Architecture.* New York: Longmans, 1942.

Bailey, Alfred Dunlop. *Alligators, Buffaloes, and Bushmasters: The History of the Development of the LVT through World War II.* Washington, D.C.: History and Museums Division, Headquarters U.S. Marine Corps, 1986.

Barger, Melvin D. *Large Slow Target: A History of the LST.* Toledo, Ohio: U.S. LST Association, 1986.

Bartlett, Merrill L. *Lejeune: A Marine's Life, 1867–1942.* Columbia: University of South Carolina Press, 1991.

———, ed. *Assault from the Sea: Essays on the History of Amphibious Warfare.* Annapolis, Md.: Naval Institute Press, 1983.

Baxter, James Phinney III. *Scientists against Time.* Boston: Atlantic Monthly Press, 1946.

Beall, Wellwood E. "Design Analysis of the Boeing B-17 Flying Fortress." *Aviation* 44, no. 1 (January, 1945): 121–44.

Bijker, Wiebe E., Thomas P. Hughes, and Trevor Pinch, eds. *The Social Construction of Technological Systems.* Cambridge, Mass.: MIT Press, 1987.

Bilstein, Roger E. *Orders of Magnitude: A History of the NACA and NASA, 1915–1990.* Washington, D.C.: Scientific and Technical Information Division, NASA, 1989.

Binkin, Martin, and Jeffrey Record. *Where Does the Marine Corps Go from Here?* Washington, D.C.: The Brookings Institute, 1976.

Bittner, Donald F. *Curriculum Evolution: Marine Corps Command and Staff College, 1920–1988.* Washington, D.C.: History and Museums Division, Headquarters U.S. Marine Corps, 1988.

Blum, John Morton. *From the Morganthau Diaries: Years of Urgency, 1938–1941.* Boston: Houghton Mifflin, 1965.

"Boeing Test Bomber, Model 299." *Air Corps Newsletter* 18 (15 July 1935): 18.

Borowski, Harry R., ed. *The Harmon Memorial Lectures in Military History, 1959–1987.* Washington, D.C.: Office of Air Force History, 1988.

Bouché, Georges G. "Grandpappy: The XB-15." *Aerospace Historian* 26, no. 3 (fall, 1979): 171–81.

Boylan, Bernard L. "The Search for a Long Range Escort Plane, 1919–1945." *Military Affairs* 30, no. 2 (summer, 1966): 57–67.

Brewer, Leighton. *Riders of the Sky.* Boston: Houghton Mifflin, 1934.

Brooks, Harvey. "The Military Innovation System and the Qualitative Arms Race." In *Arms, Defense Policy, and Arms Control*, ed. Franklin A. Long and George W. Rathgens. New York: W. W. Norton, 1976.

Burck, Gilbert. "Mr. Higgins and His Wonderful Boats." *Life*, 16 August 1943, 100–12.

Cameron, Craig M. *American Samurai: Myth, Imagination, and the Conduct of Battle in the First Marine Division, 1941–1951.* New York: Cambridge University Press, 1994.

Campbell-Kelly, Martin, and William Aspray. *Computer: A History of the Information Machine.* New York: Basic Books, 1996.

Claussen, Martin P. *Materiel Research and Development in the Army Air Arm, 1914–1945.* Air Historical Studies no. 50. Bolling Air Force Base, Washington, D.C.: Army Air Forces Historical Division, Center for Air Force History, 1946.

Clifford, Kenneth J. *Amphibious Warfare Development in Britain and America from 1920–1940.* Laurens, N.Y.: Edgewood, 1983.

———. *Progress and Purpose: A Developmental History of the United States Marine Corps, 1900–1970.* Washington, D.C.: History and Museums Division, Headquarters U.S. Marine Corps, 1973.

Clodfelter, Mark. "Pinpoint Devastation: American Air Campaign Planning before Pearl Harbor." *Journal of Military History* 58, no. 1 (January, 1994): 75–101.

Close, Walter R. "The B-18—A Reminiscence." *Aerospace Historian* 29, no. 2 (summer, 1982): 90–92.

Coffey, Thomas M. *Hap: The Story of the U.S. Air Force and the Man Who Built It, General Henry H. "Hap" Arnold.* New York: Viking, 1982.

Corn, Joseph J. *The Winged Gospel: America's Romance with Aviation, 1900–1950.* New York: Oxford University Press, 1983.

Craven, Wesley Frank, and James Lea Cate, eds. *The Army Air Forces in World War II.* Vol 1, *Early Plans and Operations: January 1939 to August 1942.* Chicago: University of Chicago Press, 1948. Reprint, Washington, D.C.: Office of Air Force History, 1983.

Cringely, Robert X. *Accidental Empires: How the Boys of Silicon Valley Make Their Millions, Battle Foreign Competition, and Still Can't Get a Date.* Rev. ed. New York: HarperCollins, 1996.

Cross, Robin. *The Bombers: The Illustrated Story of Offensive Strategy and Tactics in the Twentieth Century.* New York: Macmillan, 1987.

Del Valle, Pedro. "Boats in the Landing Attack." *Marine Corps Gazette* 17, no. 1 (1932): 30–34.

———. "Ships to Shore in Amphibious Warfare." *Marine Corps Gazette* 16, no. 4 (1932): 11–16.

de Seversky, Alexander P. *Victory Through Air Power.* Garden City, N.Y.: Doubleday, 1943.

Douglas, Susan J. "Technological Innovation and Organizational Change: The Navy's Adoption of Radio, 1899–1919." In *Military Enterprise and Technological Change,* ed. Merritt Roe Smith. Cambridge, Mass.: MIT Press, 1985.

DuBuque, Jean H., and Robert F. Gleckner. *The Development of the Heavy Bomber, 1918–1944.* Air Historical Studies no. 6. Bolling Air Force Base, Washington, D.C.: U.S. Air Force Historical Division, Center for Air Force History, 1951.

Dupree, A. Hunter. *Science in the Federal Government: A History of Politics and Activities.* 1957. Reprint, Baltimore: Johns Hopkins University Press, 1986.

Edwards, Paul N. *The Closed World: Computers and the Politics of Discourse in Cold War America.* Cambridge, Mass.: MIT Press, 1996.

Emme, Eugene M. *The Impact of Air Power: National Security and World Politics.* New York: D. Van Nostrand, 1959.

———. "Technical Change and Western Military Thought, 1914–1945." *Military Affairs* 24, no. 1 (spring, 1960): 6–19.

Evangelista, Matthew. *Innovation and the Arms Race: How the United States and the Soviet Union Develop New Military Technologies.* Ithaca, N.Y.: Cornell University Press, 1988.

Finney, Robert T. *History of the Air Corps Tactical School, 1920–1940.* Air Historical Studies no. 100. Bolling Air Force Base, Washington, D.C.: U.S. Air Force Historical Division, Center for Air Force History, 1955.

"Flying Fortresses on Exhibition at Golden Gate Fair." *Air Corps Newsletter* 22 (1 March 1939): 9.

Forman, Paul. "Behind Quantum Electronics: National Security as Basis for Physical Research in the United States, 1940–1960." *Historical Studies in the Physical and Biological Sciences* 18, pt. 1 (1987): 149–229.

Foulois, Benjamin D., and C. V. Glines. *From the Wright Brothers to the Astronauts: The Memoirs of Major General Benjamin D. Foulois.* New York: McGraw-Hill, 1968.

Fuller, Ben H. "Mission of the Marine Corps." *Marine Corps Gazette* 15, no. 3 (1930): 7–8.

Furer, Julius Augustus. *Administration of the Navy Department in World War II.* Washington, D.C.: Department of the Navy, 1959.

Futrell, Robert Frank. *Ideas, Concepts, Doctrine: A History of Basic Thinking in the United States Air Force, 1907–1964.* 2 vols. Maxwell Air Force Base, Ala.: Air University, 1971.

Gilpin, Robert, and Christopher Wright, eds. *Scientists and National Policy-Making.* New York: Columbia University Press, 1964.

Goldbert, Alfred, ed. *A History of the United States Air Force, 1907–1957.* Princeton: D. Van Nostrand, 1957.

Greer, Thomas H. *The Development of Air Doctrine in the Army Air Arm, 1917–1941.* Maxwell Air Force Base, Ala.: USAF Historical Division, Air University, 1955. Reprint, Washington, D.C.: Office of Air Force History, 1985.

Hackmann, Willem D. "Sonar Research and Naval Warfare 1914–1954: A Case Study of a Twentieth-Century Science." *Historical Studies in the Physical and Biological Sciences* 16, pt. 1 (1986): 83–110.

Hallion, Richard P. "Philanthropy and Flight: Guggenheim Support of Aeronautics, 1925–1930." *Aerospace Historian* 28, no. 1 (spring, 1981): 10–21.

Hansell, Haywood S. "The Keystone Bombers: Unhonored and Unloved." *Air Force Magazine,* September, 1977, 131–36.

Hastings, Max. "The Bomber as the Weapon of Choice." Paper presented at the National Air and Space Museum Symposium on the Legacy of Strategic Bombing, Washington, D.C., 11 January 1990.

———. *Bomber Command.* New York: Simon and Schuster, 1979.

Heatherington, Norriss S. "The National Advisory Committee for Aeronautics: A Forerunner of Federal Governmental Support for Scientific Research." *Minerva* 28, no. 2 (spring, 1990): 59–80.

Heinl, R. D. "The Cat with More than Nine Lives." U.S. Naval Institute *Proceedings* 80, no. 6 (June, 1954): 659–71.

———. *Soldiers from the Sea: The United States Marine Corps, 1775–1962.* Annapolis, Md.: Naval Institute Press, 1962.

Heron, S. D. *Development of Aviation Fuels.* Boston: Division of Research, Graduate School of Business Administration, Harvard University, 1950.

Hill, Walter N. "The Employment of a Marine Corps Expeditionary Force in a Major Emergency." *Marine Corps Gazette* 15, no. 5 (1931): 16–20.

Holley, Irving B. *Ideas and Weapons: Exploitation of the Aerial Weapon by the United States during World War I; A Study in the Relationship of Technological Advance, Military Doctrine, and the Development of New Weapons.* New Haven, Conn.: Yale University Press, 1953. Reprint, Washington, D.C.: Office of Air Force History, 1983.

———. "Technology and Strategy: A Historical Overview." In *Technology, Strategy and National Security,* ed. Franklin D. Margiotta and Ralph Sanders. Washington, D.C.: National Defense University Press, 1985.

Hough, Frank O., Verle E. Ludwig, and Henry I. Shaw Jr. *History of U.S. Marine Corps Operations in World War II.* Vol. I, *Pearl Harbor to Guadalcanal.* Washington, D.C.: Historical Branch, Headquarters U.S. Marine Corps, 1958.

Howard, Michael, ed. *The Theory and Practice of War: Essays Presented to Captain Sir Basil Lidell Hart.* London: Cassell, 1965.

Hoyt, Edwin P. *The Airmen: The Story of American Fliers in World War II.* New York: McGraw-Hill, 1990.

Hughes, Thomas P. *American Genesis: A Century of Innovation and Technological Enthusiasm, 1870–1970.* New York: Penguin, 1989.

———. *Elmer Sperry: Inventor and Engineer.* Baltimore: Johns Hopkins University Press, 1971.

———. "The Evolution of Large Technological Systems." In *The Social Construction of Technological Systems,* ed. Wiebe E. Bijker, Thomas P. Hughes, and Trevor Pinch. Cambridge, Mass.: MIT Press, 1987.

———. "The Seamless Web: Technology, Science, etcetera, etcetera." *Social Studies of Science* 16 (1986): 281–92.

Hurley, Alfred F. *Billy Mitchell: Crusader for Air Power.* New York: Franklin Watts, 1964.

"An Indiscreet General." *New York Times,* 14 February 1925.

Isely, Jeter A., and Philip A. Crowl. *The U.S. Marines and Amphibious War: Its Theory and its Practice in the Pacific.* Princeton, N.J.: Princeton University Press, 1951.

Johnson, David Eugene. *Fast Tanks and Heavy Bombers: Innovation in the U.S. Army, 1917–1945.* Ithaca, N.Y.: Cornell University Press, 1998.

———. "Fast Tanks and Heavy Bombers: The United States Army and the Development of Armor and Aviation Doctrines and Technologies, 1917 to 1945." Ph.D. diss., Duke University, 1990.

Johnson, Melvin M., Jr. "Fleet Marine Force Landing Boats." *Marine Corps Gazette* 20, no. 1 (1936): 9–10, 60–63.

Jones, Lloyd S. *U.S. Bombers: B1–B70.* Los Angeles: Aero Publications, 1962.

Kaluf, John. "The Marine Corps Equipment Board." *Marine Corps Gazette* 21, no. 3 (1937): 22–23.

Kelsey, Benjamin S. *The Dragon's Teeth? The Creation of United States Air Power for World War II.* Washington, D.C.: Smithsonian Institution Press, 1982.

Kennett, Lee. *A History of Strategic Bombing.* New York: Charles Scribner's Sons, 1982.

Kevles, Daniel J. "R&D and the Arms Race: An Analytical Look." In *Science, Technology, and the Military,* ed. Everett Mendelsohn, Merritt Roe Smith, and Peter Weingart. Dordrecht: Kluwer, 1988: 465–80.

Krulak, Victor H. *First to Fight: An Inside View of the U.S. Marine Corps.* Annapolis, Md.: Naval Institute Press, 1984.

Lane, Rufus H. "The Mission and Doctrine of the Marine Corps." *Marine Corps Gazette* 8, no. 1 (1923): 1–13.

Lejeune, John A. "The Mobil Defense of Advance Bases by the Marine Corps." *Marine Corps Gazette* 1, no. 1 (March, 1916): 1–6.

———. *The Reminiscences of a Marine.* Philadelphia: Dorrance, 1930.

———. "The United States Marine Corps." *Marine Corps Gazette* 8, no. 4 (1923): 243–54.

LeMay, Curtis E., and Bill Yenne. *Superfortress: The B-29 and American Air Power.* New York: McGraw-Hill, 1988.

LeMay, Curtis E., with MacKinlay Kantor. *Mission with LeMay.* Garden City, N.Y.: Doubleday, 1965.

Lindsay, Robert. *This High Name: Public Relations and the U.S. Marine Corps.* Madison: University of Wisconsin Press, 1956.

Long, Franklin A., and Judith Reppy, eds. *The Genesis of New Weapons: Decision-Making for Military R&D.* New York: Pergamon, 1980.

McFarland, Stephen R. *America's Pursuit of Precision Bombing: 1910–1945.* Washington, D.C.: Smithsonian Institution Press, 1995.

MacIsaac, David, ed. *The United States Strategic Bombing Survey.* 10 vols. New York: Garland, 1976.

MacKenzie, Donald. *Inventing Accuracy: A Historical Sociology of Nuclear Missile Guidance.* Cambridge, Mass.: MIT Press, 1990.

McNeill, William H. *The Pursuit of Power: Technology, Armed Force, and Society since A.D. 1000.* Chicago: University of Chicago Press, 1982.

Manchester, William. *Goodbye, Darkness: A Memoir of the Pacific War.* Boston: Little, Brown, 1980.

Manning, George C. *Manual of Ship Construction.* New York: Van Nostrand, 1942.

Mansfield, Edwin, ed. *Defense, Science, and Public Policy.* New York: W. W. Norton, 1968.

Margiotta, Franklin D., and Ralph Sanders, eds. *Technology, Strategy, and National Security.* Washington, D.C.: National Defense University Press, 1985.

Maurer, Maurer. *Aviation in the U.S. Army, 1919–1939.* Washington, D.C.: Office of Air Force History, 1987.

Mendelsohn, Everett, Merritt Roe Smith, and Peter Weingart, eds. *Science, Technology, and the Military.* 2 vols. Dordrecht: Kluwer, 1988.

Merillat, Herbert Christian. *Guadalcanal Remembered.* New York: Dodd, Mead, 1982.

Metcalf, Clyde H. *The History of the United States Marine Corps.* New York: G. P. Putnam's Sons, 1939.

Mets, David R. *Master of Air Power: General Carl A. Spaatz.* Novato, Calif.: Presidio, 1988.

Miller, E. B. "A Naval Expedition Involving the Landing of a Marine Expeditionary Force." *Marine Corps Gazette* 17, no. 4 (1933): 28–35.

Millett, Allan R. *Semper Fidelis: The History of the United States Marine Corps.* New York: Macmillan, 1980.

Millett, Allan R., and Peter Maslowski. *For the Common Defense: A Military History of the United States of America.* New York: Macmillan, 1984.

Mitchell, William. *Memoirs of World War I: From Start to Finish of Our Greatest War.* New York: Random House, 1960.

———. *Winged Defense: The Development and Possibilities of Modern Air Power—Economic and Military.* New York: G. P. Putnam's Sons, 1925.

Mondey, David. *Pictorial History of the U.S. Air Force.* New York: Arco, 1971.

Morton, Louis. "American and Allied Strategy in the Far East." *Military Review* 29, no. 9 (December, 1949): 22–39.

———. "War Plan ORANGE: Evolution of a Strategy." *World Politics* 11, no. 2 (January, 1959): 221–50.

"Much Viewed Bomber Resumes Normal Role." *Air Corps Newsletter* 22 (15 November 1939): 19.

The National Cyclopedia of American Biography. Vol. 55. Clifton, N.J.: James T. White, 1974.

Navy Department. *Annual Reports of the Navy Department for the Fiscal Year 1923.* Washington, D.C.: USGPO, 1924.

———. *Annual Reports of the Navy Department for the Fiscal Year 1932.* Washington, D.C.: USGPO, 1933.

O'Connor, Raymond G. "The U.S. Marines in the 20th Century: Amphibious Warfare and Doctrinal Debates." *Military Affairs* 38, no. 3 (October, 1974): 97–103.

Olmsted, Merle C. "The Martin Bomber: First of the U.S. Heavies." *Aerospace Historian* 20, no. 3 (fall, 1973): 150–54.

"Our Gallant Marines Drive 2½ Miles; Storm Two Towns, Capture 300 Prisoners." *New York Times,* 8 June 1918.

Paret, Peter, ed. *Makers of Modern Strategy from Machiavelli to the Nuclear Age.* Princeton, N.J.: Princeton University Press, 1986.

Parker, William D. *A Concise History of the United States Marine Corps, 1775–1969.* Washington, D.C.: Historical Division, Headquarters U.S. Marine Corps, 1970.

Parton, James. *"Air Force Spoken Here": General Ira Eaker and the Command of the Air.* Bethesda, Md.: Adler and Adler, 1986.

Phillips-Birt, Douglas H. C. *The Naval Architecture of Small Craft.* New York: Philosophical Library, 1957.

———. *Ships and Boats: The Nature of Their Design.* New York: Reinhold, 1966.

Posen, Barry R. *The Sources of Military Doctrine: France, Britain, and Germany between the World Wars.* Ithaca, N.Y.: Cornell University Press, 1984.

Quester, George H. *Deterrence Before Hiroshima: The Airpower Background of Modern Strategy.* New York: John Wiley and Sons, 1966.

Rae, John B. *Climb to Greatness: The American Aircraft Industry, 1920–1960.* Cambridge, Mass.: MIT Press, 1968.

Raudzens, George. "War-Winning Weapons: The Measurement of Technological Determinism in Military History." *Journal of Military History* 54, no. 4 (October, 1990): 403–34.

Reber, John J. "Pete Ellis: Amphibious Warfare Prophet." *U.S. Naval Institute Proceedings* 103 (November, 1977): 53–64.

Roland, Alex. *Model Research: The National Advisory Committee for Aeronautics, 1915–1958.* Washington, D.C.: Scientific and Technical Information Branch, NASA, 1985.

Ross, Bill D. *Peleliu: Tragic Triumph: The Untold Story of the Pacific War's Forgotten Battle.* New York: Random House, 1991.

Russell, John H. "A Plea for a Mission and Doctrine." *Marine Corps Gazette* 1, no. 2 (1916): 109–22.

Schaffer, Ronald. *Wings of Judgment: American Bombing in World War II.* Oxford: Oxford University Press, 1985.

Schatzberg, Eric. "Ideology and Technical Choice: The Decline of the Wooden Airplane in the United States, 1920–1945." *Technology and Culture* 35 (January, 1994): 34–69.

Schlaifer, Robert. *Development of Aircraft Engines.* Boston: Division of Research, Graduate School of Business Administration, Harvard University, 1950.

Schmidt, Hans. *Maverick Marine: General Smedley D. Butler and the Contradictions of American Military History.* Lexington: University Press of Kentucky, 1987.

Searle, Loyd. "The Bombsight War: Norden vs. Sperry." IEEE *Spectrum* 26, no. 9 (September, 1989): 60–66.

Seidel, Robert W. "From Glow to Flow: A History of Military Laser Research and Development." *Historical Studies in the Physical and Biological Sciences* 18, pt. 1 (1987): 111–47.

Sherman, Herbert. "The Role of the Military Laboratory in Electronics Research and Development." *Transactions of the Institute of Radio Engineers Professional Group on Engineering Management.* PGEM-1 (February, 1954): 30–43.

Sherry, Michael S. *The Rise of American Air Power: The Creation of Armageddon.* New Haven, Conn.: Yale University Press, 1987.

Shiner, John F. "The Air Corps, the Navy, and Coast Defense, 1919–1941." *Military Affairs* 45, no. 3 (October, 1981): 113–20.

———. "Birth of the GHQ Air Force." *Military Affairs* 42, no. 3 (October, 1978): 113–20.

———. *Foulois and the U.S. Army Air Corps.* Washington, D.C.: Office of Air Force History, 1983.

Sledge, E. B. *With the Old Breed at Peleliu and Okinawa.* Novato, Calif.: Presidio, 1981.

Smith, Dale O. *Screaming Eagle: Memoirs of a B-17 Group Commander.* Chapel Hill, N.C.: Algonquin Books, 1990.

Smith, Herschel. *Aircraft Piston Engines: From the Manly Balzer to the Continental Tiara.* Manhattan, Kans.: Sunflower University Press, 1981.

Smith, Holland M., and Percy Finch. *Coral and Brass.* Washington, D.C.: Zenger, 1949. Reprint, Washington, D.C.: Zenger, 1979.

Smith, Merritt Roe, ed. *Military Enterprise and Technological Change: Perspectives on the American Experience.* Cambridge, Mass.: MIT Press, 1985.

Smith, Merritt Roe, and Leo Marx, eds. *Does Technology Drive History?* Cambridge, Mass.: MIT Press, 1994.

Spector, Ronald H. *Eagle against the Sun: The American War with Japan.* New York: Free Press, 1984.

Strahan, Jerry E. *Andrew Jackson Higgins and the Boats that Won World War II.* Baton Rouge: Louisiana State University Press, 1994.

Swanborough, F. G. *United States Military Aircraft since 1909.* London: Putnam, 1963.

Tate, James P. "The Army and Its Air Corps: A Study of the Evolution of Army Policy towards Aviation, 1919–1941." Ph.D. diss., Indiana University, 1976.

Taylor, Michael J. H. *Boeing.* London: Jane's, 1982.

Thayer, Lucien H. *America's First Eagles: The Official History of the U.S. Air Service, A.E.F. (1917–1918).* San Jose, Calif.: R. James Bender, 1983.

Tilford, Earl H. Jr. "The Barling Bomber." *Aerospace Historian* 26, no. 2 (summer, 1979): 91–97.

U.S. Congress. House. Committee on Appropriations in Charge of War Department Appropriation Bill for 1925. *Hearings.* 68th Cong., 1st sess. Washington, D.C.: USGPO, 1925.

———. House. Committee on Appropriations in Charge of War Department Appropriation Bill for 1923. *Hearings.* 67th Cong., 2d sess. Washington, D.C.: USGPO, 1923.

———. House. Committee on Interstate and Foreign Commerce. *Hearings before the President's Aircraft Board.* 3 vols. Washington, D.C.: USGPO, 1925.

———. House. Committee on Military Affairs. *Hearings, Aeronautics in the Army.* 63d Cong., 1st sess. Washington, D.C.: USGPO, 1913.

———. House. Select Committee of Inquiry in Operations of the United States Air Services. *Hearings.* 68th Cong. Washington, D.C.: USGPO, 1925.

U.S. Strategic Bombing Survey. Washington, D.C.: USGPO, 1945–46.

Van Creveld, Martin. *Technology and War: From 2000 B.C. to the Present.* Rev. ed. New York: Macmillan, 1991.

Walker, J. Samuel. *Prompt and Utter Destruction: Truman and the Use of Atomic Bombs against Japan.* Chapel Hill: University of North Carolina Press, 1997.

Weigley, Russell F. *The American Way of War: A History of United States Military Strategy and Policy.* New York: Macmillan, 1973. Reprint, Bloomington: Indiana University Press, 1977.

———, ed. *New Dimensions in Military History.* San Rafael, Calif.: Presidio, 1975.

Werrell, Kenneth P. "The Strategic Bombing of Germany in World War II: Costs and Accomplishments." *Journal of Military History* 73, no. 3 (December, 1986): 702–13.

Westenhoff, Charles M. *Military Air Power: The CADRE Digest of Air Power Opinion and Thoughts.* Maxwell Air Force Base, Ala.: Air University Press, 1990.

Williams, Dion. "Discussion of Marine Corps War College." *Marine Corps Gazette* 1, no. 4 (1916): 364–65.

———. "The Fleet Landing Force." *Marine Corps Gazette* 11, no. 2 (1926): 116–27.

———. "The Temporary Defense of a Fleet Base." *Marine Corps Gazette* 15, no. 4 (1931): 9–13, 53–62.

———. "The Winter Maneuvers of 1924." *Marine Corps Gazette* 9, no. 1 (1924): 1–25.

York, Herbert. *Race to Oblivion: A Participant's View of the Arms Race.* New York: Simon and Schuster, 1970.

Index

General Headquarters (GHQ) Air Force, 60, 163; established, 59

George, Harold L., 61, 66

Georgia School (Institute) of Technology: aeronautics program, 39

Gibbons, Floyd, 102

Glenn L. Martin Company: early bomber aircraft, 44. *See also* Martin, Glenn L.; Martin B-10 bomber; Martin B-12 bomber

Greenport boat. *See* landing craft: Cape May boats

Guadalcanal, 167

Guam, 167

Haiti, 128

Hamilton Standard Company: variable pitch propellers, 43

Hansell, Haywood S., 8, 66; and ACTS precision bombing doctrine, 64

Haynes, Caleb V., 71

Higgins, Andrew Jackson, 146, 150–62; and Cape May trials, 151; and doctrine for amphibious operations, 161–62; marketing skill, 155; and production engineering, 159; shallow draft boat designs, 151; tank lighter dispute with Bureau of Ships, 167–68; and technical innovation, 158; and threat of foreign sales, 154; and wooden landing craft, 157–59. *See also* landing craft: Higgins boat

Higgins Industries, 150, 162; Boat Operators and Marine Engine Maintenance School, 161

Hiroshima, 170

Hitler, Adolf, 96

Honeywell Regulator Company, 90, 93

Hoover, Herbert: and air mail fiasco, 56; and coast defense controversy, 55; and tensions with Marine Corps, 127–29

Howell Commission, 59

Hughes, Thomas P., 117

IBM, 3–4

Inglis, Henry B., 50, 83

institutional culture, 5–6, 172, 177; and technology, ix–xi, 3–4, 7–9, 11, 101. *See also* U.S. Army Air Corps; U.S. Marine Corps

isolationism, 6

Iwo Jima, 167, 170; as Marine Corps icon, 4, 101, 162

Japan: U.S. war plans against, 10. *See also* War Plan Orange

Jobs, Steve, 6

Joint Action of the Army and Navy, 125, 148–49

Joint Army-Navy Board, 54, 107–108, 125, 149; created, 106; and Marine Corps representation, 111

Kármán, Theodore von, 39

Kennedy, Joseph P., 96

Keystone, 68–69

Keystone B-1 bomber, 48

Klystra, Jack, 70

Krulak, Victor H., 161

Kuter, Laurence: on defeating Chennault at ACTS, 66

Kwajalein, 167

Lampert Committee, 25–26

landing craft: A-boat, 120, 140–41, 146, 149; B-boat, 120, 149; Beetle Boat, 120; bow ramp, 160–61; Bureau boat, 145–46, 149, 159; Cape May boats, 142–46, 149, 151; C-boat, 120, 149; Higgins boat, 151–62, 170, 175; Higgins tank lighter, 167–68; Landing Craft, Vehicle, Personnel (LCVP), 162; Landing Ship, Tank (LST), 170; Landing Vehicle, Tracked (LVT), 170;

seamless web metaphor, 175–76

Seversky, Alexander P. de, 82–83, 164

Seversky C-1 bombsight, 82. *See also* bombsights: Seversky

Smith, Holland M., 111; and Andrew Jackson Higgins, 157

Smith, Lotha A., 66

Snavely, Ralph A., 66

Spaatz, Carl A., 35, 163–64; early proponent of air force concept, 24; and Boeing B-17 bomber, 74; and coast defense controversy with U.S. Navy, 55

Sperry bombsights, 9, 87; A-1 autopilot, 85; A-5 autopilot, 88, 90; C-4, 83; S-1, 91–93. *See also* bombsights: Sperry

Sperry Gyroscope Company, 50; bombsight development, 82–85, 90–91

Sperry-Inglis L-1 bombsight, 83

Stanford University: aeronautics program, 39–40, 73

Star Trek, x

strategic bombing. *See* precision bombing

Strategic Bombing Survey, 164–66

Sutton, Harry, 36

synchronous method. *See* bombsights: synchronous method

Taft, William H., 104

Tarawa, 167

technological determinism, 174–75

technological enthusiasm, 7

Tentative Manual for Landing Operations, 134–39, 147, 166–67. *See also* Marine Corps Schools

terror bombing, 8

timing method. *See* bombsights: timing method

Tinian, 167

Treaty of Versailles, 104, 107

Trenchard, Hugh, 28–29, 31

Tydings-McDuffie Act, 109

University of Akron: aeronautics program, 39

University of Michigan: aeronautics program, 39–40

University of Washington: aeronautics program, 39–40

U.S. Air Force, 3–4; created, 97, 171

U.S. Army, Air Corps independence from. *See* U.S. Army Air Corps: seeking independence from U.S. Army

U.S. Army, as Air Corps patron, 8, 58–60, 94–95

U.S. Army Air Corps, x, 3–4, 126; air mail fiasco, 56–59; bombsight rivalry with U.S. Navy, 86, 88, 93; bureaucratic stress on, 17, 53; creation, 18, 26; institutional culture, 20–21; institutional culture and high technology, 6–8, 9, 79, 85, 93, 170, 172–73; institutional culture and precision bombing, 65, 97, 101; research and development network, 33–41; seeking independence from U.S. Army, 8, 22–23, 27, 59; technology and public relations, 46–47. *See also* precision bombing: and Air Corps culture

U.S. Army Air Forces: aircraft, ix; created, 163; procurement of Norden bombsights, 93; in World War II, 97

U.S. Army Air Service: in World War I, 19–20

U.S. Marine Corps, x, 3–4; and advance base mission, 105–106, 110; bureaucratic stress on, 9–10, 102–104, 111–12, 126–29, 135, 148–49; Division of Operations and Training, 111–12; institutional culture, 130; institutional culture and amphibious operations, 101, 112; institutional culture and low technology, 6–7, 9–11, 101, 157, 170, 172–73; public relations, 110–11; record in